I Never Knew That
About

ENGLAND'S
COUNTRY CHURCHES

BY THE SAME AUTHOR:

I Never Knew That About England
I Never Knew That About Ireland
I Never Knew That About Scotland
I Never Knew That About Wales
I Never Knew That About London
I Never Knew That About the English
I Never Knew That About the Irish
I Never Knew That About the Scottish
I Never Knew That About Britain: the Quiz Book
I Never Knew That About the Lake District
I Never Knew That About Yorkshire
I Never Knew That About the River Thames
I Never Knew That About Royal Britain
I Never Knew That About New York

Christopher Winn

I Never Knew That

About

ENGLAND'S COUNTRY CHURCHES

ILLUSTRATIONS
BY
Mai Osawa

EBURY
PRESS

1 3 5 7 9 10 8 6 4 2

Published in 2014 by Ebury Press, an imprint of Ebury Publishing

A Random House Group Company

Text © Christopher Winn 2014
Illustrations © Mai Osawa 2014

Christopher Winn has asserted his right to be identified as the author of this Work
in accordance with the Copyright, Designs and Patents Act 1988

The Random House Group Limited Reg. No. 954009

Addresses for companies within the Random House Group can be found at
www.randomhouse.co.uk

A CIP catalogue record for this book is available from the British Library

The Random House Group Limited supports the Forest Stewardship Council® (FSC®), the leading
international forest-certification organisation. Our books carrying the FSC label are printed
on FSC®-certified paper. FSC is the only forest-certification scheme supported by the leading
environmental organisations, including Greenpeace. Our paper procurement policy can be found at
www.randomhouse.co.uk/environment

To buy books by your favourite authors and register for offers visit www.randomhouse.co.uk

Series design by Peter Ward

Typeset by Palimpsest Book Production Limited,
Falkirk, Stirlingshire

Printed and bound by CPI Group (UK) Ltd, Croydon, CR0 4YY

ISBN 978 0 09 194525 1

This book is in memory of two people who loved their churches and who helped and inspired me so much in life.

Basil Guy, Bishop of Gloucester,
and
Diana de la Rue

And for Mai
You inspire me every day

Acknowledgements

All my thanks to Carey Smith for her invaluable advice and enthusiasm for this book and for all her encouragement and support.

A special thanks to Nicki Crossley for her help, patience, imagination and good humour, her hard work and dedication, and for bringing everything together so beautifully.

Thanks also to Steve Dobell for making sense of it all and for his suggestions and fine editing work.

Particular thanks to my agent Kevin and all his wonderful team at Tibor Jones for looking after us so well.

Contents

Preface

As the historian A.J.P. Taylor was wont to say, 'The (country) churches of England constitute its greatest treasure'. And, indeed, England's country churches have something for everyone. Fortress, refuge, lighthouse, landmark, mausoleum, museum, market-place, school-room, court-room, concert hall, theatre, House of God. England's country churches are, and have been, all these things.

They are England's most visible and tangible links to the past. They are England's timeline, present since the dawn of England itself, witnesses to historic events and everyday happenings, births and deaths and marriages, triumphs and sorrows. Through the centuries they keep watch over the memories and monuments of England's sons and daughters, the grand and the modest, the noble and the disreputable.

They are galleries of the very best of English craftsmanship and design, in wood and stone, in carvings, sculptures and stained glass. They reflect the tastes and skills of generations of England's artisans and architects. They guard treasures that would grace palaces and museums.

England's country churches are as integral to the English landscape as the rose bush or the oak tree, the chalk down or the hedgerow, and even more varied. Some churches achieve beauty from their location, some are a thing of beauty in themselves; some live in legend and literature.

There are Saxon churches, reflective of simple faith, Norman churches with rugged arches and powerful pillars, stamping their authority, Gothic churches with their soaring arches and huge windows, Puritan chapels, plain and honest, Georgian churches, spacious, galleried, filled with rich oak furnishings, Victorian churches, resplendent with imperial pomp, eccentric Arts and Craft churches – every one of them with illuminating wonders to show and remarkable tales to tell, wonders and tales that will move you to exclaim, again and again . . . I never knew that!

SCOTLAND

Northumberland

Durham

Cumbria

Yorkshire

Lancs

Cheshire

Derbys

Notts

Lincs

Shropshire

Staffs

Norfolk

Leics

1

Northants

Cambs

2

Suffolk

WALES

Hereford

Worcs

Warwicks

Beds

Herts

Essex

Glos

Oxon

Bucks

London

Wilts

Berks

Surrey

Kent

Somerset

Hants

Sussex

Devon

Dorset

Cornwall

1... Rutland
2... Huntingdonshire

England's Country Churches

County by County

John Betjeman wrote of churches that are 'worth bicycling twelve miles against the wind to see'. For me, all of England's ten thousand country churches can justify that ride but I can only find room in this book for some three hundred of them. So, how to choose?

To begin with I have featured only village churches or those that stand alone in the countryside – there are some glorious churches in country towns, but these must wait for another book.

Next, I have ordered the book by county. England's counties are almost as ancient as her churches, and since each county's churches are distinctive and different, not just in style and building materials, but in accent and feel, using counties ensures variety.

In respect of the counties, I have elected to use, as far as possible, England's traditional counties, as they existed at the time the churches were built (other perhaps than some of the earlier Saxon and Norman churches). However, Cumberland, Westmorland and the Furness district of Lancashire I have combined into the present-day Cumbria. I have treated the three Ridings of Yorkshire as the one county of Yorkshire. Huntingdonshire has its own chapter separate from Cambridgeshire. Rutland, of course, has been reborn. Poor Middlesex has been largely subsumed by London and has lost most of the churches that could once have been described as country churches – only Harefield could perhaps still qualify – and so, sadly, does not feature in the book.

Otherwise the choice of church has been purely random. It may be a church I know personally or happen to have read about or has been recommended. There is nothing calculated or wilful in my choice – how I wish I could have included all ten thousand.

BEDFORDSHIRE

Elstow Abbey – John Bunyan's church

Cardington

St Mary the Virgin

A Heady Brew

Much of this stately 15th-century Perpendicular church was rebuilt in 1898 but it still retains an abundance of interesting features old and new, such as the SAXON SUNDIAL on the outside south wall of the tower. Such sundials are extremely rare and this one is in exceptionally good condition.

Inside, the church is full of monuments, the oldest being two beautiful canopied tomb chests that sit beneath 16th-century arches on either side of the chancel. One is to SIR WILLIAM GASCOIGNE, Comptroller of the Household of Cardinal Wolsey. He died in 1540 and his brass portrait is set between those of his two wives. The other is to SIR JARRATE HARVYE (d.1638), THE FIRST MAN TO ENTER CADIZ in the siege of 1596. He was married to Dorothy Gascoigne and the two of them lie here together.

Whitbreads

Everywhere there are monuments to Cardington's most famous family, the WHITBREADS, who settled in Cardington in the 1650s in a house called The Barns, and many of whom lie beneath the church in the family vault. The finest of the Whitbread memorials is a splendid marble sculpture in the north transept, completed by John Bacon in 1799 in memory of SAMUEL WHITBREAD I, founder of WHITBREAD'S BREWERY.

Standing on a plinth beneath the monument is a BLACK BASALT FONT MADE BY JOSIAH WEDGWOOD in 1783, ONE OF ONLY FIVE SUCH FONTS IN EXISTENCE AND ONE OF ONLY TWO TO BE FOUND IN AN ENGLISH CHURCH, the other being in St Mary's, Essendon in Hertfordshire.

World's First Major Air Disaster

In the south aisle there is a memorial to the 48 men who lost their lives in the WORLD'S FIRST MAJOR AIR DISASTER, when the *R101* airship crashed in France, on 5 October 1930, while on its way to the Imperial Conference in India, with the Air Minister, Lord Thomson, on board. The *R101* was constructed in one of the enormous Cardington Sheds that can be seen across the fields on the edge of the village, the largest building in the world when it was put up by Shorts Brothers in the First World War, and it was from here that the airship departed at the start of its fateful voyage.

Above the memorial in the church, hanging in a glass cabinet on the wall, is the torn and scorched ROYAL AIR FORCE ENSIGN that flew proudly from the stern of the airship. It was salvaged from the wreckage and brought back to Cardington. The funeral of the men who died was held in St Mary's, and they are all buried together in the graveyard across the road from the church, beneath a fine monument designed by Sir Albert Richardson.

SAMUEL WHITBREAD (1720–96) was born in Cardington into a Bedfordshire farming family. He invested a modest inheritance from his father in a small brewery at a time when beer was being promoted as a healthy alternative to the demon gin, which was wreaking havoc among the poor. The business flourished and in 1750 Whitbread opened BRITAIN'S FIRST LARGE-SCALE PURPOSE-BUILT BREWERY, in Chiswell Street in London. It soon became THE BIGGEST BREWERY IN THE COUNTRY.

Whitbread was one of the first people in Britain to make a fortune through trade, much looked down upon by 18th-century society, but he was also one of the first great philanthropists who believed in using the fruits of his success for the benefit of everyone. He was always concerned with the welfare of his workforce and his great contribution to the Industrial Revolution, of which he was a pioneer, was the template he created for honest business practice and good relations between owners and workers. In 1768 Whitbread was elected as MP for Bedford, a post he held for over 20 years. He is particularly remembered as THE FIRST MAN TO SPEAK OUT IN PARLIAMENT AGAINST SLAVERY.

The company Whitbread founded in 1742 is today a multi-national concern that owns a number of well-known names in the hospitality business including Costa Coffee, Premier Inns and Beefeater. The Whitbread family still live in Bedfordshire, 5 miles from Cardington, at Southill Park.

Cockayne Hatley

St John the Baptist

Quite Continental

This is Bedfordshire's far east, a landscape of big skies, open fields and distant views. The tower of St John's peeps above a bower of trees standing on a gentle hill at the end of a lonely lane. From the outside this unassuming, 13th-century brownstone church creates a picture of England at its most tranquil and serene. Step inside, however, and you are suddenly in continental Europe.

Before you is a feast of heavy, dark, elaborately carved woodwork, THE MOST WONDROUS AND UNEXPECTED COLLECTION OF ECCLESIASTICAL FURNISHINGS TO BE FOUND IN ANY COUNTRY CHURCH IN ENGLAND. It was all was accumulated by HENRY COCKAYNE CUST, lord of the manor and rector here from 1806 to 1861, at a time when the monasteries and churches of northern Europe were selling off their treasures in the aftermath of the Napoleonic occupations.

The choir stalls that fill the chancel date from 1689 and come from the Abbey of Oignies, near Charleroi in what is now Belgium. They boast exquisite misericords, and the backs of the stalls are carved with the garlanded busts of popes and saints – an extraordinary display of Roman Catholic papal imagery to find in an Anglican country church. There are more of these stalls, with misericords, facing each other in the nave.

The Communion rail, decorated with carvings of harvesting cherubs, was bought from a church at Malines in Belgium, and the impressive screen under the west tower came from Louvain.

A quite lovely small window in the north aisle contains GLASS DATING FROM 1250, showing four saints of Saxon England, Edmund, Ethelbald, Oswald and Dunstan. This came from a demolished church in Yorkshire.

Cockaynes

There are also a number of fine brasses to the Cockayne family, including one to SIR JOHN COCKAYNE, Baron of the Exchequer, who bought the manor of Hatley in 1417, enlarged the church and built the hall next door. The Cockaynes held the manor until 1745, when it passed by marriage to the Custs, and they adopted the name Cockayne Cust. LADY DIANA COOPER, the actress and socialite who was regarded as the most beautiful woman of her day, spent a

---

William Henley

As a poet, Henley is best known for his poem 'Invictus', which includes the famous lines, quoted by Nelson Mandela while a prisoner on Robben Island,

> '... *Under the bludgeonings of chance*
> *My head is bloody but unbowed*
> *... I am the master of my fate:*
> *I am the captain of my soul.*'

---

part of her childhood at Cockayne Hatley Hall, the home of her natural father Henry Cust, and wrote of it in her autobiography as 'a house in Bedfordshire that must always be remembered as a place where the clouds cast no shadows, where grass was greener, taller, strawberries bigger and more plentiful and above all where gardens and woods, the house and family, the servants and villagers, would never change'.

Long John Silver and Wendy

Cockayne Hatley holds one more surprise. Standing under a tree in the windswept churchyard is the austere grey tombstone of the Victorian poet WILLIAM HENLEY (1849–1903) and his family, friends of Henry Cust. As a boy Henley caught tuberculosis and had to have one of his legs amputated. While he was recovering in hospital in Edinburgh he got to know a sickly young writer called Robert Louis Stevenson, who later in life would model one of his most famous characters, the peg-leg villain from *Treasure Island*, LONG JOHN SILVER,

on his boyhood friend William Henley.

On the reverse side of the tombstone it says:

> '*Nothing is here for tears*
> *Nothing to wail or beat the breast*
> *Nothing but what is well and fair ...*'

These words refer to Margaret, Henley's much-loved daughter, who died at the age of five. Known to everyone as the 'golden child', with her flaxen hair, bright eyes and merry laugh she captivated all who met her, including Henley's good friend J.M. Barrie. Margaret noticed how her father referred to Barrie as 'my friend', and whenever he visited she would fling herself into his arms crying 'Fwendy! Fwendy!' And so Barrie came by the name WENDY.

Elstow

Abbey Church of St Mary St Helena

John Bunyan's Church

ELSTOW ABBEY, ONCE THE THIRD LARGEST ABBEY IN ENGLAND, was founded in the 11th century by William the Conqueror's niece Judith. In 1539, during the Dissolution of the Monasteries, most of the gigantic abbey church was demolished leaving just the nave to serve as the parish church of today.

The east end of the church is supported on massive round Norman piers, while at the west end there are two Early English bays, added in the 13th century. On the floor of the south aisle there is a brass portrait of an ABBESS OF ELSTOW, ELIZABETH HERVEY (D.1527), ONE OF ONLY TWO BRASSES IN ENGLAND OF AN ABBESS WITH HER CROSIER. Down some steps and through a door in the south-west corner of the church is a beautiful 13th-century room, now used as a vestry, which has a vaulted ceiling of stone ribs resting on a slim central pillar of Purbeck marble.

Immortal Tinker

But Elstow Abbey's greatest treasure is JOHN BUNYAN (1628–88), author of the first English bestseller, *The Pilgrim's Progress*. He was born, the son of a tinker, in a little cottage outside the village and was baptised in the font that stands in the north aisle of the church, on 13 November 1628. The font is still used today. Bunyan's two daughters were also baptised in this font, Mary, who was born blind, in 1650, and Elizabeth in 1654. The small chapel at the end of the south aisle is called the Bunyan Chapel and preserves the rails and altar table before which Bunyan knelt and received Communion. Victorian windows in the north and south aisles portray scenes from *The Pilgrim's Progress,* and also the fight

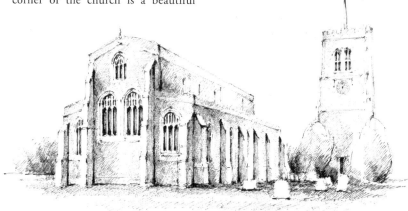

between good and evil from another of Bunyan's books, *The Holy War*.

Outside the church there is a small door in the west wall which is thought to have been the inspiration for the 'Wicket Gate' through which Christian, the main character in *The Pilgrim's Progress*, flees in search of deliverance.

To the north-west of the main church is the 13th-century DETACHED BELL TOWER, one of only two in Bedfordshire (the other is at Marston Mortaine). As a young man, Bunyan came here to ring the bells, gazing nervously upwards in case they fell down on his head as punishment for his sins.

To the south-west of the church are the remains of a house built in 1616 by Thomas Hillerson out of the abbey ruins. Hillerson lies in the church, and his house, which was still standing in Bunyan's day, became the House of the Interpreter, where Christian found a good man who could explain the mysteries of life to him.

Across the road, on the village green, is the 15th-century timber-framed MOOT HALL where Bunyan went to school. It was built by the nuns from the abbey as a stall for the Elstow Market Fair and is now a museum in Bunyan's memory.

Everywhere in Elstow there are memories of England's 'Immortal Tinker'.

Well, I never *knew this*
about

BEDFORDSHIRE CHURCHES

Bletsoe – St Mary the Virgin. A mainly 13th and 14th-century church of Norman origins, much restored in the 19th century, St Mary's, Bletsoe would have been familiar to some of the pivotal characters in the dramatic story of the great Tudor royal dynasty, for here worshipped LADY MARGARET BEAUCHAMP, grandmother to Henry VII. She lived in BLETSOE CASTLE, which still exists next door to the church at the core of a 17th-century manor house. In 1443 she gave birth there to a daughter, Margaret, who would grow up to marry Edmund Tudor, son of Henry V's widow Catherine de Valois, and half-brother to Henry VI. Margaret and Edmund had a son, Henry, who defeated Richard III at the Battle of Bosworth Field in 1485 and ascended the throne as Henry VII. Perhaps we owe our Tudor monarchs to the prayers that Lady Margaret Beauchamp put up in Bletsoe's country church.

Felmersham – St Mary's. Best approached via the old stone bridge across the Ouse, St Mary's Church stands proudly on a bluff above the river, a supreme example of Early English Gothic architecture and one of the most beautiful buildings in Bedfordshire. Built in just 20 years between 1220 and 1240, it has an imposing Early English tower, with a

Perpendicular upper stage, and a simple interior of marching pointed arches, those of the crossing being impressively tall and set upon ornate, multi-shafted pillars. The superb 15th-century rood screen still glows brightly with its original colouring. But the glory of Felmersham is its dramatic and decorative west front, a gallery of Gothic arches and blind arcading in three tiers. Any cathedral would be proud of such craftsmanship.

Northill – St Mary's. High up on the tower of this church is a one-handed clock made by England's first and

greatest clockmaker, THOMAS TOMPION (1639–1713), who was born in a tiny thatched cottage, still standing, in the next-door village of Ickwell Green.

Tompion, whose clocks and watches are among the most valuable timepieces in the world, was christened in St Mary's in 1639.

BERKSHIRE

St Mary's, Aldworth – where giants sleep

Aldworth

St Mary's

'They shall grow not old,
as we that are left grow old
Age shall not weary them,
nor the years condemn
At the going down of the sun
and in the morning
We will remember them'
LAURENCE BINYON, 'For the Fallen'

The ashes of LAURENCE BINYON (1869–1943) are scattered in the churchyard here and he is commemorated, along with his wife Cicely, by a slate gravestone under a hedge. He was born in Lancaster and for most of his life worked for the British Museum, as an expert on Oriental art. His book *Painting in the Far East*, published in 1908, was the first book ever to be written on the subject. 'For the Fallen' was composed in 1914, while Binyon was walking on the cliffs of North

Cornwall, in response to the appalling number of casualties suffered by the British Expeditionary Force on the Western Front, and his poem is recited every year at Remembrance Day services. Binyon was too old to enlist himself, but in 1915 he went to France as a volunteer hospital orderly.

Also in the churchyard is a railed enclosure containing the tombs of a number of ALFRED LORD TENNYSON'S IN-LAWS, THE SELLWOODS, who lived at nearby Pibworth Manor. Tennyson and Emily Sellwood were married not far away at Shiplake in June 1850, and they often stayed in Aldworth and worshipped at St Mary's. Tennyson obviously liked the village, for he gave the name Aldworth to the house he built for himself on Blackdown, near Haslemere in Surrey.

The attractive little church sits, quite alone, on an undulating hilltop at a fork in the road. A little further on is the village well, 365 feet (111 m) deep and said to be THE DEEPEST WELL IN ENGLAND. The yew tree on the south side of the church is anything between 600 and 1,000 years old. The oldest part of the church itself is the late Norman tower, which is 12th-century and sports a quaint, red-tiled Bavarian-style roof. Most of the rest of the building is 13th and 14th-century. All quite straightforward so far.

Aldworth Giants

But wait until you go inside. Here is a sight so spectacular and so astonishing that Queen Elizabeth I herself commanded the Earl of Leicester to ride with her the 15 miles to Aldworth from Ewelme, where she was staying, so she could see what everyone was talking about.

What they were talking about was the ALDWORTH GIANTS, a remarkable collection of nine huge stone effigies, all of the DE LA BECHE family, and all dating from between 1300 and 1350. They are unsurpassed in England and constitute THE GREATEST NUMBER OF MEDIEVAL MONUMENTS TO ONE FAMILY IN ANY ENGLISH PARISH CHURCH. Queen Elizabeth was fortunate to see the giants intact, for they were later defaced by Oliver Cromwell's iconoclasts.

Even so, what is left is magnificent. The de la Beche family came over with William the Conqueror and built themselves a castle at Aldworth, where Beche Farm now stands. They rose to prominence during the reigns of Edward II and Edward III, and the effigies here represent five generations of the family of that period. Six of the effigies lie under ornate Decorated canopies along the north and south walls, while two more are located under the arches of the arcade.

The biggest and most striking is that of SIR PHILIP DE LA BECHE (d.1336) on the north side. He was valet to Edward II and appears to have been over seven feet tall. The dwarf at his feet was his page, who accompanied his master everywhere to emphasise Sir Philip's height and importance. Sir Philip is seen reclining, a most unusual pose for a medieval effigy.

The earliest monument is that of Sir Philip's grandfather, SIR ROBERT DE LA BECHE, who was knighted by Edward I in 1278 and died around 1298. The latest one is that of SIR NICHOLAS DE LA BECHE (d.1345), who rests under the arcade and was the third son of Sir Philip. He was Constable of the Tower of London and tutor to the Black Prince, eldest son of Edward III.

The villagers of Aldworth nicknamed three of the giants John Long, John Strong and John Never Afraid. Another, John Ever Afraid, was buried inside a niche cut into the church wall because he was afraid that the Devil would come and claim him if he was left exposed. Alas, his hiding proved futile and he has vanished, no doubt seized by the dark forces.

All in all, Aldworth is an exhilarating place to visit. Fit, one might almost say, for a Queen.

Avington

St Mark & St Luke

Norman Chancel Arch and Font

Here is BERKSHIRE'S MOST COMPLETE AND LEAST SPOILED NORMAN CHURCH. It lies in a field beside the River Kennet, in the grounds of a great house, and is shaded by a magnificent cedar tree. The building is a simple two-cell structure, entirely Norman except for the Tudor south porch, which was added in the 16th century to protect the splendid Norman doorway, with its two orders of traditional chevron carving. The wooden door itself is also 16th century.

Inside, one's eye is immediately drawn to the marvellous CHANCEL ARCH, garnished with flowers, zigzags, various animals and beak-heads. It covers the whole width of the church and sags delightfully in the middle as if about to buckle under the weight of ages. There are truncated pillars on either side of the chancel, which suggest that it was intended to have a stone vault, but this was never built, perhaps because the money ran out.

Some of the deeply splayed Norman windows have Victorian stained glass, installed by the REVEREND JOHN JAMES, who was rector here in the 1850s. The window in the south wall of the chancel commemorates his daughter BARBARA WILBERFORCE JAMES who, as the inscription tells us, was the grand-daughter of William Wilberforce the abolitionist.

The jewel in the crown of this delectable church is the early Norman font decorated with an arcade of 11 arches containing 13 figures of saints, bishops, lawyers and other learned men. One shows the Kiss of Judas, another a cloven-footed Devil tempting said Judas. Although the carvings are worn and crude, this is one of the BEST NORMAN FONTS IN ENGLAND.

Lower Basildon

St Bartholomew's

Some Interesting Memorials

Down a leafy lane in water meadows by the Thames, with just a group of farm buildings for company, St Bartholomew's occupies a blessed spot. It is a bit untidy looking, with an 18th-century grey stone and red-brick tower, and a 13th-century nave and chancel with uneven roof lines. The chancel arch inside is high and Gothic, resting on clustered pillars. The pews face each other, college style, and the pulpit has some interesting carvings.

There is a small 15th-century brass to JOHN CLERK, possibly the MP for Reading, and his wife, and several tablet memorials of interest on the wall. One of them, to SIR FRANCIS SYKES (d.1804), is a sculpture in high relief of a weeping woman leaning against an urn. It is the work of JOHN FLAXMAN and echoes his famous Wedgwood designs. Sykes is actually buried outside, in an elaborate 14th-century canopied chest tomb borrowed from inside the church and built into the south external wall of the chancel.

Near the porch is a moving sculpture of two boys in swimming costume, commemorating HAROLD AND ERNEST DEVERELL, brothers who lived in the adjoining farmhouse and drowned while swimming in the Thames in 1886.

SIR FRANCIS SYKES (1732–1804) was a merchant with the East India Company who made a fortune in Bengal and became Governor of the Bengali state of Kasimbazar. MP for Wallingford, he was responsible in his final years for building BASILDON PARK, a huge Palladian mansion by John Carr, which sits not far from the church and is now run by the National Trust. Basildon Park gave its name to the well-known brand of writing paper BASILDON BOND, after the directors of Millington and Sons, the company that developed the product, stayed there in 1911.

Also lying somewhere in the churchyard is JETHRO TULL, inventor of the seed drill. He is remembered by a gravestone which states that he died in 1740 rather than 1741, but this is explained by the fact that he died during the last days of the Julian calendar and his gravestone was carved after the introduction of the Gregorian calendar in 1752.

Well, I never knew this *about*

BERKSHIRE CHURCHES

Appleford – St Peter & St Paul. Buried somewhere in the churchyard of this 12th-century riverside church is JOHN FAULKNER, THE WORLD'S OLDEST JOCKEY. He rode his first winner at the age of eight in the year that Queen Victoria came to the throne (1837) and rode his last race when he was 74. He lived in Appleford, fathered 32 children, and died in 1933, aged 104.

Boxford – St Andrew's. Boxford is a delightful village of red brick and thatch, with an old mill house by a bubbling stream. The attractive grey-walled church is mostly 15th-century, handsomely rebuilt by the Victorians. The chancel is Saxon, and during renovations in 2010, workmen removing the concrete rendering from the outside of the chancel wall uncovered a small oak-framed window with a wooden shutter, which turned out to date from before the Norman Conquest. Over 1,000 years old, it is THE ONLY WORKING SAXON WINDOW IN BRITAIN.

Bucklebury – St Mary's. Jonathan Swift preached from the Jacobean

JETHRO TULL (1674–1741) was born in Basildon, at his mother's family home, and baptised in St Bartholomew's. He originally studied for the law but because of financial difficulties was forced to help out on his father's farm at Howberry near Wallingford. In those day crops were sown by hand, which was slow and inefficient, and Tull hated the grinding manual labour, so he set about devising a machine that would do the work for him.

In 1701, using pieces of an old pipe organ, he came up with THE WORLD'S FIRST SEED DRILL, a rotating cylinder with grooves cut into it that allowed seed to fall from a hopper into a funnel. This directed the seed into a furrow cut by a plough at the front of the machine, which was then covered over with soil by a harrow fixed to the back. The contraption was pulled along by a horse and could sow up to three rows at once.

In 1709 Tull moved to Prosperous Farm near Hungerford and continued to perfect the design. He also produced a horse-drawn hoe for clearing weeds and loosening the roots of crops, which enabled them to absorb water more efficiently. In 1731 he published his theories on farming and plant nutrition in a book called *The New Horse Hoeing Husbandry*. His inventions revolutionised farming and anticipated the beginnings of the Industrial Revolution.

Some 200 years later the name Jethro Tull was made famous again by a rock band. They were given the name Jethro Tull by their agent, who happened to see a copy of Tull's book on the shelf in the office of a record company where he was pitching the new band.

pulpit of this Norman church, where the family of a future Queen of England worships today. Perhaps as a child, to pass the time during sermons, the Duchess of Cambridge tried to flick away the fly from the window above the Squire's box pew in the chancel – THE ONLY WINDOW IN AN ENGLISH CHURCH DECORATED WITH A FLY. Designed to illustrate the notion that 'Time Flies', it was painted on in the 17th century, with the wings on one side of the glass and the body and legs on the other, and looks so realistic you can almost hear it buzz. The south doorway of St Mary's is one of the finest in Berkshire, with four arches of rich carvings surmounted by a strange cross with a man's head at the base. On the south-east buttress of the church tower

is a 16th-century carving of a man combing a wheel, or winch. This is a pun on the name of England's first factory owner, clothier JOHN WINCHCOMBE, otherwise known as JACK O' NEWBURY, whose descendants lived in Bucklebury House in the 16th and 17th centuries.

BUCKINGHAMSHIRE

St Lawrence's, West Wycombe – home of the Hellfire Club

Hillesden

All Saints

An Architect's Inspiration

This is one of ENGLAND'S FINEST PERPENDICULAR CHURCHES. It stands on a hilltop at the end of a country lane and is utterly beautiful, so beautiful in fact that the architect SIR GEORGE GILBERT SCOTT, born nearby in the village of Gawcott, was inspired in his love of Gothic architecture by seeing it. A drawing he made of All Saints can be seen in the vestry, and he later restored the church for free.

All Saints was built by the monks of Notley Abbey at the end of the 15th century when Perpendicular was at its height, and their church encapsulates all that is glorious about this style, huge walls of glass that fill the church with light, graceful tracery in the windows, tall Gothic arches, elegant arcades.

The most notable feature, from the

outside, is an exquisite OCTAGONAL STAIR TURRET that rises on the north side, with a delicate stone crown of pinnacles and flying buttresses. The staircase inside gives access to a vestry and, above it, a private chapel that was once linked to Hillesden House next door by a bridge.

The north porch of the church has a lovely vaulted roof and a door that is pockmarked with bullet holes. During the Civil War, Hillesden House belonged to the Denton family, staunch Royalists, and was besieged by Oliver Cromwell himself and razed to the ground. There is nothing left of the house, but the battered front door was rescued and installed in the church.

Treasures inside include a traceried, 15th-century wooden chancel screen, a frieze of angels carrying scrolls or musical instruments running around the top of the chancel walls, and some splendid monuments to the Dentons of the 16th century.

Medieval Comic

Most of the medieval glass was destroyed in the Civil War but what remains is magnificent, particularly THE EAST WINDOW OF THE SOUTH TRANSEPT,

WHERE THE LIFE OF ST NICHOLAS IS DEPICTED IN BRIGHTLY COLOURED 16TH-CENTURY FLEMISH GLASS. The pictures, which cover four windows, are so extraordinarily lifelike and full of action that this could almost be a medieval comic strip. In the top left-hand panel a boy falls from a ship into the sea, and in the next panel to the right he is miraculously saved by St Nicholas. In the bottom panel of the third window another boy is strangled by the Devil, and he too is revived by the hard-working St Nicholas in the panel next door. A very happy time can be spent reading this window – perhaps the most unusual and enjoyable storybook you will find in any English church.

Stoke Poges

St Giles'

'The curfew tolls the knell of parting day,
The lowing herd wind slowly o'er the lea
The ploughman homeward plods
his weary way,
And leaves the world to darkness
and to me.'
THOMAS GRAY, 'Elegy Written in
a Country Churchyard'

The church of St Giles sits in a cherished patch of green where the Chilterns begin to break against the suburbs of London. It is a most satisfying church to look at, with lots of gables and a square tower with a pyramid cap. It was in this country churchyard that THOMAS GRAY (1716–71) wrote what must be one of the best-loved poems in the English language, 'Elegy Written in a Country Churchyard', and despite the closeness to London it is still possible to experience here some of the solitude and peace that inspired his masterpiece. There are a few more trees, perhaps, and the spire that rose above the tower in Gray's day is gone, taken down in 1924 because it was unsafe, but the churchyard is still countryfied and the famous lea is now owned by the National Trust and safe from harm.

Thomas Gray is buried with his mother Dorothy and her sister Mary in a red-brick chest tomb outside the east wall of the Hastings Chapel, which was added to the south-east corner of the church in 1558 by lord of the manor Lord Hastings. Gray's name does not appear on the actual tomb since there was no room for an inscription, but a tablet on the wall of the chapel records his interment there.

Near the south-west door of the church is the YEW TREE UNDER WHICH THOMAS GRAY SAT WHILE WRITING HIS ELEGY. A short walk away, on the lea, is a large monument erected in Gray's memory by a local landowner, JOHN PENN, grandson of William Penn, the founder of Pennsylvania.

Some of the lines and phrases that have
passed into the English language from
'Elegy Written in a Country Churchyard':

The paths of glory lead but to the grave

Full many a flower is born to blush unseen
And waste its sweetness on the desert air

Far from the madding crowd's ignoble strife

Some kindred spirit shall enquire thy fate

St Giles' Church itself has Saxon and
Norman origins, and inside there are
some sturdy round Norman pillars
supporting the arches of the nave. The
Norman chancel arch has been replaced
by a slim Gothic arch and most of what
we see in the main body of the church
today is 13th-century work, although
there is a Norman window in the north
wall of the chancel and a small square
window next to it, which may have
been the window of a hermit's cell. The
Chantry was built in 1338 by lord of
the manor Sir John de Molyns and
boasts a RARE DOUBLE PISCINA.

The Naked Cyclist

The west window commemorates those
who fell in the Second World War and
is called the BICYCLE WINDOW, as it
incorporates a fragment of glass dating
from 1643 which shows a nude man
blowing a trumpet while riding an early
form of bicycle known as a hobby horse.
It is THE EARLIEST KNOWN PICTURE OF
A BICYCLE IN THE WORLD.

In the south aisle is a pair of Victorian
windows of 1871, commemorating a
child of the local Howard-Vyse family.
It is most unusual and very lovely,
showing a child slipping from the arms
of his mother and being received into
the arms of an angel.

A singular feature of the church is
the OAK-PANELLED CLOISTER, accessed
through a door in the north wall. This
once provided a private entrance to the
church from the manor house, which
can be glimpsed not far away across a
smoothly mown lawn.

Hastings Chapel

At the south-east corner of the church
the HASTINGS CHAPEL, with its Tudor

mullioned windows, was founded to serve both as a private chapel for the inmates of the almshouse that Lord Hastings had built next door, and as a burial place for him and his family. It was originally cut off from the main church but was opened up in the 18th century with the removal of the south wall of the chancel.

Although the chapel is festooned with monuments there is strangely no memorial to Lord Hastings himself. A staunch Catholic, he was Queen Mary's Master of the Horse, and during her coronation procession in 1553 he led the Queen's horse by the bridle through the streets of London from the Tower to Westminster Abbey. When Mary died, Hastings was sent to Hatfield to inform Princess Elizabeth that she had become queen, and to accompany her back to London. After Elizabeth's accession he retired to the manor house at Stoke Poges, where he died without heirs in 1573.

Bond

Back outside, on the other side of the pink brick wall lining the western edge of the churchyard, is the Stoke Park Golf Club where James Bond, played by Sean Connery, took part in a golf match against Auric Goldfinger, played by Gert Frobe, in the 1964 film *Goldfinger*. The statue at the entrance to the clubhouse, beheaded by the bowler hat of Goldfinger's sidekick Odd Job, has since been replaced.

James Bond's wife, Tracy, was buried in St Giles' churchyard, not far from Thomas Gray. We see Bond visiting her

grave in the pre-title sequence of *For Your Eyes Only*.

Wing

All Saints

Saxon Apse and Crypt

This Saxon church was begun in the 8th or 9th century and enlarged in the 10th century by Aelfgifa, sister-in-law of King Edgar, the first crowned King of England. As such it is ONE OF ENGLAND'S OLDEST COUNTRY CHURCHES. It is also unique in that it retains not only its Saxon nave, aisles and west wall but also an apse with a crypt beneath it – THE ONLY SAXON APSE AND CRYPT SURVIVING COMPLETE IN ENGLAND.

The apse is very prominent in the church exterior. It has seven sides, each side separated by vertical pilasters and decorated with a blind arcade, while the window arches of the crypt below peep intriguingly just above ground level. The entrance to the crypt is in the south wall and the crypt itself is very well preserved, largely because it was sealed for hundreds of years before being opened up again in the 19th century. It consists of a passageway or ambulatory that runs round a small chamber accessed by three narrow archways. The whole ensemble is stone vaulted and has walls of rough flint.

Apart from the apse and crypt, the church hides its Saxon origins well, appearing to be a mainly 15th-century Perpendicular affair with battlements, tower, clerestory, Gothic windows and a particularly handsome porch all dating from that period.

Widest Saxon Arch

Inside, the Saxon becomes more obvious – spectacularly so. The nave is typically long and narrow and tall with unsophisticated round arches, plain and simple. And the chancel arch is just breathtaking – 21 feet (6.4 m) wide, it is THE WIDEST SAXON ARCH IN EXISTENCE. Unfortunately, a 16th-century

carved wooden screen fills the arch, and while a fine piece in itself, it does rather spoil the full Saxon effect.

Above the arch is a double-headed Saxon window divided by a central shaft, ONE OF ONLY FOUR SUCH SAXON WINDOWS TO BE FOUND IN THE NAVE OF AN ENGLISH CHURCH, the other three all being at Worth, in Sussex (*see* page 281).

The 15th-century roof is superb, festooned with carvings of angels, kings, saints and numerous medieval characters.

Renaissance Splendour

Putting on quite a show in the north aisle is possibly THE EARLIEST RENAISSANCE MONUMENT IN ENGLAND, certainly one of the very best. SIR ROBERT DORMER (d.1552) lies in a stone sarcophagus garlanded with bull's heads beneath a vast canopy supported on Corinthian columns. The observer is transported straight to Ancient Rome. The other Dormer tombs, which anywhere else would be considered noteworthy, are made to look somewhat ordinary in comparison.

In the wall of the south aisle is a rather simpler memorial, a brass to THOMAS COATES (d.1648), who was a porter at the Dormer's home, Ascott Hall. He is recorded as having '. . . (alas) left his key, lod, fyre, friends, and all to have a roome in Heaven . . .'

Well, I never knew this
about
BUCKINGHAMSHIRE CHURCHES

Clifton Reynes – St Mary the Virgin.
This sweet little church, which gazes across the River Ouse at the tall spire of Olney, could almost be made of Lego building blocks. The elements of square Norman tower, 13th-century aisles, and 15th-century battlemented nave and clerestory, all seem to slot together like a Christmas toy. Inside are four 14th-century wooden effigies, all of members of the Reynes family, THE LARGEST NUMBER OF WOODEN EFFIGIES IN ANY PARISH CHURCH IN ENGLAND. THOMAS REYNES (d.1385) has a stone effigy, and his feet rest on a little dog with the name BO on his collar – THE ONLY PET NAMED IN STONE ON A MEDIEVAL TOMB IN ENGLAND.

Fingest – St Bartholomew's. Here is a marvellously unspoiled Norman church with a mighty 12th-century tower crowned by a distinctive DOUBLE

SADDLEBACK ROOF, ONE OF ONLY TWO SUCH ROOFS IN ENGLAND. The lower part of the tower inside once served as the nave and is consequently wider than the present nave, which was originally the chancel, while the huge Norman arch spanning the whole width of the church was once the chancel arch.

West Wycombe – St Lawrence's. A prominent landmark in the Chilterns, this medieval hilltop church was renovated in the 18th century by SIR FRANCIS DASHWOOD, Chancellor of the Exchequer and noted rake. The unique 'GOLDEN BALL' on top of the tower, reached by a precarious ladder, was large enough inside for Dashwood and eight of his friends to sit down to dinner or cards. The view from it is stupendous and includes Dashwood's stately home across the valley, West Wycombe Park, the lovely old village of West Wycombe itself at the foot of the hill, and the long, dead-straight stretch of road into High Wycombe that Dashwood built out of material mined from the hill below the church. The worked mines were fashioned into caves where Dashwood's notorious Hellfire Club would party, gamble and very probably indulge in orgies.

CAMBRIDGESHIRE

St Mary's, Swaffham Prior – the oldest octagonal tower in Cambridgeshire

Barton

St Peter's

Some Rare Saints

Here is a UNIQUE GALLERY OF SAINTS AND BIBLICAL SCENES PORTRAYED IN 14TH-CENTURY WALL PAINTINGS. We see the Annunciation, the Baptism in the River Jordan, the Marriage at Cana where Jesus turns the water into wine, and the Last Supper. We see St Christopher, John the Baptist with the Lamb, a knight in armour attacking a waiting demon with his lance, and St Michael weighing up souls while the

Virgin Mary, wearing a large crown, tips the opposing scales with her rosary. While superb, these scenes are relatively commonplace, but on the north wall there is some rather more unusual imagery.

ST ANTHONY, patron saint of animals, is seen with a pig, representing the sins of the flesh tamed by Anthony's piety. This is THE BEST EXAMPLE OF AN IMAGE OF ST ANTHONY AND HIS PIG THAT SURVIVES IN ENGLAND.

On the same wall is a lovely picture of ST DUNSTAN, patron saint of armourers and gunsmiths, pinching the Devil's nose with a pair of tongs. Dunstan was Archbishop of Canterbury in the 10th century, and it was he who devised the traditional coronation ceremony we use today, for the crowning of King Edgar as the first King of England at Bath Abbey in AD 978. THIS IS THE ONLY KNOWN PORTRAIT OF ST DUNSTAN IN AN ENGLISH COUNTRY CHURCH.

There is also a rare portrait of ST THOMAS OF CANTELUPE, 13th-century Bishop of Hereford, and the last Englishman to be canonised before the Reformation.

St Peter's is a fine example of an ordinary country church bedecked with imagery with which to educate its simple village folk, and although these wall paintings are not the finest or the best preserved, they nonetheless form a wonderfully spirited and diverse gallery of characters and story-telling.

Ickleton

St Mary Magdalene

Norman Wall Paintings

Ickleton is a sweet old village caught in a tangle of motorways. It has long been an important crossroads, at the point where the ancient Icknield Way crosses the River Cam. The Romans were not far away at Chesterford, while the village still follows a Saxon layout and the church is, at its core, Saxon and 12th-century Norman, enhanced by a fine 15th-century lead broach spire.

There is a plain Saxon west doorway leading to a nave that is long, tall and narrow, in the Saxon way. The arcades are of superb round Norman arches resting on plain cushion capitals above slender columns, SOME OF WHICH MAY BE ROMAN – monolithic pillars salvaged from the nearby Roman ruins by the Saxons and re-used by the Normans. There is an unusual DOUBLE CLERE-STORY, with splayed Norman windows just above the apex of the arches, and 15th-century windows above that, put there when the roof was raised but out of phase with the arcade. The wonderful rood screen is 14th-century, as is the

painted font cover, while several carved poppy-head bench ends survive, one of them showing St Michael weighing up souls.

Ickleton is but one of England's many fine Norman churches, and it might have remained just that had it not been for a fire in 1979. The subsequent restoration uncovered an extensive set of EXTREMELY RARE NORMAN WALL PAINTINGS on the north and east walls of the nave, dating from about 1170, and rivalled only by those at Kempley, in Gloucestershire (*see* pages 105–6). The paintings between the clerestory windows show the four Passion scenes: the Last Supper, the Betrayal, the Flagellation, and Christ carrying the Cross. Lower down we see the martyrdoms of the saints.

Above the chancel arch there is a Doom, a painting showing the Last Judgement. This dates from the middle of the 14th century and includes a somewhat startling picture of the Virgin

Mary baring her breasts to Jesus in a show of supplication, THE ONLY PICTURE OF A BARE-BREASTED MARY IN ANY OF ENGLAND'S CHURCHES.

Swaffham Prior

St Cyriac & St Julitta and St Mary's

Two Churches

Not content with just the one ancient church, this pretty village has two of them, sharing the same hilly churchyard as if to flaunt the fact that here is one of Cambridgeshire's few heights. Both churches sit atop a well-tended grassy mound dotted with trees and both have Norman foundations, although the original St Cyriac & St Julitta was probably there first since it occupies the higher ground and has the more central position. They were built by different patrons and served different parishes until 1667, when the parishes were merged under one vicar and St Mary's became the sole parish church.

St Cyriac & St Julitta

Founded by three Norman knights in the 12th century, this is ONE OF ONLY SIX ENGLISH CHURCHES DEDICATED TO THE CHILD SAINT, CYRIAC, AND HIS MOTHER JULITTA, who were both martyred by the Emperor Diocletian in AD 304. The extraordinary octagonal tower was added in 1493, and all that seems to prevent it from rotating on its square base like a post mill in the wind is the outside stair turret. After St Mary's became the parish church in 1667, St Cyriac's was left to decay, until required again at the end of the 18th century when a lightning strike damaged St Mary's.

Apart from the tower, St Cyriac's was completely rebuilt in 1810 in neo-Gothic style, and when it was abandoned again in 1902 all the Georgian wood furnishings and box pews were removed, leaving just a bare empty space which, apparently, has the most wonderful acoustics.

St Mary's

The glory of St Mary's is the SUPERLA-TIVE 12TH-CENTURY OCTAGONAL TOWER, which presumably was the inspiration for the octagonal tower of St Cyriac and St Julitta, which was added in 1493. Indeed, since St Mary's originally belonged to the Abbot of Ely, it is possible that the tower here was also the model for the celebrated octagonal lantern of Ely Cathedral, built some 200 years later. It begins with a colossal square base that blends into an octagonal second stage, both of which are Norman. The third stage is 13th-century Early English with lancet windows and has 16 sides. At the top is a shallow ring of blind arches, restored in the mid 20th century, and a fibre-glass needle spire that neatly catches the sun.

After entering the church through the western porch you pass under the tower, which is open to the roof, and from this exhilarating perspective you can see the cleverly engineered 'squinches' that allow the structure to change shape as it rises.

The nave with its

tall arcades has been adequately restored after being left to decay for most of the 19th century, and a set of rather fine medieval brasses has survived, while the chancel was rebuilt in 1878 and has a 20th-century screen. The windows of the aisles commemorate the First World War and show pictures of weapons from that conflict, including a fighter plane, submarines, a Zeppelin and even the Statue of Liberty. The pictures are simple and unsophisticated but somehow strangely moving.

Westley Waterless

St Mary the Less

Unusual Early Brass

This little church lies tucked away behind some farm buildings in flat fields not far from Cambridge. It has a petite 19th-century bell turret in place of a Norman round tower that fell

down in 1855, and looks small and unimportant from the outside. Inside, however, it is surprisingly spacious, with an early 13th-century chancel and a 14th-century nave with graceful white painted Gothic arcade, and a black-and-white beamed roof. There is a rugged, roughly carved 13th-century octagonal font and a 13th-century stone effigy of a layman in the south aisle.

Next to him, in the floor, is a matchless treasure, the detailed and amazingly well-preserved brass of Sir John de Creke and his wife Lady Alyne, dating from 1324. This is THE EARLIEST BRASS IN ENGLAND OF A MAN AND HIS WIFE AND THE EARLIEST OF JUST SIX BRASSES IN ENGLAND THAT SHOW A KNIGHT WEARING A CYCLAS, which is a type of sleeveless tunic worn over armour by knights of the 14th century. In addition it is ONE OF ONLY TWO BRASSES IN ENGLAND THAT BEAR THE MARK, AS OPPOSED TO THE SIGNATURE, OF THE CRAFTSMAN, in this case believed to be one WALTER LE MASUN.

Well, I never knew this about
CAMBRIDGESHIRE CHURCHES

Guyhirn Chapel. Set in a generous churchyard across the road from an embankment holding in the River Nene, and surrounded by modern bungalows, this tiny church of brick and stone may have an inauspicious setting but is worthy of respect as a rare

and precious example of an untouched Puritan chapel. It was completed in 1660, at the end of the Commonwealth, and there is nothing showy or unnecessary here, just one small room with four big windows of clear glass. The walls are bare of any ornamentation and the lovely old silvered oak benches are crammed closely together so that there is no room to kneel – kneeling, after all, was a Papist outrage. The Jacobean pulpit seems almost vulgarly ostentatious. After the richness of so many of our country churches this plain and uncomplicated place serves to cleanse the palate. The real treasure here is the simple faith that built it.

Isleham Priory Church. Built around 1090 as the chapel for a Benedictine priory, this lovely building has been described as THE BEST EXAMPLE OF A SMALL UNALTERED NORMAN CHURCH IN ENGLAND. The priory was abandoned in 1254 and after years of neglect the chapel was passed into the possession of Pembroke College, Cambridge. After the Reformation the roof was raised so that the church could be used as a barn, and a cart door was inserted in place of the Norman doorway. While these privations are regrettable, at least the chapel was preserved from rebuilding and retains its simple, classic form of nave, chancel and semi-circular apse. There are no furnishings at all inside,

which means that you can see the Norman architecture at its best. There are said to be tunnels leading under the road to Isleham's 14th-century church of St Andrew, noted for its high angel roof of 1495.

Willingham – St Mary's All Saints. Here is a 13th-century church famous for its WALL PAINTINGS, discovered beneath the Puritan whitewash during renovations in the 1890s. At the west end of the south aisle is an Early English lancet window, and painted on to the splayed jambs are pictures of two 7th-century saints, ST ETHELDREDA, founder of the abbey at Ely, and her sister ST SEXBURGHA. These date from about 1250. Above the north arcade of the nave is a splendidly vivid 14th-century depiction of ST CHRISTOPHER carrying Jesus across a tumultuous river teeming with fish. The colours, reds, greens and ochres, are bold and vibrant. Next to him is a less well-preserved picture of ST GEORGE AND THE DRAGON. Above the chancel arch is a 15th-century DOOM, and there are also paintings from the 16th and 17th centuries scattered throughout the church, making a colourful gallery spanning some 400 years. Enclosing two bays of the north aisle is a BEAUTIFULLY CARVED AND TRACERIED SCREEN, decorated with green popinjays on a red background, which has been dated to 1320 and is possibly THE OLDEST SCREEN IN ENGLAND.

CHESHIRE

St Mary's, Acton has the oldest stone church tower in Cheshire, 80 feet high and dating from 1180

Astbury

St Mary's

Unique Layout

A battlemented castle with a soaring spire, St Mary's stands in an elevated position at the head of the village green and watches over the chocolate-box scene below with a quiet grandiloquence. There is so much that is unusual about this glorious church that it is hard to know where to begin. THE LAYOUT, FOR INSTANCE, IS UNIQUE, WITH TWO TOWERS AND A SPIRE. The original 13th-century tower stands on Norman foundations off to the north-west of the main church and is attached to the north aisle by a covered passageway. Its elegant spire was added in the 14th century. At the west end of the church, where you would expect to find the tower, there is a 15th-century three-storey porch that to all intents and purposes is a second tower. And on the south side of the

church there is another porch, this time of two storeys, with a priest's room on the top floor.

The body of the church is basically two churches, one upon the other, the lower 13th-century church having an aisle either side, the upper storey, added in the 15th century, being formed of magnificent clerestory windows that rise in glory above the nave. There is no structural arch between the nave and the chancel, and the aisles continue through to the chancel where they form two chapels. At the west end the nave is 40 feet (12 m) wide, wider than Chester Cathedral, and THE WIDEST NAVE OF ANY PARISH CHURCH IN CHESHIRE. Most unusually for a Gothic church, IT NARROWS TOWARDS THE EAST END, accentuating the length.

Fixtures and Fittings

St Mary's is deemed to possess MORE MEDIEVAL FIXTURES AND FURNISHINGS THAN ANY OTHER CHURCH IN CHESHIRE. Revealed above the arcade on the north wall of the nave, during restorations by

Sir George Gilbert Scott in 1857, is a rare 15th-century painting of two scenes from the life of St George. In one he is being blessed by the Virgin Mary, while in the other he is receiving the adulation of a maiden, no doubt a princess he has saved from the dragon. In the middle stands his white horse, saddled and champing to go. THIS IS THE ONLY KNOWN PAINTING IN THE WORLD OF THESE SCENES FROM ST GEORGE'S LIFE.

Dating from 1500 are the choir stalls, which have hinged seats but have lost their misericords, the impressive chancel screen, sumptuously carved with birds and foliage, and the oak lectern, ONE OF THE OLDEST EAGLE LECTERNS IN ENGLAND.

The box pews and octagonal pulpit are Jacobean, as is the spectacular painted ceiling, resplendent with richly carved bosses and pendants.

The dazzling east window, almost as tall as the church itself, contains Victorian glass of 1858.

Outside in the churchyard, which is entered through a large 17th-century stone gateway, is the ASTBURY YEW, 2,000 years old and not surprisingly leaning on a wooden support; also the badly weathered 13th-century canopied tomb, originally that of a member of the VENABLES family but apparently claimed in the 16th century by the BRERETONS. It contains two figures, one male, one female, their hands clasped in prayer. IT IS THE ONLY TOMB OF ITS KIND IN CHESHIRE.

Daresbury

All Saints

Wonderland

The church here is an oasis of peace, set among the trees on the edge of the village and withdrawn from the busy, encircling roads and industries of Runcorn and Warrington. In the 12th century this was a chapel for Norton Priory, then a pink sandstone parish church, built in 1550, from which the tower remains.

In 1832 a baby boy was baptised in this church who would grow up to create characters that would never die and write stories that would enchant children everywhere. Son of the curate, he was born in the All Saints vicarage, of which just the gateposts remain. He was christened Charles Lutwidge Dodgson, but would be known to the world as LEWIS CARROLL. 'This happy place where I was born' is how he described Daresbury, where he lived until the age of 11. The church was restored in 1870 and is much changed since he knew it, but he would recognise the big yew tree by the door and the beautiful Jacobean pulpit carved with angels' heads and strange animals from where his father preached. Were any of the strange creatures from Wonderland or *Through the Looking Glass* inspired by these carvings?

In 1935, three years after the centenary of his birth, a striking memorial window to Carroll was erected in the east wall of the Daniell Chapel, designed by Geoffrey Webb and paid for by subscriptions from his devotees around the world. The window, of five lights, depicts the Scene of the Nativity. Carroll appears with Alice in the far left panel, while at the bottom of each panel are figures from his stories, as pictured by Sir John Tenniel, including the White Rabbit, the Mad Hatter, the Cheshire Cat and the Queen of Hearts. It is most diverting to while away the time by searching out all the characters in this colourful wonderland.

Mobberley

St Wilfrid's

Because It's There

This noble church stands proudly above the road across from the pretty red-brick Church Inn, with a cluster of attractive houses for company, making a welcome sight to gladden the hearts of passengers descending into nearby Manchester airport. The Saxons worshipped here but the oldest part of the present church dates from about 1245. The splendid Perpendicular tower was rebuilt in 1533.

St Wilfrid's is reputed to have THE BEST WOODEN ROOD SCREEN IN CHESHIRE, carved in 1500 and decorated with coats of arms and a variety of faces, including that of a Green Man.

On the north wall inside there is a medieval mural showing St George and the Dragon, while a faded St Christopher can be seen above the arcade in the nave.

Throughout the church there are memorials to the Mallory family, including a glorious window in memory of Mobberley's most famous son, GEORGE MALLORY, who died on Mount Everest in 1924, 'lost to human sight between earth and heaven', as it says on the inscription.

There is also a brass plate in the church in memory of George Mallory's younger brother, SIR TRAFFORD LEIGH-MALLORY, who was Commander-in-Chief of the Allied Expeditionary Air Force, in charge of the Allied air forces during the Normandy landings in 1944. He was killed, along with his wife, in an air crash in the French Alps in 1944 while on his way to take up the post of Commander-in-Chief of South East Asia Command.

GEORGE MALLORY, born in 1886, grew up at Mobberley Old Hall, a handsome Jacobean house half a mile from the church across the fields. His father was the last of five Mallory rectors of St Wilfrid's, and there are stories that George practised his climbing skills by clambering up the church tower. He went on three expeditions to Mount Everest, the last in the summer of 1924, when he was spotted by a member of the support team further down the mountain, along with his companion Sandy Irvine, just 800 feet (244 m) from the summit. They disappeared into a snow squall and were never seen alive again. Mallory's body was lost on the mountain for 75 years, but in 1999 it was finally found at 27,000 feet (8,230 m) on Everest's north face and he was buried beneath a cairn on the spot where he lay.

Were George Mallory and Sandy Irvine the first men to conquer Everest? A Kodak camera they had with them with which to take pictures from the roof of the world may hold the answer, but it has never been found. It is undoubtedly Mount Everest's most sought-after treasure.

George Mallory was the source of one of the great English quotes. When asked why he wanted to climb Everest, he replied, 'Because it's there.'

Black-and-White Churches

As well as some of the finest black-and-white half-timbered houses in England, Cheshire can lay claim to the best of England's handful of timber-framed churches, too.

Lower Peover – St Oswald's

St Oswald's sits at the end of a narrow cobbled lane off the main road called, rather cleverly, the Cobbles, and presides over a quaint little grouping of cottages, school, water mill and the Bells of Peover pub. There has been a church here since 1269, but most of the lovely timber-framed building we see today, with its overhanging eaves and black-and-white gables, is 14th-century, THE OLDEST ARCADED WOODEN CHURCH IN EUROPE. The projecting sandstone tower was added in 1582.

The inside is breathtaking, a wealth of wood, with massive wooden arcades and wooden arches supporting the raftered roof, all hewn from trees that were growing in Saxon England. The furnishings of screens, pulpit, choir stalls and lectern are all 17th-century, as are the box pews, many of which retain their original half-doors, with only the top section opening and the bottom half fixed to hold in the rushes that were strewn along the floor to keep the congregation's feet warm on cold days. Three different pews bear the crests of three grand families who endowed the church, the SHACKERLEYS, the CHOLMONDELEYS and the LEYCESTERS.

In the SHACKERLEY CHAPEL at the south-east corner of the church there is a huge 'bog oak' chest, sculpted out of a Cheshire oak tree and reputed to be older than the church itself. The chapel contains tombs and monuments of the Shackerleys, including that of the Royalist SIR GEOFFREY SHACKERLEY,

who distinguished himself fighting for Charles I at the Battle of Rowton Heath in 1645. When hurrying to get orders from the King, rather than take a diversion up river to the bridge he rowed himself across the River Dee in a barrel, with his horse swimming alongside.

Peover, by the way, is pronounced 'Peever'.

Marton – St James & St Paul

Sitting atop a small knoll on the edge of the village, St James & St Paul is the prettiest church imaginable, a picture in black and white, with a shingled wooden tower and spire, low slate roof, crooked porch and walls of upright timbers infilled with white rendered brick. Massive beams support the tower inside, while the nave arcades stand on great pillars of wood. There is a Jacobean pulpit and on

St James & St Paul, Marton

either side of the door are two large 18th-century paintings of Moses and Aaron by Edward Penney, said to be THE BEST PORTRAITS OF THEIR KIND IN CHESHIRE.

Founded by Sir John de Davenport in 1343, and little altered since, ST JAMES & ST PAUL IS THE OLDEST AND BEST-PRESERVED HALF-TIMBERED CHURCH STILL IN USE IN EUROPE.

Well, I never knew this about
CHESHIRE CHURCHES

Acton – St Mary's. This magnificent church boasts the oldest church tower in Cheshire, built by the Normans in 1180 to a height of 100 feet (30 m). In 1757 the top portion of the tower fell down in a storm and was replaced in Gothic style to a height of 80 feet (24 m). A rare survival inside is the original stone seating around the walls.

Bunbury – St Boniface. First a wooden Saxon church then a stone Norman church, St Boniface as we see it now dates mainly from the 14th century. It was rebuilt then at the expense of SIR HUGH CALVELEY, who died in 1394 and is buried in the chancel beneath THE OLDEST ALABASTER TOMB IN CHESHIRE. He was reputed to be seven feet tall and he fought for the Black Prince with the strength of ten men. Sir Hugh's descendant, SIR GEORGE BEESTON, is buried under an elaborate, red, green and gold painted tomb in the sanctuary. Born in 1499, he lived through the whole of the 16th century, besieged Boulogne for Henry VIII, fought against the Scots at Musselburgh for

Edward VI, and at the age of 89 commanded the *Dreadnought*, which helped to break the line of the Spanish Armada in 1588 – for which he was knighted. He died in 1601 at the age of 102. The stone screen at the entrance to the 16th-century Ripley Chapel is THE ONLY PAINTED MEDIEVAL STONE SCREEN SURVIVING IN CHESHIRE.

Gawsworth–St James's. This has perhaps THE MOST CLASSICALLY PICTUR-ESQUE SETTING OF ANY CHURCH IN ENGLAND. The approach is along a fine avenue of elms with glimpses of a stately Elizabethan black-and-white hall through the trees and the prettiest Old Rectory in Cheshire, built in 1470 with a crooked porch and an oriel window. The backdrop is emerald green parkland. The noble Perpendicular church tower is mirrored in the lake, so clearly that you can tell the time by the reflection of the church clock. Inside, kneeling alongside her six sisters and three brothers in front of the tomb of her father, Sir Edward Fitton, and mother Anne, is MARY FITTON, Maid of Honour to Elizabeth I and 'Dark Lady' of Shakespeare's sonnets.

Mellor – St Thomas's. It is a steep climb to get to St Thomas's, which stands next to Mellor Hall on a ridge overlooking the village. The tower, which from a distance appears to have a slight tilt, is 15th century, while the rest is early 19th-century rebuild. It has two treasures of which any church could be proud, a carved EARLY NORMAN FONT and THE OLDEST WOODEN PULPIT IN THE WORLD, dating from the reign of King Edward II in the early 14th century and sculpted from a single block of oak. It has six sides, one for the entrance, one left plain, and four carved with tracery and foliage. For this pulpit alone, it is worth the climb.

CORNWALL

St Winwaloe's Landewednack, England's most southerly church

Landewednack

St Winwaloe's

Last Cornish Sermon

ENGLAND'S MOST SOUTHERLY CHURCH sits in a hollow embowered in trees bent to the wind. To the west is England's most southerly village, the Lizard. Beyond, and to the south and east, only sea. The sounds and smells of the ocean are all around. In the churchyard is a memorial to Cornishmen lost at sea. Tombstones are carved with seagulls. The rest of the world seems very far away. It is said that THE LAST SERMON SPOKEN IN THE CORNISH TONGUE WAS PREACHED HERE, in 1674.

A wooden church was established here in about AD 600 and dedicated to St Winwaloe (460–532), a Celtic saint of Cornish ancestry who spent much of his life in Brittany. The stone church was begun by the Normans, and enlarged in the 13th and 14th centuries.

The result is a very beautiful little church. The sturdy tower could be made of Lego, an irregular patchwork of granite bricks and massive, rough-hewn blocks of grey, blue and dark green serpentine, a local stone found only on the Lizard. The whole is flecked with golden lichen.

The gabled south transept throws a protective arm around the tiny embattled square porch, which shelters a 15th-century doorway sitting underneath the oldest remaining feature of the building, a mossy Norman arch carved out with crosses, rings and chevrons.

The interior is simple and unpretentious but has a strange AMBULATORY, supported by a round pillar, running between the transept and the chancel, which gives the church a rather endearing lopsided appearance. There are some interesting carvings on the chancel seats.

The square font, made of serpentine, sits on four legs and bears the inscription 'Master Richard Bolham made me'. He was rector here in the early 15th century.

Launcells

St Swithin's

An Unspoiled Church and a Forgotten Genius

Just up the lane from St Swithin's Well, this stately building was considered by John Betjeman to be the 'least spoiled church in Cornwall'. It is tucked away in a dell down its own sunken lane, just the tips of the high-pinnacled tower visible above the hedgerows. The Victorian restorers missed it and what we see today is the unblemished artistry of our 14th and 15th-century builders.

The heavy ancient door swings open to reveal a church that is nearly as wide as it is long, with a nave and two aisles each with their own lovely waggon roofs, the aisles boasting elaborately carved ribs and bosses, the nave roof plain. The arcades are different from each other, the north one of granite, the south made with Cornish stone from the quarries of Polyphant, near Launceston to the south.

The floor of the chancel is set with 15th-century glazed tiles from Barnstaple showing lions, griffins, pelicans and flowers. Next door, at the east end of the south aisle, is the grand Jacobean monument of SIR JOHN ESMOND (d.1624), who is shown in effigy lying sideways, with his head on his hand and a rather puffy look on his face. There is a Georgian pulpit with tester and some box pews in the north aisle, and high on the north wall are traces of a painted text, part of a letter written by Charles I in 1643 in which he thanks his loyal Cornish subjects for their support against the Roundheads.

But what really takes the breath away is THE DAZZLING CARVING ON THE TUDOR PEWS, rich and sumptuous as icing on a chocolate cake. Cornish churches are renowned for their wood carvings and these are amongst the best. The first and last pews are decorated along their front and backs while the others, some 30 in all, are decorated at each end. The carvings show the Instruments of the Passion, such as the Crown of Thorns, the Nails of the Cross and the Thirty Pieces of Silver, and allegories of biblical stories, such as the Ascension (with Christ's feet disappearing into the clouds) and Easter Day, with Christ the gardener represented by a spade. There is not a human figure among them. It is great fun to go around the pews attempting to interpret the pictures, although the temples do start to throb after a while.

If you need to take a break then you could do worse that go out into the churchyard and have a look at the grave of the inventor, SIR GOLDSWORTHY GURNEY, Cornwall's forgotten genius (see opposite).

Morwenstow

St Morwenna's

'King James's men shall understand
What Cornish lads can do!
And have they fixed the where and when?
And shall Trelawny die?
Here's twenty thousand Cornish men
Will know the reason why!'
ROBERT STEPHEN HAWKER,
'The Song of the Western Men'

Everything peters out at the church here. The road peters out into a cliff path. Cornwall peters out into Devon, this being Cornwall's most northerly parish, and England peters out altogether, as there is no more land to the west between here and America, just ocean. This is the wild West Country, bare fields, tall, broken cliffs, Atlantic rollers, seagulls.

The robust, grey-pinnacled 15th-century tower of St Morwenna's peeps

Goldsworthy Gurney

Born at Treator near Padstow in 1793, GOLDSWORTHY GURNEY was a distant cousin of the Norfolk Gurneys, who founded what later became Barclays Bank, and so was wealthy enough to devote himself to science and invention. A meeting with fellow Cornishman, steam pioneer Richard Trevithick, fired his enthusiasm and his first invention was the blast-pipe, a high pressure steam jet (later adapted by George Stephenson for his Rocket) which he used to power a road-going steam engine with a passenger carriage in tow called a Gurney drag. In 1829 this travelled from London to Bath at an average speed of 15 mph (24 kph) in THE FIRST LONG JOURNEY BY A SELF-PROPELLED VEHICLE AT A SUSTAINED SPEED ANYWHERE IN THE WORLD. Gurney established a daily service between Cheltenham and Gloucester, THE WORLD'S FIRST REGULAR STEAM-PROPELLED COACH SERVICE, but was bankrupted when rival horse carriage owners forced the government to impose a ruinous tax on his enterprise.

Gurney returned to Cornwall and set about building himself a family home on the dunes of Bude beach, for which he devised a concrete raft to provide firm foundations. The result, BUDE CASTLE, still stands today, THE FIRST PERMANENT HOUSE IN THE WORLD EVER TO BE BUILT SUCCESSFULLY ON SHIFTING SANDS. His concrete raft technique is still widely used in the construction of some of the world's tallest buildings.

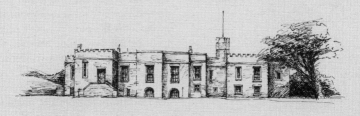

Gurney lit his new house with a new lighting system created by forcing a mixture of oxygen and hydrogen through a blowpipe to produce a hot flame and then adding lime to make the light burn especially bright – LIMELIGHT. Using just one limelight and a series of mirrors and lenses he was able to light the whole house, and he developed just such a set-up to light the Houses of Parliament in place of the thousands of candles required previously. His limelight was also used in a revolving frame to improve the intensity and visibility of lighthouses, saving thousands of lives, and in the theatre – the origin of the phrase to be 'in the limelight'.

Amongst his other inventions were the steam cleaner, ventilation systems for mines and sewers, and the Gurney stove for heating large buildings, still in use in Tewkesbury Abbey and Chester, Ely and Durham cathedrals. Indeed, we owe much of our modern world to the brilliant mind that lies in the churchyard of St Swithin's, Launcells.

out from a fold above a steep combe that runs down to the sea. There was a Celtic church here, from which comes the gorgeously primitive tub font, with carved cable moulding tied round the middle like a belt, that stands at the west end of the present building. You enter the church through a rugged Norman doorway sheltered by a rugged Norman porch, both having rugged Norman arches carved with any number of zigzags, flowers, pine cones and beasts, such as a mermaid, a dragon, a dolphin and a whale.

Three bays of the north arcade are Norman, consisting of some of Cornwall's best Norman arches, each adorned with many heads, including those of a monk, an antelope and a hippopotamus. One of the capitals of the Perpendicular south arcade is inscribed with the words, 'This is the House of the Lord', carved upside down so that it can be read by the angels in

Heaven. There are over one hundred medieval bench ends and a wealth of wonderfully carved wooden roofing.

On the north wall of the chancel are traces of a 15th-century wall painting, thought to be of the church's patron saint and founder MORWENNA, one of the many children of the 6th-century Celtic King Brychan who spread the Word throughout Cornwall.

A Poet Parson

In the south aisle is the HAWKER MEMORIAL WINDOW, dedicated in 1904 and showing Morwenstow's famous parson with his dog. ROBERT STEPHEN HAWKER was vicar of Morwenstow from 1834 until his death in 1875. When he arrived the church and parish had been long neglected. Remote and inaccessible, they were battered by Atlantic storms and populated mainly by smugglers and wreckers, who enjoyed rich pickings from the many ships that were cast on to the rocks of this merciless coastline. Hawker put a stop to the wreckers and made sure that seamen washed up on the shore were given a Christian burial in St Morwenna's churchyard. The figure-head of the *Caledonia*, wrecked on the coast in 1842 in the first major disaster of Hawker's tenancy, hangs on a wall inside the church as a memorial.

As well as his compassion Hawker is remembered for his eccentricities. He talked to the birds, wore fishermen's boots under his cassock, sometimes dressed up as a mermaid with seaweed for hair, took his pigs for long walks and brought his nine cats into church, excommunicating one of them for catching mice on a Sunday.

He built the nearby vicarage and modelled the chimneys on the towers of churches he had served: Tamerton, where he was curate, Welcombe, next door in Devon, Morwenstow, and the tower at Magdalen, his Oxford college.

One of his many accomplishments was THE INVENTION OF HARVEST FESTIVAL. In 1843, on 1 October, he invited his parishioners to a special service of Thanksgiving for the harvest, at which he served Communion bread made from the first cut of corn and for which he encouraged them to decorate the church with their home-grown produce. The idea was copied at other churches in Devon and Cornwall and then spread rapidly throughout England.

Hawker was also something of a poet and he built himself a small hut on the edge of the cliffs, made out of driftwood, where he could sit and meditate, 'communing with St Morwenna' (usually

while smoking opium). He even enter-tained fellow poets such as ALFRED, LORD TENNYSON and CHARLES KINGSLEY in his hut, which can still be reached via a path over the stile opposite the church porch. It is now looked after by the National Trust – THE SMALLEST PROP-ERTY OWNED BY THE NATIONAL TRUST.

Not far away, half-way down the Hennacliff, second tallest sheer cliff in England after Beachy Head, is MORWENNA'S WELL, a little stone dwelling where Morwenna lived in perfect isolation 1500 years ago. Until recently it was possible to reach it down a steep path with the help of a rope, but the way is now overgrown with brambles and it is almost inaccessible, except for those with a bit of local knowledge.

Trebetherick

St Enodoc's

Betjeman's Rest

St Enodoc's 12th-century church is plugged in a bunker in the middle of

a golf course, only its stubby, arthritic 13th-century stone spire peeking above the dunes that protect it from the sea. Not too long ago the church was full of sand and the vicar and congregation had to be lowered in through the roof to attend services. St Enodoc is an eternal part of the landscape and the spectacle from the top of the dunes of church and greensward, sand and sea, is one of those classic views of England that lift the heart.

It seems only fitting that the man who did more than most to save and celebrate the country churches of England should be buried here in one of the loveliest churchyards of them all.

The grave of SIR JOHN BETJEMAN (d.1984) is by the path near the lich-gate. His mother lies nearby and a memorial to his father is inside the church.

Also in the churchyard, in the far corner from the entrance gate, is a memorial tablet to FLEUR LOMBARD (1974–96), THE FIRST FEMALE FIRE-FIGHTER TO DIE IN CIVIL ACTION IN GREAT BRITAIN.

Standing on the seat in the south porch is the slate memorial of JOHN MABLY and his daughter ALICE, who died within days of each other in 1687. This is THE LAST KNOWN SLAB INCISED WITH EFFIGIES IN ENGLAND.

Well, I never knew this
about
CORNISH CHURCHES

St Endellion – St Endelienta's. 'St Endellion! St Endellion! The name is like a ring of bells,' said Sir John Betjeman. Music certainly to the ears of British Prime Minister David Cameron and his wife Samantha, who named their daughter FLORENCE ROSE ENDELLION after this Cornish village. They were on holiday near here when she was born. The large 15th-century Perpendicular village church of St Endelienta, a mile from the sea, is now famous as the home of two annual music festivals. St Endelienta was another of the daughters of the Celtic King Brychan (*see* Morwenstow).

St Just in Roseland – St Just & St Mawes. 'And did those feet in ancient time / Walk upon England's mountains green / And was the holy Lamb of God / On England's pleasant pastures seen . . .' Once you have experienced the magical atmosphere of this lovely 13th-century church, enveloped in sub-tropical gardens beside a dazzling blue creek on the River Fal, you may well find yourself susceptible to the legend that Jesus did indeed set foot on England's pleasant pastures, right here, while accompanying Joseph of Arimathea on one of his voyages to buy Cornish tin. There is a stone by the riverbank said to be the one on to which Jesus stepped when coming ashore.

Zennor – St Senara's. On a bench end in the chancel of St Senara's is a celebrated carving of a rather Rubenesque mermaid holding a mirror and a comb. She was a comely local girl who became infatuated with one of the choristers, a boy called Matthew, whom she lured down on to the beach at Pendour Cove and then out to sea. The two were never seen again, but their voices can be heard singing across the water when all is quiet.

CUMBRIA

Cartmel Priory – England's only angled church tower

Barton

St Michael's

Unknown Delight

This church is an undiscovered gem that seems to have passed many guidebooks by. It sits, with only farm buildings for company, on a small mound in the centre of a circular churchyard of prehistoric origins, down a minor lane just off the road from Penrith to Pooley Bridge north of Ullswater. Countless holiday makers must hurry past every summer, but St Michael's crouches low behind its screen of trees

and escapes all but the most fervent church seeker's eye, slumbering on in a kind of timeless glow.

The rewards for finding St Michael's are ample. The setting is Cumbrian scenery at its loveliest, with wide pastures, distant mountains and gleaming lakes. The church is pleasing to the eye with elegant lines and proportions, a view made all the more satisfying when you realise that you are looking at THE ONLY MEDIEVAL CHURCH IN CUMBRIA WITH A NORMAN CENTRAL TOWER. And what a tower, low and chunky and perfectly square, protruding from the body of the church like a vicar's head poking through a dog collar with shoulder pads.

Inside, the massive stone wall of the tower is pierced by a UNIQUE DOUBLE ARCH, formed of a narrow Norman arch below which has been set, not quite centrally, a broader 14th-century arch, the latter created when the chancel was extended beyond the tower. The effect is both eccentric and exhilarating and there is nothing quite like it in Cumbria. The evening light plays upon the scene through a west window by Charles Kempe.

To add to the atmosphere, St Michael's is full of memorials to relatives of the Lakeland poet WILLIAM WORDSWORTH, from his grandfather Richard, who lived in nearby Sockbridge Hall and was buried in the chancel in 1760, to his cousin John with his two wives Anne and Elizabeth, and Wordsworth's aunt Anne, who married the curate of Barton.

Brougham

St Ninian's, Ninekirks

Lost in Paradise

St Ninian's, the old parish church of Brougham, known by local people as 'Ninekirks', is not easy to find. A visit there requires stamina, sturdy walking boots, a map, a sense of adventure and a large bar of Kendal Mint Cake. The challenge begins at the car park, which lies hidden off a straight, fast-moving stretch of the A66 and requires precision and lightning reactions to reach without causing a pile-up. Once you are parked, however, the walk to the church will soothe the most shredded of nerves, for it passes along tranquil country paths through fields of cows and buttercups, with views of distant mountains. The track winds on and on above the slow, murmuring River Eamont until eventually, long after you have forgotten, or care, why you came, an old gate appears, the path drops down into a sunken field and there, on the far horizon, lost in trees and garlanded with wild flowers, is the sweetest church imaginable.

There has been a church here since Saxon times, but the Ninekirks we see today was made new in 1660, one of the few churches built during the Commonwealth under Oliver Cromwell. It is made of dark red sandstone, low and rugged with a crooked porch and a bellcote.

Inside is a revelation, an almost perfect, unaltered 17th-century country church interior, bathed in sunlight that pours in through clear glass windows. There are box pews made of oak, with those belonging to the squire and the more important families caged in with wooden screens. There is a double-deck pulpit, still with its canopy or 'tester'. In plaster above the altar is the date 1660 and the initials AP, standing for Anne Pembroke, otherwise known as Lady Anne Clifford, who lived at Brougham Hall and was responsible for saving the church. She inherited many northern estates and spent her later years restoring and improving them all. Of Ninekirks she said, 'It would in all likelyhood have fallen downe, it was soe ruinous, if it had not bin now repaired by me.' And all who come to this blessed spot are grateful to her.

In 1846, during repairs, the graves under the chancel were excavated and the bodies found of two Norman warrior knights, UDARD DE BROHAM, who died in 1185, and the six-foot giant GILBERT DE BROHAM, complete with the stirrups he used when fighting in Normandy with King John. Udard and Gilbert were reburied and lie beneath the chancel still.

Burgh by Sands

St Michael's

Two Towers

St Michael's is a Norman church with Saxon foundations and incorporates Roman stones from Hadrian's Wall, traces of which can still be seen in and around the village. The church actually stands on the site of the Roman fort of Aballava and looks north across marshes and the Solway Firth to Scotland.

EDWARD I knew this church well, stopping off here to pray before marching north to confront Robert the Bruce in 1307. You can still see the marks left by his men on the stones of the east end where they sharpened their arrows. The King returned sooner than he intended, for he died a few days later of dysentery, one mile to the north on Burgh Marsh, at a spot marked by a monument. His body lay in state in St Michael's before being taken back to London.

Not long afterwards the church was fortified against the avenging Scots with two mighty towers, one at the west end and one at the east end, THE ONLY CHURCH IN ENGLAND TO HAVE TWO FORTIFIED TOWERS. The east tower is hard to identify as it was reduced in the early 18th century and its thick walls no longer rise above the chancel roof. It is accessed through a door in the east wall to the right of the altar and is now used as a vestry. The west tower is strong as a castle, plain, squat and heavily battlemented with open belfry windows leaving the 600-year-old bells exposed to the elements. The entrance to it is guarded by a bolted iron door in the nave.

St John's Newton Arlosh

There are three notable fortified churches of the 14th century worth visiting in this border area of Cumbria, of which St Michael's is the earliest. The others are ST CUTHBERT'S AT GREAT SALKELD, 15 miles south of Carlisle, which has a pele tower built in 1380 with a narrow iron door at the entrance, and ST JOHN'S NEWTON ARLOSH, 10 miles west of Burgh by Sands, which also has a pele tower accessed through a very narrow doorway, less than three feet (1 m) wide.

Cartmel

Priory Church of St Mary & St Michael

A Different Angle

Undoubtedly the grandest parish church in Cumbria, Cartmel Priory lords it over a petite village nestled in a wooded valley amongst the secluded Furness hills, unaffected by time or bustle. The mountains of the Lake District rise to the north while the flat, shifting sands of Morecambe Bay lie to the south.

Cartmel will forever be celebrated for its unique 14th-century bell tower, set diagonally on the low central tower, THE ONLY BELFRY OF ANY CHURCH IN ENGLAND TO BE SET AT AN ANGLE TO THE TOWER ON WHICH IT SITS.

The Priory was founded as a house for Augustinian Canons in 1189 by William Marshall, later the Earl of Pembroke. He insisted that an altar within the church be given to the people of the village, and so a small chapel next to the chancel called the TOWN CHOIR was set aside for their use. When the priory was dissolved at the Reformation, the villagers were permitted to keep the Town Choir as their parish church and the building was saved from destruction, although the roof was stripped from the main body.

Plenty of good work survives from the Norman church. There is a splendid deeply recessed Norman south doorway of round arches and pillars, while the richly decorated round arches of the chancel rest on mighty Norman piers. High above the Norman arcade a lovely 13th-century arcade runs around the walls. The glorious east window, 45 feet (13.7 m) high and 24 feet (7.3 m) wide, is 15th century and retains some fragments of medieval stained glass.

The seats of the 15TH-CENTURY OAK CHOIR STALLS have superb MISERICORDS displaying carvings of various creatures, a mermaid, a dragon, a peacock, a monkey, a unicorn, a Green Man, an elephant and castle. The bench ends are weathered by the wind and rain having spent 83 years under the open sky while the church was roofless after the Dissolution. The roof was repaired in 1620 at the expense of George Preston of nearby Holker Hall. Preston also provided the MAGNIFICENT FLEMISH OAK SCREEN that surrounds three sides of the chancel. Rambling vines laden with grapes climb the posts, the frieze abounds with animals and foliage, the panels are filled with latticework and tracery. It is considered ONE OF THE MOST SUPERLATIVE PIECES OF 17TH-CENTURY RENAISSANCE WOODWORK TO BE FOUND IN ANY CHURCH IN ENGLAND.

Filling a small arch between the sanctuary and the Town Choir is the EXTRAORDINARY AND UNIQUE DECORATED TOMB OF LORD HARRINGTON who died in 1347. He lies in chain mail beside his wife, a lion at his feet, while above them rises a stone screen alive with mourners and angels bowing over the effigies and stroking their faces, while more carved figures gaze heavenwards from the roof of the tomb.

In the north aisle there is a memorial in gleaming white Carrara marble to LORD FREDERICK CAVENDISH, whose family still own Holker Hall. Chief Secretary for Ireland in William Gladstone's government, he was assassinated by terrorists in Phoenix Park, Dublin, in 1882.

The priory has a noted library and owns a RARE 1596 FIRST EDITION OF EDMUND SPENSER'S FAERIE QUEENE, which was stolen in 1929 but eventually recovered in Suffolk and is now in the library of Lancaster University.

But perhaps the oddest antiquity owned by the priory is one of the very FIRST UMBRELLAS KNOWN IN ENGLAND. Dating from 1760, it has a painted canvas cover and oak ribs and was used for sheltering the vicar from the rain during funerals.

St Bees

Priory Church of St Mary & St Bega

The Power of Snow

This is the story of THE ONLY TWO CHURCHES IN ENGLAND DEDICATED TO ST BEGA, an Irish princess of the 9th century who was forced to flee her homeland to avoid a forced marriage. She sailed single-handed across the Irish Sea and landed on the Cumberland coast below St Bees Head, where she petitioned the local landowner, Lord Egremont, for land on which to establish a religious community. Now he was a canny chap and promised her that she could have as much land as

was covered with snow the following day – Midsummer Day. Picture his dismay when he woke up next morning to find a huge chunk of his land deep in snow. Nonetheless, he kept his word and allowed St Bega to build her nunnery.

In 1120 a later Lord Egremont founded a Benedictine priory at St Bees on the site of St Bega's original nunnery. The dark red sandstone Benedictine priory church he built still dominates the tiny village from every direction. Church and village both huddle in the lee of ST BEES HEAD, THE WESTERN-MOST POINT OF NORTHERN ENGLAND and THE ONLY SIGNIFICANT SEA CLIFF BETWEEN WALES AND SCOTLAND, and stand aloof from the huge caravan parks that litter the nearby coastline. Much of the priory was destroyed at the Dissolution although the cruciform priory church was spared and became the parish church of St Bees. It was much restored in the 19th century by William Butterfield but retains some splendid Norman pillars in the spacious nave and THE FINEST NORMAN DOORWAY IN CUMBERLAND, at the west end, with four glorious arches carved with chevrons and beakheads of men and serpents. Outside the west door, forming the lintel of an alcove in the wall of the vicarage garden, is a relic from the original nunnery, a carved stone known as the BEOWULF STONE, which shows an armoured figure battling a snarling dragon.

Inside the church are some exceptional modern treasures. THE VISION

OF ST BEGA in the Lady Chapel is a sensuous tableau consisting of a statue of St Bega kneeling in supplication to a statue of the Virgin Mary, sculpted by JOSEFINA DE VASCONCELLOS, a renowned artist from Brazil who lived in Cumbria and was at one time the world's oldest living artist. She died in 2005 at the age of 101. She was also the inspiration for the SLEEPING CHILD GARDEN in the priory grounds, where three of her sculptures of sleeping children are displayed.

School Screen

Back inside the priory, inserted between the nave and the chancel, is an astonishing ART NOUVEAU SCREEN BY WILLIAM BUTTERFIELD, a feast of soaring, swirling metalwork that fills the chancel arch with red and gold. The original chancel, noted for its fine lancet windows, was blocked off at the Reformation and is now part of St Bees School, alma mater of such luminaries as EDWARD CHRISTIAN, brother of the *Bounty* mutineer Fletcher Christian, CAPTAIN WILLIAM LEEFE ROBINSON, who won a VC in 1916 for being the first to shoot down an airship over Britain, and the comic actor and creator of Mr Bean, ROWAN ATKINSON.

The beach at St Bees is where Alfred Wainwright's Coast to Coast Walk begins, while the priory is the starting point of ST BEGA'S WAY, a 36-mile walk linking the two St Bega's churches, at St Bees and Bassenthwaite Lake.

Bassenthwaite

St Bega's

'The bold Sir Bedivere uplifted him,
Sir Bedivere, the last of all his knights,
And bore him to a chapel nigh the field,
A broken chancel with a broken cross,
That stood on a dark strait of barren land'
From *Morte d'Arthur* by
ALFRED, LORD TENNYSON

Alfred, Lord Tennyson, set the opening of his poem 'Morte d'Arthur' here at the little chapel of St Bega's, 'nigh the field' on the east bank of Bassenthwaite Lake. He wrote much of the poem while staying at MIREHOUSE, the big grey mansion that can be seen from the church through the trees, and used Bassenthwaite Lake as inspiration for the scene where Sir Bedivere throws King Arthur's sword Excalibur into the lake. On summer evenings members of the Tennyson Society give occasional readings of 'Morte d'Arthur' in a small open-air theatre by the lake below the church.

The setting of St Bega's is certainly bewitching and it is likely that St Bega herself chose this secluded, magical spot as a place to retire to in her later years. She may even be buried here – there is certainly no other reason for a church to be here. It stands alone, near the water's edge, in a lush water meadow with a little stream running by, encircled by a stone wall and looking very small beneath the great grey bulk of Ullock Pike. And it can only be reached on foot, via a farm track leading through fields full of sheep.

The church we see today, which was sympathetically restored in 1874, is mainly Norman, with signs of some early Saxon stonework and also some large uneven stones in the walls that could be Roman, meaning that the present building probably stands on the site of a much earlier construction.

Inside there are two delightfully crooked arches that appear to be pre-Norman, a 13th-century font, and the royal coat of arms of George II hanging above the doorway, put there in 1745 apparently to reassure the local people of their loyalty to the Hanoverian king. There are also a number of memorial windows and tablets to the Spedding family, who have lived at the nearby Mirehouse for over 200 years.

This is one of England's most romantic churches and it is hardly surprising that the poet Wordsworth featured St Bega's in his *Guide to the English Lakes*.

Wasdale Head

St Olaf's

Superlative in Every Way

ST OLAF'S, in the Lake District's far west, is ENGLAND'S SMALLEST PARISH CHURCH, if you count the number of parishioners, which was 24 when I visited in the spring of 2013. It stands all by itself behind a clump of yew trees in a green, green meadow at the head of ENGLAND'S DEEPEST LAKE, WASTWATER, up to 258 feet (79 m) deep, surrounded by ENGLAND'S HIGHEST MOUNTAINS, in an area that has been voted 'BRITAIN'S FAVOURITE VIEW'. On a fine day, which is rare and precious in these parts, the setting is sumptuous.

The church is a long, low, grey building dug into the turf, with a roof of enormous slate tiles that almost touches the ground, and it might be mistaken for a school-room or a croft were it not for the tiny bellcote. It is thought to date from 1550 but there are roof beams inside that may have come from a Viking longship, indicating that this has been a place of worship for 1,000 years or more. In fact, standing inside St Olaf's is a bit like standing in an upturned boat, with its sloping walls, V-shaped roof of wooden beams and jumble of wooden pews. And the whole place seems to rock gently in the swell. It is most soothing.

Etched on to one of the tiny diamond-shaped window panes is an image of NAPES NEEDLE, a dramatic, 65 ft (20 m) high pillar of rock on the flank of GREAT GABLE, one of the mountains that looms above the church. Below the image are the words from Psalm 121, 'I will lift up mine eyes unto the hills, from whence cometh my strength'. It serves as a memorial to the members of the Fell and Rock Climbing Club who gave their lives in the First World War and is said to be THE SMALLEST INSCRIBED GLASS WINDOW IN ENGLAND.

Along the window sills are brass memorial plaques to climbers who have perished in the mountains, not just in the Lake District, but all over the world. Wasdale Head is regarded as the 'BIRTHPLACE OF ROCK CLIMBING' – in the 19th century the world's first sporting rock climbers came here to practise on the challenging rocks of Great Gable and Scafell Pike, and in 1886 W.P. HASKETT SMITH, known as the FATHER OF ROCK CLIMBING, made a solo ascent of Napes Needle in what is regarded as THE WORLD'S FIRST OFFICIAL SPORTING ROCK CLIMB.

Outside in the tiny churchyard are the graves of some of those who died on the surrounding fells, which are more treacherous than they look. Also there is ALEXANDRA WILSON, who died in 1947, the last teacher in Wasdale Head.

Well, I never knew this about

CUMBRIAN CHURCHES

Aldingham – St Cuthbert's. What a location for a church, on the edge of the world, with the waters of windy Morecambe Bay lapping against the churchyard walls, the Lake District and the Lancashire Fells frowning across the choppy sea, a sinister Victorian Gothic mansion looming in the background. Most of the village was washed away on a tidal wave in 1553, but the sturdy 12th-century Norman church with its 15th-century tower stood its ground. A Norman font survives along with some rugged round pillars in the nave and a WONDERFULLY CROOKED CHANCEL ARCH – not, it is claimed, the result of subsidence or poor construction, but because it represents the head of Christ leaning in prayer. Five hundred years before even this ancient building was made, the monks of Lindisfarne brought St Cuthbert's relics here, seeking safe haven from the marauding Vikings. They chose a lovely spot.

Bolton – All Saints. Approached along an avenue of yew bushes, this small Norman church enjoys a delightful setting above the River Eden and flaunts a number of curious features. Filling the Norman chancel arch inside is a most UNUSUAL WOODEN SCREEN OF EXQUISITE OPEN TRACERY. Outside, the stone figure of a lady who once lay upon a 14th-century coffin lid stands in the wall next to the Norman south doorway, which itself has a capital carved with a crude picture of a man wielding a hammer and an axe. But the most extraordinary item of all can be found in the outer wall, above the blocked-up north doorway, a wonderfully vivid sculpture of two jousting knights in helmets and chain mail, one bearing a shield and lance, the other a lance and banner, all of a style as used in the 12th century. An almost unreadable inscription on a stone next to it would seem to suggest that the sculpture is a gift to the church to commemorate a local tournament. It is THE ONLY SCULPTURE OF AN ACTUAL JOUST TO BE FOUND ON ANY COUNTRY CHURCH IN ENGLAND.

Boltongate – All Saints. Gazing across the River Ellen at Skiddaw far to the south, All Saints was built by the Earl of Westmorland in about 1400 on the site of a Norman church. The setting is picturesque and the church attractive, but this in no way prepares you for the sensational interior, where you will find yourself standing in awe beneath THE ONLY STONE BARREL-VAULTED CHURCH ROOF IN ENGLAND. Supported by massive, thick walls and rising in a high pointed arch, the nave was built this way for defence against attack and fire. In the south wall there is a window by Charles Kempe.

Brampton – St Martin's. Commissioned by the Earl of Carlisle St Martin's is THE ONLY CHURCH EVER DESIGNED BY THE FATHER OF ARTS AND CRAFTS ARCHITECTURE PHILIP WEBB. It is especially noted for its 12 dazzling windows by Edward Burne-Jones.

Bridekirk – St Bridget's. Built in 1868, St Bridget's stands beside the ruins of the Norman church it replaced. A fine tympanum bearing the carved head of Christ was rescued from the old building and now sits above the south door of the new church. Inside is perhaps THE FINEST NORMAN STONE FONT IN ENGLAND, carved on four sides and THE ONLY FONT IN ENGLAND KNOWN TO HAVE A DEPICTION OF THE SCULPTOR HIMSELF ON IT. He is shown working with his hammer and chisel along with the runic inscription 'Richard he me wrought, and to this beauty me brought'. 'Richard' is thought to be the famous 12th-century sculptor Richard of Durham. On the other sides of the font are shown the baptism of Christ, the expulsion of

Adam and Eve from the Garden of Eden, and various animals and beasts. All the carvings display the influence of an older Nordic design. It is a stunning piece.

Warwick on Eden – St Leonard's. Embowered in trees and tucked away at the end of a lane close to the bridge over the Eden, this little red sandstone Norman church boasts a fine chancel arch of about 1130 with enormous capitals and a rare rounded apse. The outer wall of the apse is decorated with projecting pilaster strips and arches, a common feature in Europe, but as seen here it is THE ONLY EXAMPLE OF SUCH A DESIGN ON A MEDIEVAL ENGLISH CHURCH.

DERBYSHIRE

St John the Baptist, Tideswell – the largest country church in England

Ashover

All Saints

All Sorts of Treasures

Ashover is rightly proud of its slender OCTAGONAL CHURCH SPIRE, 128 feet (39 m) high and a prominent landmark in the lovely Amber valley. It was built by THOMAS BABINGTON in 1417 to celebrate his safe return, and that of the men of Ashover, from the Battle of Agincourt. The inn beside the church is named the Crispin Inn after St Crispin upon whose day, 25 October, the battle was fought.

A later Thomas Babington, who provided All Saints with its fine wooden rood screen and died in 1518, is buried inside the church by the chancel in a superb alabaster tomb regarded as THE BEST 16TH-CENTURY TOMB IN DERBYSHIRE. All Saints also boasts a Norman font of about 1150, which is THE ONLY LEAD FONT IN DERBYSHIRE AND ONE OF ONLY 30 LEAD FONTS IN ALL OF ENGLAND. This one is UNIQUE IN THAT THE INSIDE IS MADE OF STONE, while all the others are of solid lead or are made of stone outside with a lead lining. It was saved from destruction during the Civil War by being buried in the rector's kitchen garden.

Hanging in the tower is a bell that bears an inscription saying that it 'rung the downfall of Bonaparte and broke April 1814', THE ONLY BELL IN ENGLAND THAT BEARS THE NAME OF NAPOLEON BONAPARTE.

Across the road from All Saints, the BASSETT ROOMS commemorate the BASSETT SISTERS, members of the family who produced BASSETT'S LIQUORICE ALLSORTS and who were great benefactors of the church. The liquorice recipe that is used in Liquorice Allsorts was first mixed in Ashover.

Hathersage

St Michael's

Jane Eyre and Little John

This handsome 14th-century church stands high above the village, its spire a prominent landmark for miles around. Of special note is the imposing east window, which is by Charles Kempe and was salvaged from Derwent Chapel before it was submerged beneath the waters of the nearby Ladybower Reservoir.

Over the church porch are the arms of the EYRES, lords of the manor here for 800 years or more, while inside there is a fine array of brasses commemorating them. Particularly endearing is the brass above the altar tomb of ROBERT AND JOAN EYRE in the chancel, which shows their son Robert and his wife kneeling, with their four sons lined up on their knees behind them.

In 1845 CHARLOTTE BRONTË attended services here while staying in the old vicarage next to the church with her friend Ellen Nussey, whose brother had just become the new vicar of Hathersage. There seems no doubt that she found the name for her heroine JANE EYRE here and used many local landmarks for the places in her novel. Hathersage became Morton, while NORTH LEES HALL, an atmospheric Elizabethan tower house on the edge of the village that was a seat of the Eyres, became Mr Rochester's Thornfield Hall. Henry Nussey, the vicar, is almost certainly the kind clergyman St John Rivers who rescues Jane Eyre when she is destitute.

In the churchyard, beside an old yew tree, there is a large grave reputed to be that of Robin Hood's giant right-hand man LITTLE JOHN, whose cap and bow once hung in the church and who, it is said, lived in a cottage that stood near the church. A thigh bone nearly three feet (1 m) long was found in the grave, indicating that the man who is buried there would have been nearly eight feet (2.5 m) tall.

North Lees Hall

Repton

St Wystan's

'Holy air encased in stone'
Sir John Betjeman

Repton speaks to us from before the dawn of England. Today, it is a serene middle English village slumbering by Trent water meadows, a reassuringly tranquil scene of mellow cottages, church and school. Thirteen hundred years ago, it was the capital of Mercia the most powerful Saxon kingdom of the day and a cradle of English Christianity, for Repton's market cross marks the spot where, in AD 653, King Peada, son of the powerful pagan King Penda, was converted to Christianity.

Repton's school, partly housed in old priory buildings, has been a seat of learning since Tudor days and forms a graceful backdrop to St Wystan's Church, the needle spire of which, 212 feet (64.6 m) high, soars above one of England's most thrilling and precious ancient places.

The main body of the church is spacious and light with lofty 13th-century arcades leading to an 11th-century Saxon chancel illuminated by a huge Decorated east window. Either side of the chancel, steps lead down to perhaps THE OLDEST UNALTERED PLACE OF CHRISTIAN WORSHIP IN ENGLAND, a tiny, exquisite crypt made up of vaults supported by eight grooved pilasters, and four pillars decorated with barley sugar swirls based on the design of the pillars that held up the canopy of St Peter's tomb in Rome. Pevsner describes it as 'the most perfect example of Anglo-Saxon architecture on a small scale now extant'.

The original bare structure was built in about AD 750 as a royal mausoleum for KING ETHELBALD OF MERCIA, who was laid to rest here in AD 757. The columns and vaulting were installed some 80 years later by KING WIGLAF, who was also interred here after his death in AD 840. The custom was for the bodies to be buried in the soil until the flesh had rotted away and then for the skull and bones to be put in a mortuary casket and placed on a shelf in one of the recesses of the crypt.

In AD 850, Wiglaf's grandson WYSTAN, to whom the church is dedicated, was murdered by his own body-guard before he could inherit the crown of Mercia and was buried in the crypt. Miracles were ascribed to his remains and the crypt became a place of pilgrimage. The two staircases were

constructed at that time to allow for large numbers of pilgrims to pass easily through the chamber, in through one door and out the other. Wystan was later made a saint and his relics were moved to the abbey at Evesham by King Canute in the 11th century.

Guarding the northern staircase to the crypt is the 14th-century alabaster effigy of SIR ROBERT FRANCES, who was the lord of the nearby manor of Foremark.

All Rounder

Buried in the churchyard is one of Repton School's most distinguished old boys C.B. FRY (1872–1956), described as ENGLAND'S GREATEST SPORTING ALL-ROUNDER. He played soccer for England, appeared in an FA Cup Final for Southampton FC, played rugby for the Barbarians, held the world record for the long jump in 1893 and captained the England cricket team, never losing a Test Match and scoring six centuries in successive innings. He was also offered the throne of Albania.

Youlgreave

All Saints

Derbyshire's Finest Perpendicular Tower

The majestic, battlemented church of All Saints sits right at the heart of this busy, straggling village, forcing tourist traffic to zigzag around it. Its princely 100 FT (30 M) HIGH-PINNACLED

Recently discovered near Repton's church is a mass grave containing the bones of men from the Viking invasion force known as the GREAT HEATHEN ARMY, which set up a winter camp at Repton during its conquest of Mercia in AD 873/4. Repton is THE ONLY PLACE IN ENGLAND WHERE SUCH AN ENCAMPMENT HAS BEEN FOUND.

The Great Heathen Army was a Viking army of some two to three thousand men led by Ivar the Boneless, which originated in Denmark and invaded England in AD 865. The army landed in East Anglia and from there pillaged its way across England, conquering Northumbria and Mercia. They were eventually stopped in the south by King Alfred the Great at the Battle of Ethandun in AD 878.

PERPENDICULAR TOWER dominates the scenery, summoning visitors down from the Peaks to sample its delights, which are considerable. The wide, late Norman nave is flanked with round pillars and carved capitals, carrying round arches to the south and pointed arches to the north. The oak roof is 15th century. The beautiful east window is by BURNE-JONES.

Right in the middle of the chancel, placed so that newly wed couples must separate and pass either side as they process down the aisle, is an EXQUISITE MINIATURE ALABASTER TOMB adorned with angels and crowned with the recumbent figure of a knight in plate armour. His feet rest on a lion while his head rests on a cockerel, the pertinent crest of the Cokayne family. He is THOMAS COKAYNE of Harthill Hall, who died in 1488 after a fight with another fellow over a family matter. Since he died before his father, Thomas's effigy is made smaller than life-size, just three and a half feet (a metre and a bit) long.

On the north side of the sanctuary is the 14th-century tomb of Thomas's ancestor SIR JOHN ROSSINGTON, who married a Cokayne and died in 1325. He is shown cross-legged and holding a heart in his hands.

Behind the altar at the east wall of the north aisle is a remarkable monument to ROBERT GYLBERT, who died in 1492. It is a stunning piece of medieval artwork, an alabaster panel showing Gylbert and his seven sons facing his wife and ten daughters with the Virgin Mary standing between them holding the Holy Child.

On the wall of the north aisle is a memorial to SIR ROGER ROWE, who died in 1613, showing him kneeling in prayer opposite his wife, who wears a tall hat. Below them are effigies of their six sons and two daughters, all in Elizabethan ruffs.

Also in the north aisle is a window containing fragments of medieval glass collected from the ruined cathedral at Ypres, by the brother of a man who died at Gallipoli.

In the wall of the north arcade,

opposite the entrance, there is a small STONE CARVING OF A FIGURE WITH A CENTRE PARTING, holding a staff. Thought to be a pilgrim, he is possibly a remnant from a previous Saxon church.

Unique Font

Last, but certainly not least, is YOULGREAVE'S UNIQUE TREASURE, actually the first thing you see as you enter the church by the south door. It is a ROUND FONT FROM THE 12TH CENTURY

WITH A SMALL STOUP PROJECTING FROM THE SIDE, supported by a salamander, all carved from the same block of sandstone. It is THE ONLY FONT LIKE IT IN ENGLAND.

Well, I never knew this about

DERBYSHIRE CHURCHES

Dale Abbey – All Saints. Is that a Tudor cottage or a 13th-century chapel, set against the hillside of this beautiful deep green valley? Hard to tell, since they are all of a piece. In fact the cottage was originally the infirmary of Dale Abbey, founded here in the 12th century, to which was attached the infirmary chapel. Not quite the smallest church in England since it has an aisle, All Saints nonetheless has THE SMALLEST NAVE IN ENGLAND, with room for just three pews. A gallery for the infirm from next door runs around the nave. There are traces of a wall painting showing two saints in an embrace, probably Mary and Elizabeth. The chancel barely contains a pulpit that leans drunkenly out from the wall, an altar, a desk and a 'Bishop's Throne' given

in 1824 by Earl Stanhope, who called this place his 'little cathedral'. It is said that Dale is where ALLAN-A-DALE, the wandering minstrel of Robin Hood's band of merry men, was married by Friar Tuck to his sweetheart Ellen.

Dethick – St John the Baptist. In 1856 the bell of this lovely 13th-century church, set on a ridge high above the

Derwent valley, rang out from its tall tower to welcome home FLORENCE NIGHTINGALE, the most talked-about woman in the world, as she returned from the Crimea to her childhood home LEA HURST, in the nearby village of Holloway. Almost 300 years before that, in 1561, the bell had rung out from that same tower to celebrate the birth of an heir to one of Derbyshire's great families, the Babingtons, who lived in the manor house below. Alas, the ANTHONY BABINGTON whose arrival the bell saluted was destined to bring his family to ruin. In 1586 he became THE LAST ENGLISHMAN TO BE HUNG, DRAWN AND QUARTERED, executed for his leading role in the Babington plot to murder Elizabeth I and put Mary Queen of Scots on the throne. So distressed was Queen Elizabeth by the horror of Babington's death that she decreed that such a means of execution should be banished for ever.

Foremark – St Saviour's. This little church, THE FIRST CHURCH TO BE BUILT IN ENGLAND AFTER THE RESTORATION, is DERBYSHIRE'S BEST KEPT SECRET. It sits at the end of a farm track in the grounds of the Palladian FOREMARK HALL, built in 1760 by SIR ROBERT BURDETT, ancestor of the philanthropist Baroness Burdett-Coutts, and now the home of Repton Preparatory School. St Saviour's Church was constructed in 1662 by SIR FRANCYS BURDETT, and its gorgeous 17th-century interior is little changed, with iron altar rails by ROBERT BAKEWELL, wooden box pews, wood panelling along the walls, a high three-decker pulpit and tester

and an extraordinary pedimented wooden chancel screen, the latter probably Victorian.

Anchor Church. A short walk through woods from St Saviour's brings you to Anchor Church, a hermit's cell cut into the rocks above Black Pool, by the River Trent. Local tradition has it that this was the cell of St Hardulph of Breedon, in Leicestershire (*see* page 164), who hid himself away here during the reign of the pagan King Penda of Mercia (AD 625–55). In the 18th century the Burdetts of Foremark Hall used the caves as a summerhouse for parties and picnics.

Norbury – St Mary & St Barlock. There is no scene as English as this, a heavenly church set beside a 14th-century stone hall and Tudor manor house, all embowered in trees on the banks of that most English of rivers, the Dove. The church is oddly but beautifully formed, its 15th-century western half appearing symmetrical when viewed from the south, with a small graceful tower rising above the central south porch. The eastern half is the earliest part of the church and is made up of a large and lofty 14th-century chancel, with four huge Decorated windows on each side filled with THE FINEST COLLECTION OF MEDIEVAL GLASS IN DERBYSHIRE. It is justly described as a 'lantern in stone'. Inside, in the chancel, are the superb and immaculate chest tombs of SIR NICHOLAS AND SIR RALPH FITZHERBERT, LORDS OF NORBURY, considered amongst THE BEST ALABASTER TOMBS IN ENGLAND. Sir Nicholas, who died in 1473, wears the White Lion pendant of Edward IV, while his son Sir Ralph, who died in 1483, wears that of Richard III, THE ONLY SURVIVING REPRESENTATION OF RICHARD III'S WHITE BOAR PENDANT IN ANY CHURCH IN ENGLAND.

ROBERT EVANS, father of the novelist GEORGE ELIOT, was born near Norbury, at Roston Common, sang in the choir at Norbury church, and is buried in the churchyard along with his wife and his parents.

Tideswell – St John the Baptist. Standing high in the Peak District, 1,000 feet (300 m) above the sea, the majestic 14th-century Decorated church of St John is reputed to be THE LARGEST COUNTRY CHURCH IN ENGLAND and is known as the CATHEDRAL OF THE PEAK.

St Mary & St Barlock, Norbury

Devon

St Pancras, Widecombe in the Moor, Cathedral of the Moors

Brentor

St Michael's

England's Highest Church

The views from Brentor are arguably THE WIDEST AND MOST SPECTACULAR FROM ANY CHURCHYARD IN ENGLAND, with Bodmin Moor and half of Cornwall to the west, Exmoor to the north, Whitsand Bay to the south and, to the east, bleak Dartmoor, a vast panorama of green and gold rising majestically to a tor-strewn skyline – Devon, lush and wild all around. Joyous and uplifting on a clear summer's day, romantic and mysterious as the sun is setting, terrifying and yet exhilarating as the mist descends and the driving rain stings your face and the wind howls.

St Michael de Rupe sits right on top of a volcanic cone, on the edge of a precipice, at a height of 1,110 feet (338 m) above sea level, THE HIGHEST WORKING CHURCH IN ENGLAND.

Churches on heights are often dedicated to St Michael, the Chief of Angels, with perhaps the most famous being St Michael's Mount, near Penzance on the south Cornish coast.

Legend tells us that this St Michael's was built by a rich merchant rescued at sea, who vowed to build a church on the most prominent piece of land he saw on his safe return to Plymouth. Church and tor are certainly a distinctive landmark for miles around, in particular for sailors coming into Plymouth Sound – how Drake and Raleigh, Gilbert and Grenville must have been cheered to see St Michael's distant embattled tower welcoming them home from their adventures.

The first church was actually put here by SIR ROBERT GIFFORD, in 1130 – and he was indeed a wealthy merchant, so there could be some truth in the story. It is certainly an ancient site, with the remnants of an Iron Age fort scattered around the foot of the tor. During one of many renovations a number of skeletons were found under the church floor, laid north to south, indicating that this was a pagan burial place.

The church as we see it today is mainly 13th-century and measures only 37 feet (11 m) by 15 feet (4.6 m), making it one of ENGLAND'S TEN SMALLEST CHURCHES. The walls are solid and thick, a fortress against the elements. It is astonishing how quiet it is inside and how cosy and secure beneath the low roof beams. St Michael himself watches over the church from the modern east window.

There are still services held at St Michael's in the summer. It is a steep climb to get there, even for the casual visitor, but how much more so for the bride at her wedding, the mother carrying her baby to be christened or the coffin bearers at a funeral. Their reward is a matchless view and an unforgettable experience.

Sheepstor

St Leonard's

White Rajahs

The little 15th-century granite church of St Leonard, on the southern edge of Dartmoor, lies right beneath the granite tor that gives the village its name. This

is quintessential Devon, but there is also a whisper of the romantic East about the place. Hanging on a wall inside the church is a Pua Kumba or ceremonial cotton blanket, a gift from the Malaysian state of Sarawak to the final resting place of Sir James Brooke, Charles Brooke and Charles Vyner Brooke, the three legendary White Rajahs of Sarawak, who are buried in the churchyard.

James Brooke (1803–68), born of Devon stock, was a British East India Company officer who helped quash an uprising against Sarawak's ruler, the Sultan of Brunei, and in return was granted the title Rajah of Sarawak. Under his rule, which lasted 26 years from 1842 until his death, Sarawak prospered, with Brooke overseeing the suppression of slavery and piracy and developing trade. He was succeeded by his nephew Charles Brooke (1829–1917), who founded schools, parliamentary government and railways, and who was in turn succeeded by his own son

Charles Vyner Brooke (1874–1963). Sarawak was occupied by the Japanese during the Second World War, after which, much against the will of Charles Vyner Brooke, it became a British colony. Granted independence in 1963, it is now part of the Federation of Malaysia.

A window in the south wall of St Leonard's was donated by the Association of the Sarawak Civil Servants in memory of those from Sarawak who died in the Second World War, and shows a pitcher plant from Sarawak and a butterfly, Papilio Brooklana, named after James Brooke.

Staverton

St Paul de Leon

A Village Cathedral

This is a huge and lovely church in a small and lovely village. In medieval times Staverton drew its congregation

from a multitude of small farming communities that were dotted about the surrounding countryside, and would have been packed every Sunday. Its big, empty spaces are harder to fill in these modern times.

It is THE ONLY CHURCH IN ENGLAND DEDICATED TO ST PAUL DE LEON, a 6th-century Welsh-born saint who was one of the founders of the Celtic nation of Brittany, and apparently lived to be 140 years old. He sailed up the River Dart and constructed a wooden church here, above a crossing place on the river. This was replaced by a Norman stone church, which almost fell down through neglect. In the 14th century the villagers were scolded for this by the Bishop and told to build a new church – they built what was almost a cathedral just to spite him.

The church we see today is splendid and stately and looks as though it has been here for ever. A rare feature is an outside brass, set in the south wall of the chancel, in memory of John Rowe. The narrow, square tower rises 70 feet (21 m), tapering slightly towards the top. A tiny statue of St Paul de Leon occupies a little niche above the entrance to the embattled porch, which has a priest's room above it.

The interior is cavernous, and dominated by one of THE FINEST 15TH-CENTURY WOODEN ROOD SCREENS IN ENGLAND, which stretches across the whole width of the church and is 57 feet (17 m) long – THE THIRD LONGEST SCREEN IN ENGLAND, after Uffcumbe in Devon (67 feet/20 m) and Dunster in Somerset (58 feet/18 m). It was beautifully restored in the 19th century and a replica of the gallery destroyed in the 17th century was put back. The carving across the whole screen and gallery is superb.

On the north wall of the Worth Chapel, now an organ chamber, is a delightful monument of the Worth family of 1629, unusually showing the eight Worth children kneeling or standing *above* their parents. This handsome treasure is easily overlooked as it is tucked away in a corner, but should not be missed.

Indeed, St Paul de Leon as a whole should not be missed. It is a sublime example of the kind of country church, unpretentious and yet full of history and unexpected treasure, that makes England so seductive.

Torbryan

Holy Trinity

A Gallery of the Saints

Another mighty Devon village church, this time with no village at all, just the old church house next door, now an inn, both of them lost down a tangle of deep Devon lanes. Holy Trinity was built in less than 20 years, between 1450 and 1470, and is a superb example of undiluted Perpendicular architecture, tall,

elegant windows with fine tracery and a high, powerful tower of three stages, with five-sided stair turret, emerging dramatically out of a hidden fold.

The porch, which sports its own outside stair turret, has a rare and gorgeous stone roof with fan vaulting and angels carved on the ribs. Inside, unexpectedly and thrillingly, is THE BEST-PRESERVED MEDIEVAL ROOD SCREEN IN ENGLAND. Dating from the 15th century, it covers the whole width of the church and on its panels are painted 40 of the saints, including a rare depiction of ST CATHERINE OF SIENA.

The intricate carving of the screen is reflected in the fine tracery of the windows, some of which still retain their lovely 15th-century stained glass, showing angels and saints and shields. The screen and glass were saved from Puritanical destruction by the rector here during the Civil War, EDWARD GOSEWELL, who whitewashed the screen and hid the glass until after the Restoration. He is buried with his father, who preceded him as rector, in front of the altar.

In the 19th century parts of another old screen were used to make the red and gold painted pulpit, while the original pulpit was made into an altar. Rising out of the 15th-century benches, which have been encased as box pews, are elegant arcades of Beer stone with exquisitely carved capitals. All is watched over by a nicely curved wagon roof.

In August 2013 this beautiful church was desecrated when thieves hacked out and stole two of the screen panels, leaving ugly gaps and at the same time damaging a third panel. It is feared that the panels, which show St Victor of Marseilles and St Margaret, have disappeared abroad for ever. Iconoclasts are with us still.

Widecombe in the Moor

St Pancras

'Tom Pearce, Tom Pearce,
lend me your grey mare.
All along, down along, out along lea.
For I want for to go to Widecombe Fair,
With Bill Brewer, Jan Stewer,
Peter Gurney, Peter Davy,
Dan'l Whiddon, Harry Hawke,
Old Uncle Tom Cobley and all,
Old Uncle Tom Cobley and all'

Devon folk have been coming to WIDECOMBE FAIR, held annually in September in the lee of the great church of St Pancras, CATHEDRAL OF THE MOORS, since at least as far back as 1850, and probably for centuries before that. Church and village nestle in a deep green vale ringed by desolate moorland hills. From the top of the surrounding heights, the distant view

of the landmark Perpendicular tower, 135 feet (41 m) high to the tips of its pinnacles and rising out of a comfortable patch of trees, is one of the most stirring sights in Devon, a beacon promising welcome and refuge from the hardships of the moor.

The church was first built in the 15th century, constructed from locally mined granite, and it has been enlarged and restored over the years thanks in part to the riches from Dartmoor's tin mines. In 1638, during a great thunderstorm, it was struck by a fireball and badly damaged. Four people attending afternoon service were killed, and over 60 injured.

The interior is bright but fairly bare, like the moors, with just a font to fill the west end, high arcades supported by SINGULAR MONOLITHIC PILLARS OF GRANITE, and wagon roofs above the nave and aisles. There are some quaintly carved roof bosses including ONE OF THE ONLY SIX ROOF BOSSES IN ENGLAND DEPICTING ST KATHERINE, and another of three hares sharing three ears between them, known as the TINNER'S RABBITS, a symbol of the Holy Trinity adopted by the tin miners of Devon and Cornwall and found in a number of Dartmoor churches.

A plaque on the north wall at the west end in memory of MARY ELFORD (d.1642) includes an anagram of her name, 'Fear my Lord'.

Well, I never knew this about
DEVON CHURCHES

Hartland – St Nectan's. The tower of this noble 14th-century church high above the sea is 128 feet (39 m) tall, THE SECOND TALLEST CHURCH TOWER IN DEVON and a beacon for sailors. Inside is a Norman font decorated with interlacing arches and DEVON'S BIGGEST AND MOST COMPLETE MEDIEVAL ROOD SCREEN, beautifully carved and painted, 45 feet (13.7 m) across, 12 feet (3.6 m) high and 6 feet (1.8 m) wide at the top. Buried outside in the churchyard is publisher ALLEN LANE, FOUNDER OF PENGUIN BOOKS, the man who published the unexpurgated version of D.H. Lawrence's *Lady Chatterley's Lover* in 1959 (which led to a famous obscenity trial) and the original publisher of the incomparable PEVSNER ARCHITECTURAL GUIDES.

Molland – St Mary's. For anyone who loves Georgian interiors the two Exmoor churches of Molland and Parracombe, have the best in Devon. Molland's mainly 15th-century church sits on a hill below the high moors and looks down on the valley of the River Yeo. It completely escaped restoration by the Victorians, largely because the THROCKMORTONS, lords of the manor at the time, were Catholics and little interested in this Anglican church on the far edge of their estates.

All that survives of Molland's Norman church is the splendid font, which struggles to be seen amongst the sea of shoulder-high 18th-century box pews that threaten to swamp the leaning, clustered pillars of the central arcade. The lovely THREE-DECK PULPIT sports an immense sounding board, while the chancel is enclosed by a wooden screen, above which is a plastered tympanum bearing a royal coat of arms and a board bearing the Ten Commandments. In the north aisle are three fine mural monuments to the COURTENAYS, lords of the manor in the 17th and 18th centuries.

Parracombe – St Petrock's. This church in the north-western wilds of Exmoor sits on a hillside high above the village, reached by a farm track from the main road. They were going to pull it down at the end of the 19th century, but a national outcry and a cheque for £10 from John Ruskin saved it for posterity while a new church was built closer to the village, leaving St Petrock's gloriously unrestored. The rugged square tower is 12th century, the chancel 13th century and the nave 15th century, while the interior is an 18th-century Georgian feast, all except for the gated screen separating the nave from the chancel, which is 15th century. Above it the wall is painted with the Royal Arms, the Creed, the Ten Commandments and the Lord's Prayer. There are benches and box pews with hat pegs and a three-deck oak pulpit. St Petrock's is THE LAST CHURCH IN DEVON TO HAVE USED LIVE MUSICIANS TO ACCOMPANY THE HYMNS. They sat in the raised pews at the back, and there is a hole in one of the pews to allow elbow room for the bow of the base viol.

Swimbridge – St James's. The church has a 90 FT (27 m) HIGH LEAD-COVERED BROACH SPIRE FROM 1310, ONE OF ONLY THREE IN DEVON, a precious 15th-century rood screen, 44 feet (13.4 m) wide, with fan vaulting and masses of delicate tracery, a rare 15th-century stone pulpit and a UNIQUE FONT COVER consisting of a tall octagonal carved oak cupboard with doors that open to give access to the font, and a crown-shaped canopy. Buried in the churchyard, and vicar here for almost 50 years from 1832 until 1880, is PARSON JOHN 'JACK' RUSSELL, the hunting parson who bred a strain of small, hardy hunting dogs from his fox terrier bitch Trump. They became known as JACK RUSSELLS.

DORSET

*St Andrew's, Winterborne Tomson – one of only four surviving single-cell
Norman churches with an apsidal east end*

Bere Regis

St John the Baptist

Where Did They Go?

Ethelred the Unready's mother, Queen
Elfrida, came to the Saxon church that
originally stood here, to atone for her
part in the murder of her stepson
Edward the Martyr at Corfe Castle in
AD 979. That church was replaced in

the 12th century, and the new Norman
church was visited by the infamous
King John on 16 different occasions.
Then came Simon de Montfort,
founder of Parliament, and finally the
TURBERVILLES, who stayed on as lords
of the manor for the next 500 years.
They died out in the 18th century, no
one knows why, a mystery that piqued
the interest of THOMAS HARDY when
he came across the neglected Turberville
tombs in St John's, 'their carvings
defaced and broken, their brasses torn

from their matrices . . .' His answer was to write a novel about what might have happened to them, *Tess of the D'Urbervilles*.

The REMARKABLE AND UNIQUE CARVED AND PAINTED OAK ROOF OF THE NAVE, with its huge bosses and carvings of the 12 Apostles in Tudor dress, was built in 1475. It was the gift of a famous son of Bere Regis, CARDINAL MORTON, Archbishop of Canterbury and Lord Chancellor to Henry VII, in memory of his mother, who was a Turberville. The Cardinal also paid for the magnificent west tower, 64 feet (19.5 m) high, and erected in 1500.

Stinsford

St Michael's

'On afternoons of drowsy calm
We stood in the panelled pew
Singing one-voiced a Tate-and-Brady psalm
To the tune of "Cambridge New"'
THOMAS HARDY,
'Afternoon Service in Mellstock'

Stinsford is THOMAS HARDY'S CHURCH, his 'most hallowed spot', the Mellstock of his second novel *Under the Greenwood Tree*. His father and grandfather walked over the hill from their home at Higher Bockhampton, where Hardy was born in 1840, carrying their violas and cello to play in the church. Hardy himself was baptised there, attended service there throughout his boyhood years and taught at the Sunday school. His last home, Max Gate, is close by. And his heart will always be there, buried close to his two wives, Emma and Florence, his parents and his brother and two sisters. 'I shall sleep quite calmly at Stinsford, whatever happens,' he wrote, although his ashes lie beside those of Charles Dickens in Westminster Abbey, as befits one of the giants of English Literature, even if contrary to his wishes.

Also lying in the churchyard at Stinsford is the former Poet Laureate CECIL DAY-LEWIS (1904–72), who loved Dorset and so admired the works of Hardy that he asked to be buried near him.

The church itself, which is small and most attractive, sits on a hillside beside a big house and some thatched cottages, not far from Dorchester. It hails mainly from the 13th century with a plain, square 14th-century tower. Set in a niche above the west door is a modern carving of St Michael with outstretched wings, which replicates the original, rather weathered Saxon carving that once sat there and can now be seen inside the church.

The graceful nave arcades are 13th century with moulded round arches, the south arcade resting on clustered piers with capitals carved in stiff leaf, the north arcade plainer after Victorian restoration. The lovely, slightly crooked, less than central, 13th-century pointed chancel arch is continuous, with deep, shapely mouldings running all around from floor to floor, with no piers or capitals. It is very unusual and very effective.

The wooden gallery at the west end, where Hardy's father and grandfather sat with the choir and other musicians, was removed by the Victorians, much to Hardy's dismay. When there was talk of installing an organ he suggested, '. . . speaking for myself alone, that the old west gallery should be re-erected for it . . .'. Eventually it was, in 1996, thanks to an endowment in 1990 by the late Richard Purdy, professor of English at Yale University, in memory of Hardy's second wife, Florence.

In the south aisle is the THOMAS HARDY MEMORIAL WINDOW, unveiled in 1930 and illustrating Hardy's favourite Old Testament story, Elijah listening to

the 'still, small voice' of God after the tumult (1 Kings, 19:12).

Stinsford is far from tumultuous; indeed, it is far from the madding crowd, quite still and calm.

Studland

St Nicholas

Casting a Spell

The old church, like the old part of the village, withdraws demurely from the froth and gaiety of the crowds heading for Studland's golden sandy beach. The secluded churchyard offers a peep of the blue sea and the white cliffs of a distant Isle of Wight through the trees. If the scenery is pretty, the church, at first sight, is not. It is a low, grey, lumpen building dominated by a truncated tower left unfinished when the

Norman builders realised they could go no higher on such shaky foundations. And yet, the closer one looks, the more one falls under the spell of this strange and magical church.

It is THE FINEST NORMAN CHURCH IN DORSET and contains material from an earlier Saxon church in its make-up. There are Norman windows all around and a ring of bawdy corbels under the eaves. Some of the carvings are so joyously unrestrained as to bring a blush to the most broad-minded of cheeks.

Inside it is dark and cool and unspoiled, a soothing place to be. There is a homespun Norman font. The simple tower arches, which are of two orders, are early Norman, plain and unembellished and very pleasing. They rest on nicely carved capitals. The chancel, which is under the tower between the arches, is Norman perfection with a gorgeous vaulted roof

divided into four by huge ribs. The sanctuary has a similar vault lit by an east window of three lancets.

I could stay there for ever.

Winterborne Tomson

St Andrew's

I Could Kiss You, Hardy

Amidst green Dorset meadows and trees, in the valley of the Winter Bourne, sits a quite lovely little farm-yard church, beside a handsome but unpretentious old manor house. Both have been here for almost 900 years. The manor house as we see it was rebuilt in the 17th century and is now a farm-house. The single-cell church is 11th century and is ONE OF ONLY FOUR NORMAN CHURCHES IN ENGLAND WITH AN APSIDAL EAST END. Together they

form an enchanting picture of Olde England.

The form and fabric of the church are almost pure Norman. There are three 16th-century windows and one Norman, all in the south wall, and a tiny wooden belfry. In the early 18th century the Norman doorway on the north side was blocked up and a new one inserted in the west wall. The view as you enter via the west door is one of utter delight, sloping, uneven, lime-washed walls, box pews of pale bleached oak, a simple wooden screen, pulpit with sounding board. Above the door is a gallery, reached by a steep wooden staircase. THE LOVELY WAGON ROOF OF SLENDER TIMBERS AND DECORATIVE BOSSES IS UNIQUE IN THAT IT CURVES ROUND THE APSE.

The 18th-century oak furnishings

were installed and paid for by WILLIAM WAKE, ARCHBISHOP OF CANTERBURY from 1716 to 1737, who used to preach here when he was staying with his family, who lived nearby. He loved the simplicity of the church compared to the grandeur and opulence of the cathedrals he was used to.

Even the Archbishop's generosity could not save the church from a dwindling congregation, and by the end of the 19th century the only churchgoers were pigs, sheep and chickens from the next-door farm. St Andrew's was eventually saved from total ruin by the Society for the Protection of Ancient Buildings, who restored it in 1931 with funds raised from the sale of a Thomas Hardy manuscript. A wall plaque inside commemorates A.R. POWYS, Secretary of the Society, who discovered the neglected church and organised its revival. Good man.

Worth Matravers

St Nicholas of Myra

First Vaccination

This is one of Dorset's oldest churches, mainly 12th century and not much altered. It sits above the village pond, watching over this remote, windswept cliff-top village of sturdy limestone cottages. The sea glistens silver in the distance. The quarries here have provided Purbeck stone and marble for churches and cathedrals all over England, in particular Salisbury Cathedral in 1220.

The church is very pleasing to look at, with its Norman west tower and later pyramid cap, nave with two round-headed Norman windows, neat 18th-century porch and late Norman chancel. There is a blocked-up doorway with a triangular head, probably Saxon.

The inner doorway to the church has a Norman arch with chevron carvings and a badly worn carved tympanum. The windows are mostly small and set high up in the walls, protecting against both wind and raiders from the sea. Overwhelming all else is the MASSIVE NORMAN CHANCEL ARCH OF THREE ORDERS, a simple inner arch and two huge and irregular outer arches carved with bold chevrons. Above it are two small Norman windows.

Outside on the north side of the well-tended churchyard are the gravestones of a simple farmer and his wife whose courage and ingenuity have undoubtedly saved millions of lives over the years. FARMER BENJAMIN JESTY WAS THE MAN WHO DISCOVERED THE VACCINATION. HIS WIFE WAS THE FIRST PERSON EVER TO BE VACCINATED (see panel overleaf).

Worth Matravers

St Aldhelm's

Lighting the Way

This tiny 12th-century stone chapel stands on the edge of the cliffs right on the southern tip of the Isle of Purbeck, some 2 miles (3.2 km) south of Worth Matravers. To reach it one must undertake a bracing walk along a farm track and past a still-working quarry, usually into a driving headwind. It is well worth the effort, though, for this is an exhilarating place, with wide sea views, daunting cliffs plunging 350 feet (over 100 m) to the rocks below, and a most intriguing and unusual church.

St Aldhelm's is a four-square building with a pyramidal roof topped by a cross. The four corners face directly east, south, north and west, making St Aldhelm's THE ONLY CHURCH IN ENGLAND TO HAVE NO EAST WALL. The walls are buttressed haphazardly.

Benjamin Jesty

BENJAMIN JESTY (1736–1816) was the owner of Upbury Farm in Yetminster, Dorset, in the middle of the 18th century, at the time when England was ravaged by smallpox. In 1774, saddened by the loss of so many friends and neighbours, Jesty determined to find a way of protecting his wife and children from this terrible scourge. He noticed that neither of his two dairymaids, both of whom had caught a mild dose of cowpox from handling infected cows, had caught smallpox, which was highly contagious, even though they were nursing family members with the disease. From this he concluded that cowpox must give immunity to smallpox and so decided to give his family a dose of cowpox. In an open field he took some pus from an infected cow, and using the point of a knitting needle, scratched his wife's arm and injected the pus. This was THE WORLD'S FIRST KNOWN VACCINATION, the name being derived from 'vacca', the Latin word for cow.

Jesty then repeated the procedure with his two eldest sons. All three of the vaccinated suffered from cowpox for a few days, his wife quite badly, but all recovered and failed to catch smallpox – Elizabeth Jesty lived until she was 84 years old. In 1797 the Jestys moved to Downshay Manor Farm at Worth Matravers, where they lived out the rest of their lives. Over the next few years, under the watchful eye of Farmer Jesty, many of the inhabitants were vaccinated by the local doctor, although Jesty did not make his findings widely known until 20 years later, leaving the field clear for Edward Jenner to claim the first vaccination in 1796. On Jesty's gravestone at Worth Matravers are the words 'the first person known that introduced the Cow Pox by innoculation'.

One enters via a small round-arched doorway in the north-west wall. The interior is cold and dark and echoes to the sound of water dripping from the ceiling on to the uneven flagstone floor. And yet it somehow feels cosy and peaceful against the wind. At the centre of the room is a great pillar with eight ribs running off through the gloom to the sides and corners, dividing the roof into four vaults. There are a couple of old benches against the wall and a modern stone altar set diagonally across the eastern corner, barely lit by the only window, a small lancet in the south-east wall. The altar was carved out of stone from a local quarry and consecrated in 2005 by the Archbishop of Canterbury,

Rowan Williams, to commemorate the 1300th anniversary of St Aldhelm's consecration as Bishop of Sherborne.

Since the building has such a strange shape and orientation, there is speculation that it was not originally built as a chapel, but rather as a beacon or lookout for the sea approaches to Corfe

Castle. Local legend has it that the chapel was built as a memorial and warning beacon for sailors in around 1140, by a local man who had watched from here as his daughter and her new husband were drowned after their boat hit rocks and capsized off the headland.

However, the fact that it sits in the middle of a set of earthworks, indicating that this was an early Christian site, and considering the high quality of the internal vaulting, it would seem that it was always a religious place, possibly a chantry where priests would pray for the safety of sailors. It may have served as a lighthouse at the same time, and there are indications that there was a beacon on the roof where the cross is now.

Well, I never knew this about
DORSET CHURCHES

Moreton – St Nicholas. Here is THE ONLY CHURCH IN THE WORLD TO HAVE ALL WINDOWS OF ENGRAVED GLASS, and THE ONLY CHURCH IN THE WORLD TO HAVE ALL ITS WINDOWS DESIGNED BY LAURENCE WHISTLER. He designed the five windows of the apse, which were installed in 1958, and engraved the remaining nine windows personally, between 1955 and 1985. The result is a glorious interior, radiant with dappled sunlight and quite dazzling. The original 12th-century church was rebuilt in

1776 and most of the furnishings come from this period, but the building was damaged by a stray bomb in October 1940, which destroyed all the glass, hence the Whistler replacements. In the cemetery down the lane is the grave of T.E. LAWRENCE (1888–1935), LAWRENCE OF ARABIA, who lived at a small house nearby called Clouds Hill and was killed in a motorcycle accident in the Dorset lanes. His death from head injuries led to the eventual introduction of motorcycle crash helmets.

St Nicholas, Moreton

Osmington – St Osmund's. Osmington and its church are the subject of one of ARTIST JOHN CONSTABLE'S MOST FAMOUS PAINTINGS. Constable was a great friend of the vicar of Osmington, ARCHDEACON JOHN FISHER, and Constable and his wife Maria spent their honeymoon in Osmington Vicarage in 1816.

Wimborne St Giles – St Giles. Commemorated in this extraordinary country church is something to make the blood of schoolboys everywhere run cold – THE CABBAGE. St Giles House, in Wimborne St Giles, lying on the edge of Cranborne Chase, has been the ancestral home of the Ashleys, later Earls of Shaftesbury, since the 16th century, when the estate was inherited from cousins by SIR ANTHONY ASHLEY (1551–1628). He replaced the 12th-century village church with a new one, which

was rebuilt as a Georgian church by the Bastard brothers in 1732. This in turn was Victorianised and then restored in classical style by SIR NINIAN COMPER after a fire in 1908. In the Lady Chapel is the grand, elaborate, almost gaudy monument of Sir Anthony Ashley. At his feet is a spherical ball believed to be

a representation of a cabbage. According to the diarist JOHN EVELYN, cabbages were FIRST GROWN IN ENGLAND BY SIR ANTHONY ASHLEY in his garden at Wimborne St Giles. Quite a legacy. This gorgeous church boasts another unique feature – A PAINTED INSCRIPTION BY THE ALTAR COMMEMORATING A PAIR OF ROBINS found nesting in the church during the renovations of 1887 – another nest was found in the same place during repairs after the fire in 1908.

DURHAM

St John's Escomb – one of England's best Saxon churches

Bowes

St Giles'

Nicholas Nickleby

Situated in the middle of the remote but agreeable dry-stone Pennine village of Bowes, St Giles' is a simple cruciform church set in a shady churchyard overlooked by a Norman castle made ruinous by Robert the Bruce. Mainly 13th and 14th century, St Giles' has been extensively rebuilt but retains two Norman doorways and two fonts, one plain and Norman, the other a lovely

13th-century bowl carved with leaves and set on what was originally a Roman altar. Bowes stands on the site of an important Roman garrison called Lavatrae and there are several Roman remains in the church, including a stone inscribed to the Emperors Marcus Aurelius and Severus.

Under a tree in the churchyard, just to the north of the chancel, is the tombstone of GEORGE ASHTON TAYLOR, immortalised for ever by Charles Dickens as 'SMIKE' in *Nicholas Nickleby*. Taylor died here in 1822 aged just 19, a victim of the harsh conditions at the local school, SHAW'S ACADEMY. Dickens came to Bowes in 1838 to investigate for himself the truth about the infamous Yorkshire 'boy farms' (Bowes was once in Yorkshire), where unwanted children were sent to be educated by cruel and unscrupulous bullies, and when he stumbled across Taylor's grave, it 'put Smike into my mind on the spot'. The headmaster of the academy, WILLIAM SHAW, whose grave stands nearby, became WACKFORD SQUEERS in the book, and Shaw's Academy became DOTHEBOYS HALL.

After *Nicholas Nickleby* was published, Shaw was pilloried and his academy forced to close, but Shaw's family believed that he had been unfairly treated by Dickens, and in 1895 Shaw's granddaughter placed a memorial window to her grandfather in St Giles' to try to redress the balance.

While visiting Bowes, Dickens stayed in the ANCIENT UNICORN INN, said to be haunted by the spirits of two star-crossed lovers, RODGER WRIGHTSON, who died of a fever in 1713, and his sweetheart MARTHA RAILTON, who died shortly afterwards of a broken heart. Their tale is told in the *Ballad of Edwin and Emma* by David Mallet, and their gravestone can be seen up against the outside west wall of the church.

Dalton-le-Dale

St Andrew's

A Royal Ray of Sunshine

St Andrew's sits at the top of the village, just below the road that runs down through the dale to Seaham Harbour. The church sports a zigzag Norman north door dating back to the foundation of the church in 1150 and is renowned for the remains of a RAY SUNDIAL THAT IS UNIQUE IN ENGLAND. It can be found inside on the north wall where some Roman numerals are raised in relief on the plaster. Only the numbers I to VII are recognisable now, but originally all the figures I to XII would have been visible, with the passing of the hours marked by the rays of the sun shining through a slit in the roof above the window in the south wall.

Set against a recess on the north side of the chancel is a recumbent alabaster effigy of SIR WILLIAM BOWES, who fought with the Black Prince at Poitiers in 1356 and died in 1420. The Bowes coat of arms of three bows can be seen above the effigy and over the south porch. Sir William's descendant MARY ELEANOR BOWES, the richest heiress of her day thanks to her father's coal fortune, was married in 1767 to John Lyon, 9th Earl of Strathmore, laird of Glamis Castle in Scotland, and their names were united as Bowes-Lyon. Their great-great-great-granddaughter was ELIZABETH BOWES-LYON, better known as QUEEN ELIZABETH THE QUEEN MOTHER.

Escomb

St John's

Unspoiled Saxon Church

Marooned behind a ring of trees, on an island of green lawn enclosed by an old stone wall in the middle of a 1960s housing estate, one mile west along the River Wear from Bishop Auckland, there stands a remarkable treasure, THE OLDEST UNALTERED ANGLO-SAXON CHURCH IN THE NORTH OF ENGLAND, perhaps the very first church to be built in Northumbria.

Rugged and austere and utterly beguiling, it comes down to us from the earliest days of English Christianity. The round churchyard is reminiscent of religious sites in Ireland, suggesting that the church was built by Celtic Christians in the early 7th century, before the introduction of Roman Christianity at the Synod of Whitby in AD 664. There are Roman stones in the walls, taken from the fort at Binchester three miles away across the river, and one stone of the north wall has an inscription reading 'LEG VI', or 'Sixth Legion'.

The design of St John's is uncomplicated, with a long, tall nave and a tiny square chancel. There are five original round-headed windows, two on each side of the nave and one in the west wall, all placed up high for defence. The only additions and alterations to this Saxon structure are three 13th-century lancet windows in the south wall, a 13th-century porch, one pointed window in the west wall and a large east window, both inserted in 1800, and a small bellcote, probably Victorian. Otherwise the church remains almost as the Saxons made it nearly 1400 years ago.

Between the two Saxon windows in the south wall, set beneath a carved animal's head, is THE OLDEST SUNDIAL STILL IN ITS ORIGINAL PLACE IN

ENGLAND. It has three lines corresponding to the three most important times of worship in the day.

In the north wall is the original doorway into the church, lifted almost whole from the Roman fort at Binchester. It was blocked up in medieval times when it was thought that the Devil lurked in the sunless shadows on the north side of the church.

Inside, to the left of the entrance door, there is a marvellous old font, carved in the 13th century out of a Roman pillar. Some of the old cobbled floor survives.

Facing east, the lofty nave with its wide splayed windows leads to a high, narrow Roman chancel arch showing traces of medieval paintings, 12th or 13th century, on the underside. Unfortunately, almost everything has been whitewashed, making it difficult to discern the detail of the ancient stonework.

High up in the north wall, to the left of the Saxon window nearest the chancel, there is a Roman inscription on a large stone that reads 'BONO REI PUBLICAE NATO', meaning 'to the man born for the good of the state'. This probably comes from the base of a statue of the Emperor. Below, on the wall behind the pulpit, is a stone bearing an incised Celtic consecration cross.

Above the altar in the chancel is a stone carved with a cross, possibly the remnant of a Celtic preaching cross that has survived from the days before the church was built. To stand before this ancient cross, in the silence of this venerable old church, breathing in the dust of its simple, unsophisticated faith, is to be lost in time.

Seaham

St Mary the Virgin

A Marriage Programme

Founded as a Saxon mission in the 8th century and granted a village by King Athelstan in AD 930, this ancient church set above Seaham Dene in Durham's far east has looked out across the cold North Sea from the cliff-tops for well over 1,000 years. The village long ago moved south and became industrial, leaving St Mary's in the company of Seaham Hall, now a hotel, and the Old Rectory of 1830, now a private home, its grey stone bulk sheltering the church from the wind and sea spray.

St Mary's is long and low, buttressed against the elements and mottled by modern pollution. From outside, if the wind abates, it is possible to see a Saxon window above the south porch and two Norman windows with round lancets in the east wall. Also above the porch is an unusual sundial of 1773 with an almost legible inscription:

> *'The natural clockwork*
> *by the Almighty One*
> *Wound up at first,*
> *and ever since has gone,*
> *Wound up at first,*
> *its springs and wheels hold good.*
> *It speaks its Maker's praise,*
> *tho' once it stood*
> *But that was by the*
> *order of His wondrous power,*
> *And when it stands again*
> *it goes no more'*

Inside, the leaning walls of the tall, narrow, bare-stone nave, which has no aisles and is almost unchanged since Norman days, are pierced by three deeply splayed Saxon windows. The font is 700 years old, the carved wooden pulpit Elizabethan, and the gorgeous, musty, creaking box pews Georgian, some still with their brass name plates recording owners such as 'Mr Bewick Seaton, 1811'. In the south wall are two outstanding stained-glass windows by Charles Kempe, dating from 1908 and both showing his trademark wheatsheaf symbol.

A pointed arch, rebuilt in 1913, leads through to a chancel of 1180 where there are pews for the rector and the squire, and on the south wall, a double piscina decorated with elaborate nailhead ornamentation.

One couple who would have sat in those pews, and whose signatures grace the marriage register of St Mary's, are the poet LORD BYRON and his bride ANNE ISABELLA MILBANKE. On 2 January 1815 they were married in the drawing room of Seaham Hall next door, then owned by Anne's father. 'I shall never forget the 2nd of January 1815!' wrote Byron later. 'Lady Byron was the only unconcerned person present. Lady Noel, her mother, cried. I trembled like a leaf, made the wrong responses, and after the ceremony called her Miss Milbanke.' The marriage lasted not much more than a year, but long enough for the couple to produce a daughter, ADA, who would grow up to be a formidable mathematician, later recognised as THE WORLD'S FIRST COMPUTER PROGRAMMER (*see* page 209 and 243–4).

Well, I never knew this
about
DURHAM CHURCHES

Hart – St Mary Magdalene. This attractive grey stone church with distant sea views, which was founded by the fourth Robert de Brus in 1185, is mother church of the mighty St Hilda's in Hartlepool. It sits at the end of the sloping main street of Hart, a tiny village that was once an important administrative centre in Saxon England and later the site of the de Brus's fortified home. The nave of the present church follows the line of the original Saxon church and the low tower is Norman, as is the wide chancel arch inside. But the great treasure of Hart is its elaborately carved 15th-century octagonal font, made out of local limestone and considered to be THE FINEST FONT IN COUNTY DURHAM. The bowl is carved with emblems of the four Evangelists, a number of saints and a Resurrection scene, with shield-bearing angels beneath, while the shaft portrays the figures of various saints and churchmen. The base is decorated with

flowers and eight men's heads. There is also a massive square Norman font beside the door, carved from a single stone, with columns and capitals at each corner.

High Coniscliffe – St Edwin's. A graceful, mainly 13th-century church, dramatically set on a cliff on the north bank of the River Tees near Darlington, ST EDWIN'S IS THE ONLY CHURCH IN ENGLAND DEDICATED TO EDWIN, first king of Northumbria (c.586–633). It also boasts an OCTAGONAL SPIRE, ONE OF ONLY FIVE ANCIENT SPIRES IN COUNTY DURHAM.

Kelloe – St Helen's. Occupying a lovely position on the high slope of a wooded valley, just outside the small mining village of Kelloe, St Helen's has Saxon walls for the nave and a delightfully simple square Norman tower. Inside, against the north wall of the sanctuary, is a richly sculpted 12th-century Romanesque cross known as the ST HELENA CROSS, discovered during rebuilding works in 1854. Reading from the bottom upwards, the wonderfully preserved carvings illustrate the Discovery of the True Cross, Helen and her son Constantine, the first Christian Roman emperor, and, at the top, a reclining Constantine being blessed by an angel. On the south side of the church is a window inscribed in memory of the poet ELIZABETH BARRETT BROWNING, who was born at nearby Coxhoe Hall (demolished in 1956) in 1806. The circular 18th-century stone font where she was baptised still stands in place beneath the tower. In the churchyard extension is a monument marking the burial place of 26 of the 74 men and boys who were killed in the Trimdon Grange colliery explosion of 1882.

St Helen's, Kelloe

Norton-on-Tees – St Mary the Virgin. Dating from 1020, this gorgeous church is THE ONLY CRUCIFORM SAXON CHURCH IN THE NORTH OF ENGLAND and one of only two in England to have all four crossing arches of the same height and width, the other being at Stow in Lincolnshire. The four simple Saxon

arches of the crossing are rugged and quite beautiful, forming a most unusual and attractive interior. Buried in the south-east corner of the churchyard is JOHN WALKER (1782–1859), the Stockton chemist who invented the friction match in 1827.

St Mary the Virgin, Norton-on-Tees

Winston – St Andrew's. Conspicuous by its diminutive Victorian tower and conical spire, 13th-century St Andrew's has a fine 13th-century font decorated with a pair of fighting dragons. The magnificent view of the river valley from the churchyard includes WINSTON BRIDGE, built across the River Tees in 1763 and boasting what was once THE WIDEST STONE ARCH IN EUROPE, with a span of 111 feet (34 m).

ESSEX

St John the Baptist, Little Maplestead – prettiest of England's four round churches

Bradwell on Sea

St Peter's on the Wall

England's Oldest Church

Here, on the edge of the world, where the sea meets the sky, stands what could be ENGLAND'S OLDEST UNALTERED CHURCH. The land is flat, the wind whistles across the fields, the empty marshes echo to the cries of sea birds and the crashing of the waves. The village lies distant at the far end of a grassy track. Bits of brick and stone from the buried walls of a lost Roman fortress poke through the thin, sandy topsoil. This is an ancient place.

St Peter's stands alone against the elements. It is immense and majestic, simple and unadorned, and comes down to us from those turbulent times when Celtic monks from the north were roaming the land to spread Christianity amongst the heathen

Saxons. In AD 654, at the invitation of King Sigbert of Essex, a monk called CEDD, who had been a pupil of St Aidan of Lindisfarne, landed on the coast here to begin his mission to convert the Saxons of East Anglia. Here he set up a wooden church and over the next years this was steadily rebuilt in stone, using materials from Othona, the Roman fort. That church of stone, built 1300 years ago is, to all intents and purposes, the church we see today. Lost are the apse that once stood at the east end with two small rooms either side, and a porch at the west end.

Cedd's church must have been one of the biggest structures in the whole of Saxon England and is certainly BRITAIN'S LARGEST SURVIVING COMPLETELY SAXON BUILDING. Why and how it survived both structural collapse and Viking destruction is open to speculation. The church was built above the gatehouse of the Roman fort and hence has firm foundations. Also, while most Saxon buildings were made of wood, Cedd's church was made of stone, and was therefore more difficult to burn down. Or perhaps, being

so remote, it may have just been overlooked by the Viking raiders.

At the end of the 11th century there was a long period of stormy weather and the inhabitants of the settlement that had grown up around Cedd's church decided to move a few miles inland. They built themselves a new place of worship and Cedd's church became a chapel of ease, which it remained until the 17th century, when it seems the congregation finally became too small to sustain it. The apse was knocked down, large doors were inserted in the south wall of the nave, and the chapel, one of England's earliest and most significant Christian sites, became a barn.

In 1920 a passing rambler observed that this isolated building seemed rather too grand and lofty for a barn and began to look at it more closely. He noted the noble proportions, the round-headed window high up in the wall, the gables and the outlines of the arches. He realised that here was something rather wonderful. The hay bales and the horse carts were taken away and the barn was lovingly converted back into a chapel. Communion services are now held here weekly, and every year there are pilgrimages to this venerable spot from all over the country.

The church has survived in remarkably good condition, with the towering walls of Kentish ragstone and Roman bricks still solid and compact, the windows intact. The foundations of the original apse and side chapels are marked out in chalk at the east end, while the outline of the big barn door can be seen in the south wall.

Inside is a huge space, bare and impressive, lit by shafts of sunlight falling through the small windows south and west. The outline of the blocked-up chancel arches can be seen in the high east wall. There is little furniture, just a few benches, a colourful modern Crucifix on the east wall, and a modern altar with three stones embedded, one from Iona, the cradle of St Cedd's Celtic Christianity, one from Lindisfarne, where St Cedd studied, and one from Lastingham in Yorkshire, where he died and is buried.

All is peace and calm inside these old walls on the edge of the world.

Danbury

St John the Baptist

High Point

Danbury's church sits at THE HIGHEST POINT OF ONE OF THE HIGHEST VILLAGES IN ESSEX, 367 feet (112 m) above sea level, and its splendid 15th-century wooden spire is a noted landmark for miles around. St John's dates from the 12th and 13th centuries, but much of the interior is the work of George Gilbert Scott, who restored the church in 1866. The Victorian bench ends are beautifully carved into a variety of poppy-heads and animals and imitate the style of the THREE ORIGINAL 15TH-CENTURY PEWS that can be seen at the back of the nave on the north side.

Danbury's greatest treasures are set into arched recesses in the north aisle, the celebrated 'KNIGHTS OF DANBURY', two oak effigies of armoured knights dating from the 13th century and thought to be Crusaders of the St Clere family, who in 1290 endowed what is now the north aisle as a chapel, 'for the soul of William de St Clere'. There is another, slightly later wooden effigy of a knight in the south aisle. Each of the effigies assumes a slightly different demeanour; one is drawing his sword, one sheathing his sword and one has

his hands clasped in prayer. They all have their legs crossed and rest their feet on a lion. It is thought that each posture signifies something, but exactly what has been lost in time.

The Right Pickle

In 1779 workmen were digging a grave for the lady of the manor under one of the recesses when they came across a lead coffin some three feet (1 m) below the surface. When they removed the lid, instead of bones they found the body of a man, about five feet (1.5 m) tall, dressed in a linen shirt fastened at the top with lace, and preserved in almost perfect condition. The coffin in which he lay was three-quarters full of an aromatic pickling liquid, which had feathers and herbs floating in it, discoloured but still intact. In wonder, they closed the coffin and placed it back in the grave, where it has lain undisturbed ever since. Is the body of this Knight of St Clere still uncorrupted after more than 700 years?

Greensted-juxta-Ongar

St Andrew's

England's Oldest Wooden Walls

Here, set in a sleepy sylvan glade almost within the sound of London, is THE OLDEST WOODEN CHURCH IN THE WORLD. Here you can touch and run your hands along THE OLDEST WOODEN WALLS IN ENGLAND, carved from mighty oak trees that may just have existed as little acorns when Jesus was walking the earth and the Romans came this way.

It is a serene and lovely place, a Christian site since the 7th century when St Cedd was preaching to the men of Essex. Evidence of a 7th-century timber church lies beneath the present chancel.

In 1013 the body of ENGLAND'S FIRST PATRON SAINT, ST EDMUND OF EAST ANGLIA, rested here overnight on its way from London for reburial at Bury St Edmunds. A Victorian roof beam inside shows a carving of St Edmund, decapitated and guarded by a dog, while there is a 15th-century panel painting of him in the nave and a small roundel of 15th-century glass in the west window, which is also said to be of St Edmund. There is a rather beguiling suggestion, alas unproven, that the wooden covers of the Bible on the altar come from the very tree at Hoxne in Suffolk where St Edmund was martyred, tied to the trunk and shot through with arrows by the Danes.

The little church is a disorderly medley of ages and styles, with a shingled spire, white clapperboard tower, wooden nave with 19th-century dormer windows, Victorian porch and pale red-brick chancel. It is at once very amateurish and very English – and very pretty.

The oldest part of the church is the wooden nave, its walls made up of 51 oak tree trunks split down the middle, with the rounded parts on the outside and the flat parts inside. These are THE ONLY SPLIT LOG WALLS IN ENGLAND and the timbers have been most recently

dated to between 990 and 1060, making this part of the church THE OLDEST WOODEN BUILDING STILL STANDING IN THE WHOLE OF EUROPE. Originally the roof was of thatch and there was a slit in the timbers of the west wall to light the interior.

The Normans for some reason left the Saxon wooden nave more or less alone, not rebuilding it in stone as was their custom, although they did rebuild the chancel in flint. The only Norman features left now are the flint footings of the chancel and a very plain pillar piscina in a corner of the sanctuary.

Tudor builders built the brick chancel on the foundations of the Norman chancel, replaced the thatched roofs of the nave and chancel with tiles and put in dormer windows to act as a clerestory. Seventeenth-century builders put up the weatherboarded tower and belfry. Victorian builders put in new dormer windows, constructed a low brick base for the timbers and added the porch.

A Martyr and a Crusader

In 1839 JAMES BRINE, one of the TOLPUDDLE MARTYRS, was married in St Andrew's to ELIZABETH STANDFIELD, the daughter of another of the martyrs. Their names are in the marriage register on view inside the church. The Tolpuddle Martyrs were a group of Dorset farmers who were transported to Australia for forming a union, but were pardoned and allowed to return to England after a public outcry. They were then given tenancies in this area of Essex.

Outside in the churchyard, next to the porch, is the gravestone of an unknown 13th-century crusader, thought to have been an archer, who apparently arrived at the church badly wounded and died there. He was buried beneath a stone slab as befits a hero. Nearby is a battered wooden cross marking the grave of Edward Edwards, a local innkeeper, who died in 1842 after an inebriated misunderstanding with a scythe, which came to pass while he was trying to win a bet.

Hadstock

St Botolph's

England's Oldest Door

Here is THE OLDEST DOOR IN ENGLAND, still hanging on the original hinges on which it has been swinging open and shut for over 1,000 years. Saxons, Normans, Tudors and Stuarts, Georgians and Victorians have all passed through this door to worship in ONE OF ENGLAND'S OLDEST CHURCHES.

St Botolph's stands above an elevated churchyard with fine views into Cambridgeshire, and is thought to be the 'minster on a hill' built by King Canute in 1016 in gratitude for his victory against Edmund Ironside at the Battle of Assandun, which was fought nearby at Ashdon. This minster was itself built on the site of an earlier Saxon church founded by Abbot Botolph in AD 654.

The door, which is located on the north side of the church, is ONE OF ONLY TWO WORKING SAXON DOORS LEFT IN ENGLAND, the other being in Westminster Abbey. It is of plain oak held fast with three iron straps and is contained within a hefty stone arch with capitals carved in honeysuckle ornamentation. The door was once adorned with human skin, that of a 'sacrilegious Dane', which was attached to it by nails.

The west door is of a similar vintage but is no longer used. The nave too survives from Canute's church and is pierced by four Saxon windows, one of

them retaining its original Saxon wooden frame.

At the back of the church are the remnants of a 15th-century screen with an amusing picture on one of the panels of a fox preaching from a pulpit to some geese.

Well, I never *knew this*
about
ESSEX CHURCHES

Langford – St Giles'. This early Norman church standing quietly at the centre of the village is a unique treasure as it possesses THE ONLY WESTERN APSE IN BRITAIN, and one of only a very few left in the whole of Europe. St Giles' was built originally with an apse at both ends, common practice in the 11th century, but the eastern apse was demolished in the 15th century and a square extension added to the chapel in its place. The rest of the church was greatly altered and restored in the 19th century but surprisingly, and fortunately, the precious western apse was preserved.

Little Maplestead – St John the Baptist. Here is ONE OF ONLY FOUR MEDIEVAL ROUND CHURCHES REMAINING IN USE IN ENGLAND and ONE OF ENGLAND'S ONLY FIVE SURVIVING CIRCULAR NAVES. Of those round churches Little Maplestead is the smallest and the newest, but arguably the most beautiful. It was built in around 1340, on the site of an earlier church, as a hospital chapel for the Knights of St John of Jerusalem, the Knights Hospitallers, a group of warriors who in 1070 had established a hospice in Jerusalem for Christians making the pilgrimage to the Holy City. They are the direct forebears of today's St John's Ambulance. Its design was based on the circular Church of the Holy Sepulchre in Jerusalem. The round nave, encircled by an arcade of six graceful columns and an ambulatory, was originally shut off from the chancel by a screen so that the Preceptory church where the knights performed their rituals could be private. The hospital buildings were dismantled by Henry VIII at the Dissolution and the church converted for parish use.

Newport – St Mary the Virgin. Set on a hill above a colourful high street of brick-built Georgian houses and timber-framed buildings, St Mary's contains work of every century from the 13th to the 19th. Hiding in one of the 13th-century transepts is a rare PORTABLE ALTAR, made in 1250 and designed in the form of a carved chest to be carried around and used on the battlefield. The five panels of the lid, which lifts up to become a reredos (as we see it in the church now), are painted with pictures of the Crucifixion, with three saints and the Madonna kneeling at the foot of the Cross. These paintings are THE EARLIEST OIL PAINTINGS ON WOOD TO BE FOUND ANYWHERE IN ENGLAND.

Tolleshunt D'Arcy – St Nicholas. This small, mainly 14th-century church shelters the medieval tombs and brasses of the D'ARCY family who lived in the old hall next door and gave their name to the village. The most notable feature inside the church is the PAINTED CEILING OF THE NAVE, created in 1897 by a local artist. In the window of the north chapel is a small piece of stained glass dating from around 1600 and showing a red tulip. The first tulips were introduced into England at about that time and this is THE EARLIEST KNOWN PICTURE OF A TULIP IN AN ENGLISH CHURCH WINDOW. Along the path from the church to the hall is a row of rare apple trees growing the D'Arcy Spice Apple, first discovered in the garden of the hall in 1880.

GLOUCESTERSHIRE

*St Mary, Upleadon – its unique Tudor wooden tower of timbers rises
straight up from the ground with no external support or buttressing*

Coberley

St Giles'

Close to the Heart

Coberley folk regard their church as THE
FIRST CHURCH ON THE RIVER THAMES,
located as it is just downstream from
Seven Springs, the furthest direct source
from the mouth of England's longest
river. It is a picturesque and charming

place of Norman origins, with a
14th-century Decorated south chapel,
15th-century Perpendicular tower,
Victorian restored nave and chancel.

In the south wall of the sanctuary is
THE ONLY HEART MEMORIAL TO BE
FOUND IN THE COTSWOLDS, marking the
burial place of the heart of SIR GILES
DE BERKELEY. Sir Giles, who was born
in Coberley in 1240, was a close
companion of Edward I, with whom he
went on crusade. He died in 1294 and
the rest of his body lies in Little Malvern,

Worcestershire, where he expired, having gone there to take the waters. A plaque beneath the heart memorial informs us that his faithful charger, LOMBARD, is buried outside in the churchyard, and indeed, Lombard's headstone can be seen up against the outside wall of the sanctuary, in line with where his master's heart lies inside. THIS ARRANGEMENT OF A KNIGHT'S HORSE AND HEART IS UNIQUE IN ANY ENGLISH CHURCH.

Dick Whittington's Mother

Coberley's church was enlarged in the 14th century by Sir Giles' son SIR THOMAS DE BERKELEY (1289–1350), whose splendid tomb sits in the Decorated chapel he himself built. He lies in effigy on top of the tomb, clad in the armour he wore at the Battle of Crécy in 1346, his hands clasped in prayer, his head supported by angels, a lion at his feet. Lying next to him is his wife JOAN, and resting on the floor beside them, in her own miniature tomb, is their daughter.

In 1352, two years after Sir Thomas died, his wife Joan married SIR WILLIAM WHITTINGTON, of Pauntley in Gloucestershire, by whom she had a son, Richard. Sir William was outlawed for marrying a de Berkeley widow without the permission of the King and died in penury not long afterwards, so young Richard was left penniless and had to make his way to London to earn a living. He became apprenticed to a mercer and grew up to be that hero of pantomime, beloved of children all over the world, DICK WHITTINGTON, four times Mayor of London. It is quite a thrill to find Dick Whittington's mother buried in this quiet corner of Gloucestershire.

Royal Guests

St Giles has an unusual approach, through a small door beside a huge arched gateway and then along a path through the private garden of Coberley Court. Beyond the church is a high crumbling wall, all that remains of COBERLEY HALL, which was demolished after the owner lost his all in the South Sea Bubble of 1720. Charles I stayed at the hall during his retreat from the siege of Gloucester in 1643, and a few years later in 1651, on the night of 10 September, his son Prince Charles hid in Coberley's old rectory, disguised as a groom, during his flight through England after the Battle of Worcester.

Cowley

St Mary's

Rare Stone Pulpit

This is not one of England's famous churches. There are no monuments of kings or mighty lords, no fine carvings by master masons, no windows with fine tracery or medieval stained glass. St Mary's, Cowley, is just a beautiful, plain and simple, 13th-century English country church, where generations of Gloucestershire folk have worshipped and dozed and wept and prayed and married for the last 800 years.

Approached through an archway in a huge yew hedge, the church has a sturdy west tower, 13th century with a 15th-century battlemented top, and a 13th-century nave and chancel. Inside is an open 14th century wagon roof with tie beams, supported by walls that lean endearingly. The CIRCULAR LIMESTONE FONT BY THE DOOR IS 12TH-CENTURY and has an unusual band of decoration around the bowl.

There is no chancel arch. A recess in the chancel contains the stone effigy of a recumbent priest of the 14th century. Best of all is the RARE 15TH-CENTURY STONE PULPIT, carved from a single block of stone and patterned with crooked blind arcades and rough, childish shapes. There are ONLY ABOUT 60 SUCH PULPITS SURVIVING IN ENGLAND and it is truly a thing of beauty.

Anyone for Horlicks?

St Mary's Church stands right beside COWLEY MANOR, an Italianate pile built in 1855 on the foundations of an earlier 17th-century house and enlarged some 40 years later by SIR JAMES HORLICK (1844–1921), the 'J' in J. & W. Horlicks, makers of malted milk drinks. Sir James is buried in the churchyard and is reputed to revisit his old home, which is now a luxury hotel, at night, perhaps looking for a mug of Horlicks to help him sleep. He climbs in through the big window that overlooks the church-yard and has been encountered frequently over the years. He is always, apparently, impeccably polite.

Also buried in the churchyard is one ROBERT BROWNING, a Dorset innkeeper, who was an ancestor of the poet Robert Browning. Why he lies here no one seems to know.

Alice in Wonderland

In the mid 1800s ALICE LIDDELL, the inspiration for *Alice's Adventures in Wonderland*, was a regular visitor to Cowley, where her uncle was the rector of St Mary's. He was also a good friend of the REVEREND CHARLES LUTWIDGE DODGSON, otherwise known as Lewis Carroll, and it is widely thought that LEWIS CARROLL FIRST MET ALICE IN WONDERLAND AT COWLEY.

In 2013 the smiling face of church warden NORA SLY, 90 years old and a member of St Mary's congregation since she moved to Cowley at the age of three, was chosen by her fellow parish-ioners to be immortalised in stone, carved on to a new crocket, or small stone ornament, on the church roof.

Deerhurst

St Mary's

A Place of Some Importance

Here, on a low ridge above the flood meadows of the River Severn, is ONE OF THE OLDEST CHURCHES IN ENGLAND. The VENERABLE BEDE knew of it in the early years of the 8th century, and ST ALPHEGE was a monk here before rising to become Archbishop of Canterbury in 1006, and then being martyred by the Danes at Greenwich in 1012.

In 1016 the Saxon king EDMUND 'IRONSIDES' retreated to Deerhurst after being defeated at the BATTLE OF ASSANDUN by the Danish king CANUTE. The two kings then met at Deerhurst to sign a treaty dividing the kingdom between them, with Edmund keeping Wessex, while Canute got the rest. Edmund died shortly afterwards and Canute inherited Wessex as well, becoming king of a united England, the England we know today.

Unlike many very old religious sites

Deerhurst has continued to be an active place of worship for all of its 1300 years, although its importance did wane after the Norman Conquest in 1066 St Mary's contains features from almost every period of English church architecture, but is especially renowned for its Saxon work.

The Saxons' Finest Work

The core of the church is 9th-century Saxon while the tower, 70 feet (21 m) tall, is 10th-century Saxon. The belfry openings were pierced through in the 14th century. Halfway up the tower is a Saxon doorway, which gave access to an outside gallery, while at the base of the tower is the main entrance to the church, a medieval doorway with a pointed arch which was built inside the original round-headed Saxon doorway.

Inside, above the Saxon inner doorway, there is a UNIQUE 9TH-CENTURY BYZANTINE-STYLE SCULPTURE OF THE VIRGIN MARY, standing beneath a Saxon arch and holding a shield, on which there was once a painted figure of Christ, perhaps representing Jesus in the womb. The carving would originally have been painted all over.

On the far side of the doorway, at each end of the mouldings above the opening, there are CARVED BEASTS' HEADS, again 9th-century and again once painted. These heads are technically known as label-stops or dripstone terminals and were moved in from the outside of the church in 1860 to save them from weathering. Further examples of such beasts' heads can be found on the chancel arch, and these Deerhurst carvings are considered to be THE FINEST SUCH BEASTS' HEADS IN ENGLAND.

The nave of St Mary's is 8th-century Saxon in origin, as indicated by its high, narrow shape. The aisles and arcades, which are noted for the beautiful carvings on the capitals of the pillars, were added between 1180 and 1200, the clerestory in the 15th century. The west wall of the nave, which is also the east wall of the tower, is entirely Saxon, perhaps THE MOST FAMOUS SAXON WALL IN ENGLAND. High up, below a dedication stone, are two 10th-century Saxon pointed windows, forming what is described in the church brochure as 'the finest, most elaborate opening in any Saxon church'. Below is a curious triangular window next to a blocked-up Saxon doorway, which once gave access to the upper level western chapel.

The font, which can be found in the north aisle, was carved from a single block of Cotswold stone and is decorated with a rare spiral motif. It is acknowledged as THE FINEST SAXON FONT IN EXISTENCE.

Pet Names

The font stands in front of a stained-glass window commemorating the Strickland family, who built nearby Apperley Court and were great benefactors of the church. Below the window are the Strickland arms, complete with turkey crest, recalling the fact that it was a Strickland who introduced the turkey into England from North America (*see* pages 308–9).

At the east end of the north aisle are brasses to the Cassey family of nearby Wightfield Manor. SIR JOHN CASSEY, who died in 1400, was Chief Baron of the Exchequer to Richard II. His wife Lady Alice has a small dog at her feet, with his name 'Terri' inscribed underneath. This is THE ONLY EXAMPLE IN ENGLAND OF A BRASS WITH A NAMED PET ON IT.

At the west end of the south aisle is a window containing some early 14th-century stained glass, showing a famous depiction of ST CATHERINE WITH HER WHEEL, and also St Alphege.

Puritan Chancel

The chancel, which dates from 1650, the time of the Commonwealth, is THE ONLY EXAMPLE IN ENGLAND OF A PURITAN CHANCEL. It has seats running around the walls and altar rails surrounding the Communion table on all four sides, and originally the Communion table would have been arranged east–west rather than north–south.

Eastern Delights

Set into the east wall is the Saxon chancel arch, now filled in, that once led through to the eastern apse, long since gone. In 2004 the painted figure of a saint carrying a book was discovered on a panel high up on this wall. It is thought to be Saxon, dating from the 10th century, and could be THE OLDEST KNOWN WALL PAINTING IN BRITAIN (*see* Houghton on the Hill, Norfolk, page 178). Very little can be seen of it from floor level at the moment.

Outside the east end of the church, high up on the south wall of the ruined apse, is a 9TH-CENTURY SAXON CARVING known as the DEERHURST ANGEL, with fresh-faced looks and stylised curls that show a definite Celtic influence. There would have been other sculptured panels like this around the walls of the apse, alternating with small windows, but this is the only survivor and is very precious.

A walk around St Mary's is exhausting, for there is so much to treasure and every feature has a fascinating story beyond what you can initially see. But even now Deerhurst is not finished with us, for it is THE ONLY VILLAGE IN ENGLAND TO HAVE NOT ONE BUT TWO SAXON CHURCHES.

Odda's Chapel

ODDA'S CHAPEL IS a short walk down the road from St Mary's. It was discovered hidden beneath the plaster work of the half-timbered Abbot's Court farmhouse, to which it is attached, by the REVEREND GEORGE BUTTERWORTH, vicar of Deerhurst in the 19th century. It is tiny, with a nave 25 feet by 16 feet (7.6 by 4.9 m) and a chancel 14 feet by 11 feet (4.3 by 3.3 m). In 1675 a stone was found amongst the roots of an apple tree in the adjacent orchard inscribed with the words:

'Earl Odda ordered the royal hall to be built and dedicated in honour of the Holy Trinity and for the soul of his brother Aekfric who died in this place. Bishop Ealkdred dedicated it on 12 April. The Fourteenth year of Edward King of the English.'

The 14th year of Edward the Confessor would translate to 1056. THE ODDA STONE, as it became known, is now in the Ashmolean Museum, while the chapel has a replica. Earl Odda, who died not long after the chapel was dedicated, was, after King Harold's father Earl Godwin, the most powerful magnate and landowner in Saxon England during the reign of Edward the Confessor.

Kempley

St Mary's

England's Oldest Roof

This small Norman church sits deep in England's quietest countryside, on low-lying meadows surrounded by orchards. Kempley village abandoned St Mary's long ago in search of less boggy terrain and now lies over a mile away, happily clustered around a shiny new church constructed in 1903 in Arts and Crafts style by Lord Beauchamp, model for Lord Marchmain in Evelyn Waugh's *Brideshead Revisited*.

St Mary's was built early in the 12th century by Hugh de Lacy, son of William the Conqueror's friend Walter de Lacy. The roof timbers have been dated to 1120, meaning that THE ROOF OF ST MARY'S, KEMPLEY IS THE OLDEST ROOF IN BRITAIN. IT ALSO SHOWS THE EARLIEST USE OF MORTISE AND TENON JOINTING IN ENGLAND.

To look at, the church presents a classic picture, with a Norman nave and chancel and a powerful, well-buttressed tower. This was added in the 13th century as defence against the menacing Welsh, stirred up by the aggressions of Edward I. A creaking oak porch protects an ancient Norman doorway with a carved tympanum showing the Tree of Life.

Painted Glory

Inside, St Mary's is AGLOW WITH WALL PAINTINGS IN OCHRE AND RED. In Norman and medieval times most congregations were illiterate, and paintings such as these were used to explain biblical stories and religious teachings. The murals here date from the 14th century and are tempera paintings (*see* panel). They include, on the north wall of the nave, a vivid 'WHEEL OF LIFE' showing the ten stages of life: infant, boy, youth, young man, king, elderly man, blind old man, bedridden old

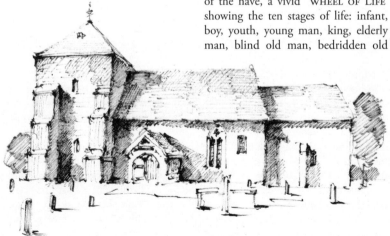

> The 12th-century paintings in the chancel and under the chancel arch at Kempley are frescoes, painted directly on to freshly laid plaster that is still wet. The 14th-century murals in the nave are tempera, a type of paint made from egg white that is painted on to plaster that is already dried.

man, a coffin and a tomb. There seems to be rather too much emphasis on the later stages of life here, but perhaps in medieval days people aged much more quickly. In the window arch next to it we see ST MICHAEL WEIGHING UP SOULS. Played out on the south wall is the MURDER OF THOMAS À BECKET in Canterbury Cathedral in 1170.

Above the glorious, rounded Romanesque chancel arch is a faded depiction of the EASTER RITUAL, showing the three Marys visiting the empty tomb of Jesus. This painting is contemporary with the arch, and dates

from the early 12th century.

Go through the arch to the chancel and you will be confronted with THE MOST COMPLETE SET OF ROMANESQUE FRESCOES IN ENGLAND. The walls and roof are almost entirely covered with depictions of Christ in Majesty beside the Virgin Mary and St Peter, the Twelve Apostles and various saints. Like the Easter Ritual in the nave, these murals date from circa 1130 and are true frescoes. THIS COMBINATION OF FRESCOES AND TEMPERA PAINTINGS IN ONE CHURCH IS EXTREMELY RARE, IF NOT UNIQUE, IN ENGLAND.

Well, I never knew this about
GLOUCESTERSHIRE CHURCHES

Duntisbourne Rouse – St Michael's. Reached through a gap in the hedge down a narrow country side lane, St Michael's sits on a steep hillside that slopes away to the east. It has a SAXON NAVE and a 12th-century NORMAN CHANCEL, with a lovely NORMAN CHANCEL ARCH and a NORMAN CRYPT underneath, rare in a small village church. Entrance to the crypt was originally via a spiral staircase from the

chancel but is now through an outside door reached by a steep flight of steps. The rough stone walls, the low rounded

roof, the heavenly views of the valley through the tiny Norman east window, all go to make this crypt one of the loveliest of England's precious peaceful places.

Elkstone – St John's. This is THE HIGHEST CHURCH IN THE COTSWOLDS, sheltered from the cold winds by tall trees and an old stone rectory. St John's is one of the finest and yet least known Norman churches in England, boasting a magnificent south door with carved tympanum, Norman carvings throughout the interior and two superb chancel arches dividing the stone vaulted chancel into choir and sanctuary. An inside stairway leads from the chancel to a first-floor pigeon loft, or columbarium, with more than 40 nesting holes in the walls. It is ONE OF

ONLY TWO SUCH COLUMBARIUMS IN ENGLAND.

Selsley – All Saints. Designed and built in 1861 by a young G.F. Bodley for the cloth manufacturer and philanthropist Sir Samuel Stephens Marling, All Saints is THE LAST OF THE GREAT WOOL CHURCHES TO BE BUILT IN THE COTSWOLDS. Its 100 ft (30 m) high tower with saddleback roof soars above the Stroud valley, a local landmark visible for miles. The windows comprise THE FIRST COMPLETE SET OF STAINED-GLASS WINDOWS PRODUCED BY THE ARTS AND CRAFTS FIRM OF MORRIS AND CO. and contain work by William Morris himself, Philip Webb, Edward Burne-Jones, Dante Gabriel Rossetti and Ford Madox Brown.

HAMPSHIRE

All Saints, East Meon – home of the finest Tournai font in Britain

Breamore

St Mary's

Saxon Church

Here is ONE OF ENGLAND'S LARGEST, MOST COMPLETE AND MOST IMPORTANT SAXON CHURCHES. It was built around AD 1000 and remains pretty much unchanged, with just the loss of the north transept, the addition of a 12th-century

Norman porch and some 15th-century rebuilding of the chancel and crossing. It sits in a field below a fine, restored Elizabethan manor house, as noble a view of England as one could ask.

From the outside the church looks rather crudely pieced together, cruciform but not recognisably Romanesque, with the south transept being neither as tall nor as wide as the tower, perhaps more of a 'porticus', or side chapel, as is more commonplace in Eastern European churches. The nave is tall,

long and narrow, as is customary for a Saxon church, and there are pilasters, some long-and-short work, and a square tower with a small square cap that is completely Saxon.

Saxon Rood

Sheltered by the Norman porch, on the wall above the inner doorway, is A RARE, PARTIALLY DEFACED, LIFE-SIZE SAXON ROOD, carved in low relief and showing Christ Bent in Suffering rather than the more traditional Christ Triumphant. The background paintings of landscapes are 15th century, as is the RARE PAINTING OF THE SUICIDE OF JUDAS on the west wall of the porch, a non-biblical subject not often illustrated in churches. THIS COMBINATION OF ROOD AND PAINTINGS IS UNIQUE IN ENGLAND.

Saxon Text

The church inside is spacious and bright with the light coming in through seven splayed Saxon windows. Only one Saxon crossing arch survives, the one leading to the south porticus, and it carries an

inscription written in six-inch (15 cm) letters picked out in red ochre paint that translates as 'Here the Covenant becomes manifest to thee'. This has been dated to the reign of Ethelred the Unready, 978–1016, and is THE LARGEST AND OLDEST SURVIVING STONE CARVED ANGLO-SAXON TEXT IN BRITAIN.

The north and east walls are festooned with hatchments, bearing the arms of the Hulse family who bought Breamore House in 1748 and still live there today. Many commentators think there are MORE HATCHMENTS HERE THAN IN ANY OTHER ENGLISH CHURCH. I shall start counting.

East Meon

All Saints

Norman Church

This imposing Norman church sits on a hillside above the village. It is of an inordinate size and splendour for a village church, no doubt because East Meon was an important country seat of the Norman Bishops of Winchester. The most notable feature of the exterior is the splendid NORMAN CROSSING TOWER, decorated with triple arcades and round windows and crowned with a broach spire from a later date. It somewhat resembles the tower of Winchester Cathedral, which is not surprising since both towers were built around 1090 for the same Bishop of Winchester, William the Conqueror's cousin BISHOP WALKELIN.

East Meon's west door is original with a Norman arch of four orders, some with zigzag carving. Inside, the sunlight pours in through the large windows of the 13th-century south aisle, illuminating four powerful Norman crossing arches that highlight the impressive scale of the church.

Finest Tournai Font

East Meon's great masterpiece sits to the right of the west door, a GLORIOUSLY CARVED FONT OF BLACK TOURNAI MARBLE, dated about 1150 and given by Henry de Blois, Bishop of Winchester and grandson of the Conqueror. This is perhaps THE BEST OF ENGLAND'S SEVEN TOURNAI FONTS, with the possible exception of the one in Winchester Cathedral. Each Tournai font was carved out of a single block of marble by Flemish craftsmen, on site at Tournai, in what is now Belgium, and then transported to England on a specially constructed boat. Every font has a different design and the East Meon font tells the story of Adam and Eve on two sides, with symbolic carvings of birds and beasts on the other two sides. The images are so detailed and so graphic that it's as good as reading a book.

Next to the church, to the south-east, is EAST MEON COURT, built around a Norman hall where the Bishops of Winchester once held court. Although most of the structure dates from a rebuilding in the 13th century, the Court is ONE OF ENGLAND'S OLDEST INHABITED HOUSES.

Hayling Island

St Mary's and St Peter's

Two Churches

HAYLING ISLAND, all 10 square miles of it, has two old churches, both quite different but both interesting. ST MARY'S IN SOUTH HAYLING is built on the highest point of the island, 20 feet (6 m) above sea level. It is mainly 13th century and has a clerestory, nave arcades with capitals carved with leaves, dragons and the heads of kings, a Saxon font from Hayling's first church, dug up from the vicarage garden, and a lovely Perpendicular east window filled with saints. In the churchyard is a yew tree 36 feet (11 m)

round, ONE OF THE OLDEST YEW TREES IN ENGLAND, and well over 1,000 years old.

ST PETER'S IN NORTH HAYLING also has an old yew, 20 feet (6 m) in girth and about 500 years old. The church itself is Norman, built in about 1170, its foundations formed of large sarsen stones deposited when the Ice Age retreated. It has three bells dating from 1350, which are said to form THE OLDEST PEAL OF THREE IN ALL OF ENGLAND.

Hayling's Princess

Buried in the churchyard is 'HAYLING'S PRINCESS', CATHERINE YOURIEVSKY (1878–1959), the youngest daughter of Tsar Alexander II of Russia, by his mistress Catherine who later became his second wife. Alexander was assassinated in 1881 and his daughter Catherine was taken to France, where she grew up. She married twice, the second time to a White Russian prince with whom she was once more forced to flee Russia, this time during the Bolshevik Revolution. In the 1920s, after her husband deserted her for the

New York heiress Alice Astor, Princess Catherine became a singer, and in 1934 settled in a house called The Haven on Hayling Island, where she remained until her death in 1959. Only two members of her family attended her funeral in St Peter's Church, her husband Prince Obolensky and her nephew Prince Alexander Yourievsky.

Nately Scures

St Swithun's

Most Perfect Church

While it may be the name that lures you here, it is the church that ensures you linger here. St Swithun's is easily missed by drivers hurrying past on the busy A30, as it crouches low among a circle of trees, on a little hill next to a farmyard, a most unlikely spot. Discovery, however, brings forth a silent scream of delight, for here is ONE OF ENGLAND'S MOST PERFECT LITTLE CHURCHES, unexpected, beautiful to gaze upon, secluded, unspoiled, with some quirky features, some interesting monuments and an air of quiet poise. It has been here for nearly a thousand years and will probably be here for a thousand more.

St Swithun's is HAMPSHIRE'S SMALLEST PARISH CHURCH, just 30 feet (9 m) long and 16 feet (5 m) wide. Except for a small bellcote put on top of the west wall in 1865 to replace a 17th-century wooden original, and a roof made new in the 18th century, there are no external additions to the structure, such as a porch or vestry, making St Swithun's THE LEAST SPOILED EXAMPLE OF ENGLAND'S FOUR SINGLE-CELL APSIDAL NORMAN CHURCHES (*see* Winterborne Tomson, Dorset, pages 77–8).

A Cautionary Tail

The church was built in 1175, and the most notable feature outside is the fine Norman doorway in the north wall, with an arch of two orders of zigzag carving resting on circular shafts. On the eastern capital is a LIVELY DEPICTION OF A VOLUPTUOUS MERMAID BOISTEROUSLY FLICKING HER TAIL, put there as a caution to the young men of Nately Scures not to be unfaithful.

Apparently one such young man from the village dallied with a mermaid while sailing the oceans and then forgot about her, and on returning to England became engaged to a local girl. As the couple came to the church for their wedding

the mermaid was waiting at the door, scooped up the young man and carried him off to sea. A warning to us all.

The original mermaid is now inside the church, safe from the weather. The one we see by the door today is a reproduction.

Skew and Scure

One enters the church beneath a substantial wooden gallery, dated to 1591 and restored in the late 18th century. Most of the furnishings are Victorian. As you look east to the lovely rounded apse you might find yourself rendered a bit boss-eyed. The reason for this is that the east window is not quite central but skewed slightly off to the north, something that is more noticeable from outside. Why is it like that? No one seems to know, probably just a mis-measurement by the builder, but it rather charmingly adds to the character of St Swithun's.

The walls are plastered with memorial tablets, one of them on the south wall dedicated to the Scures, a Norman family who owned the manor for at least 300 years and gave their name to the village. The remains of many generations of Scures are buried here.

A Fighting Family First and Last

Most of the other memorials are to members of the CARLETON family, including one on the north wall near the altar to GENERAL SIR GUY CARLETON, 1ST BARON DORCHESTER (1722–1808) who, as Governor of Quebec, repulsed the invasion of Canada by American troops in 1775–6 and later became commander-in-chief of British forces in North America during the War of Independence. Among his notable achievements was ensuring that Britain's promise to free slaves who fought on the British side was kept and, along with his brother Thomas (*see* below), overseeing the safe evacuation of British Loyalists from New York to settlements in New Brunswick.

Sir Guy Carleton's younger brother GENERAL THOMAS CARLETON (1735–1817) is also remembered. In 1784, after fighting alongside Sir Guy in Canada, Thomas was appointed the FIRST GOVERNOR OF NEW BRUNSWICK, a post he held until his death in 1817.

Next to Thomas is a wall tablet to his son CAPTAIN WILLIAM CARLETON RN (1789–1874), the last survivor of the Battle of Trafalgar, who lived on for another 69 years after the engagement.

Well, I never knew this
about
HAMPSHIRE CHURCHES

Corhampton. Here is ONE OF HAMPSHIRE'S OLDEST CHURCHES, so old that it doesn't even have a dedication. It is believed that a church was founded here by St Wilfrid while he was converting the Jutes of the Meon valley between AD 681 and 686. The present building dates from about 1020, in the reign of King Canute, and shows examples of the pilasters and the long-and-short work of the Saxon builders. Beside the south porch is a SAXON SUNDIAL, which DIVIDES THE DAY INTO EIGHT TIDES rather than hours. The main features inside are the SAXON CHANCEL ARCH, untouched and very plain, and a SAXON ALTAR STONE in the sanctuary, UNUSUAL IN THAT IT HAS SIX CONSECRATION CROSSES CARVED ON IT, RATHER THAN THE NORMAL FIVE. Both sides of the chancel wall are covered with 12th-century paintings, one showing a rare scene of ST SWITHUN MENDING A PEASANT WOMAN'S BROKEN EGGS. The church is almost entirely hidden from the road by an enormous yew tree, 23 feet (7 m) round and more than 1,000 years old – in fact, probably older than the church itself.

Itchen Stoke – St Mary's. No need to go to Paris. For glorious Gothic elegance and splendour just come to Itchen Stoke in deepest Hampshire and see this supremely beautiful Victorian village church based on that church of French kings, LA SAINTE CHAPELLE in Paris. Built in 1866, paid for by the rector, REVEREND CHARLES CONYBEARE, and designed by his architect brother HENRY CONYBEARE, the church of St Mary sits in an elevated position above the road and grabs the attention with its huge, west-end rose window, satisfying polygonal eastern apse and slate roof laid out in diamonds. The interior is quite sensational,

immensely tall with unobscured views east to the stone vaulted apse, west to a wall of delightful Gothic arcading and the red and blue hues of the rose window. Everywhere is a forest of graceful Gothic arches rising high to a richly painted roof, all flickering in a sparkling kaleidescope of colour from the sunlit stained-glass lancet windows. Marble font, clustered marble pillars and floor tiles flash like fire. Feel like a French king, in Hampshire. Who would have thought?

Selborne – St Mary's. Buried in the churchyard here is GILBERT WHITE (1720–93), ENGLAND'S FIRST ECOLOGIST and author of the bestselling *The Natural History and Antiquities of Selborne*, THE FIRST SUCH DETAILED RECORD OF THE NATURAL WORLD. White was born in Selborne and spent most of his life as curate here, devoting his spare time to observing and writing about the wildlife and plants of the village and surrounding countryside. His home in the village, The Wakes, is now a museum of his life and work and there are two memorial windows to him in the south aisle of the church, between them showing many of the birds and animals, flora and fauna that are mentioned in White's seminal book, which has never been out of print.

HEREFORDSHIRE

St Mary & St David, Kilpeck – England's finest small Norman church

Bacton

St Faith's

60 years with a Queen

In this lovely hilltop church looking down upon the Golden Valley far, far away from the intrigue of the royal court and reached only by sunken lanes, there is to be found ONE OF THE FINEST AND MOST IMPORTANT MONUMENTS IN ALL OF ENGLAND. It marks the empty tomb of BLANCHE PARRY, Chief Gentlewoman of the Privy Chamber to Elizabeth I, and her lifelong confidante. Blanche was born in Newcourt, Bacton, in 1508 and became a royal servant when Elizabeth was still in the cradle. They were together for nearly 60 years until Blanche died in 1590.

As she approached the age of 70 Blanche considered retiring to Bacton and commissioned her own monument

to be put in the church there. Made of alabaster and dated sometime before November 1578, it shows Blanche kneeling before the Queen, THE FIRST KNOWN DEPICTION OF ELIZABETH I AS GLORIANA and THE ONLY CONTEMPORARY STATUE OF ELIZABETH I IN A VILLAGE CHURCH. Blanche composed her own epitaph, which includes the line 'with maiden queen a maid did

end her life', which suggests that Elizabeth really was a virgin queen – after all, Blanche would have known. Blanche Parry never did retire and was finally buried in St Margaret's Westminster, beneath the epitaph she herself had written.

Eaton Bishop

St Michael & All Angels

Herefordshire's Best-kept Secret

This is a typical leafy village of bungalows and black-and-white houses, set above the River Wye west of Hereford. There has been a stone church here since well before the Norman invasion. The muscular Norman tower was added in the 12th century, the nave and chancel expanded in the 13th century. There is a 13th-century font, a good, wooden, wine-glass pulpit and a colourful 14th-century five-light window above the chancel arch.

St Michael and All Angels, Eaton Bridge

But it is the lower east window of five lights that we have come to see, THE FINEST MEDIEVAL STAINED-GLASS WINDOW IN ANY CHURCH IN ENGLAND, and one of the oldest, dating from 1320. The colours, predominantly greens and golds and reds, with flashes of blue, burn like jewels – and the northernmost panel, showing the Madonna and Child, is considered amongst THE MOST BEAUTIFUL PIECES OF MEDIEVAL STAINED GLASS EVER PRODUCED.

The glass was made in France and then assembled here, and the window is thought to have been paid for by Adam de Monmouth, cantor at Hereford Cathedral. It was removed for safety during the Civil War and again during the Second World War.

Where else but in England would you find one of the world's most exquisite works of art in a simple, unknown country church?

Kilpeck

St Mary & St David

A Gallery of Norman Carvings

This little church, standing in fields south of Hereford, surrounded by cottages and farmland, is one of England's gems, regarded by many as THE MOST PERFECT NORMAN CHURCH IN ENGLAND. It was built between 1130 and 1145 and follows the classic Norman pattern of nave, chancel and rounded apse. Inside, the Norman arches to the chancel and sanctuary

are sturdy and pleasing, as are the rib vaults and the three small windows of the apse.

But Kilpeck is most celebrated for its WEALTH OF SPECTACULAR NORMAN CARVINGS, all original and particularly splendid around the south doorway. The tympanum shows the TREE OF LIFE, while the inner arch is decorated with chevrons and beak-heads of birds and dragons and scary faces, and the outer arch has more birds and dragons linked together in a chain of medallions. Two soldiers entangled in creepers stand guard, one above the other, on the western shaft while serpents twist and writhe through foliage up one column and down the other. You can almost hear the leaves rustling and the serpents hissing.

Some 80 corbels encircle the church below the roof, displaying a glorious cacophany of strange animals and folk, an upside-down pig, bearded men galore, dragons, dancing figures, birds, monsters, a bear, people doing all manner of strange things, lovers entangled, priests a-praying and, my favourite, a baby rabbit cuddled up to a cute puppy dog with floppy ears, straight out of a Disney cartoon. All life is here in joyous, uninhibited detail. There are gaps now and then in the ring of corbels where Victorian sensibilities demanded the removal of the more boisterous 'exhibitionists', although they missed one brazen character whose eyes are popping with the effort of doing something unmentionable.

Kilpeck is the acknowledged masterpiece of the HEREFORDSHIRE SCHOOL OF SCULPTURE. This is a relatively modern name given to a group of master masons who worked on churches throughout the West Midland counties in the 11th and 12th centuries, mixing Celtic, Saxon and Norman influences and imagery into their exquisite carvings.

Leintwardine

St Mary Magdalene

Some Larger-than-life Characters

The church stands at the top of the hill on the site of the Roman town of Bravonium. Roman tiles and pottery have been found beneath the chancel. The original Saxon church was rebuilt by the Normans and then added to over the next three centuries, leaving us with the building as we see it today. The battlemented 14th-century tower, huge and formidable, overpowers the tangled rooflines of the nave and chapels, leaving a rather uneven profile.

Mortimer

Inside, the church is capacious and quite dark, the gloom accentuating the colour and beauty of the east window. This is a big church full of big characters – the Lady Chapel, for instance, was built as a chantry chapel by ROGER MORTIMER, who was born nearby at Wigmore Castle. It was

designed as a place where prayers could be said for his immortal soul, and indeed Mortimer's soul turned out to be much in need of prayer, for he became the lover of Edward II's queen, Isabella, deposed the King, arranged for his murder at Berkeley Castle and ruled England himself, until defeated and then executed by Edward III.

Tarleton

On the wall of Mortimer's chantry stands an impressive monument to another infamous character, SIR BANASTRE TARLETON, upon whom Mel Gibson based the cruel and villainous Colonel William Tavington in his film *The Patriot*.

Tarleton was born in Liverpool in 1754, the son of a wealthy merchant and slave trader. Having squandered his inheritance, he bought himself into the Army with the least expensive commission, that of a cavalry coronet. Strong, brave, arrogant and a born leader, he was well suited to the cavalry and volunteered for service in the American War of Independence. By 1778, a lieutenant-colonel at the age of 24, he was leading his own 'Tarleton's Legion', which he put together from several

dragoon companies. The legion had a series of astonishing successes at Charleston and Waxhaws, although it was at Waxhaws that Tarleton earned himself the name 'Bloody Ban', when many of the American soldiers trying to surrender were killed.

At Yorktown in 1781, Tarleton put forward a plan he believed would give the British victory, but it was rejected and he was forced to witness Cornwallis's humiliating surrender to the Americans. On his return to England he tarnished his war reputation by publishing a book criticising Cornwallis's handling of the war and talking up his own actions. He later became MP for Liverpool, was promoted to general, knighted in 1815 and made a Knight Grand Cross of the Order of the Bath. In his final years he came to live in Leintwardine and was buried in the church (some say along with his horse) in 1833, at the age of 78. His impressive monument was put up by his 'bereaved widow', so someone loved him.

Flossie

In 2010 a new misericord, the first of many, was unveiled in St Mary Magdalene featuring a likeness of the late FLOSSIE LANE, landlord for 74 years of the SUN INN in the village, ONE OF ENGLAND'S LAST REMAINING 'PARLOUR INNS', without a conventional counter or bar. Flossie's misericord was the first to be installed in the church for nearly 500 years, the previous ones being a set salvaged from Wigmore Abbey at the Dissolution of the Monasteries in 1540.

Whitbourne

St John the Baptist

First Man in Space

A handsome village with half-timbered cottages and elaborate chimneys, and a wonderful grouping in the east of a brown brick Old Rectory, the old garden walls of moated Whitbourne Court, and the church with its lych-gate. St John's has a Norman core with Norman brickwork in the nave and a fine 14th-century tower of rose-coloured stone. The sandstone font is 12th century, crudely carved with star patterns.

As well as a place of ancient beauty, Whitbourne is the burial place of THE FIRST ENGLISHMAN TO TAKE US TO THE MOON, BISHOP OF HEREFORD FRANCIS GODWIN (1562–1633). In about 1600, while living next door to the church,

in Whitbourne Court, then a bishop's palace, Bishop Godwin wrote *The Man in the Moon*, THE FIRST EVER SCIENCE FICTION BOOK, in which he talks about things such as human flight and the wireless.

The Man in the Moon tells the tale of a Spaniard, Domingo Gonsales, who is marooned on a island with his black companion, and escapes by training a team of wild swans to fly him to the moon. On his voyage he realises that Copernicus was right and that the earth is not the centre of the universe but revolves around the sun. He also observes that 'weights . . . are drawn by a secret property of the globe, or something within it, as the lodestone draweth iron' – some 70 years before Isaac Newton saw his apple fall from the tree, Francis Godwin accurately described gravity. On the moon, Gonsales meets a race of super-beings called Lunarians, who have no illness or doctors, no arguments and crime, hence no lawyers, and no poverty. They do, however, smoke! If the Lunarians perceive evil in one of their kind, they exile him to earth and Gonsales, realising that he can never attain their state of perfection, returns to earth himself.

Godwin did not publish *The Man in the Moon* himself, but the written manuscript was discovered in his desk in Whitbourne Court after he died and was published posthumously in 1638. The book became popular all over the world, and by 1768 at least 25 editions had been published in various languages. Daniel Defoe may have found his Man Friday and Jonathan Swift his Gulliver

in the pages of Francis Godwin's *The Man in the Moon*.

Devotees of *Star Trek* and *Dr Who* should make Whitbourne a place of pilgrimage, for here in deepest Herefordshire lies a far-seeing bishop whose imagination encouraged men to dream of one day travelling to the stars.

Well, I never knew this about

HEREFORDSHIRE CHURCHES

Clifford – St Mary the Virgin. A charming and attractive old church stands apart from the village, behind trees, with views across the Wye to the Black Mountains and the ruins of Clifford Castle, birthplace in 1140 of JANE CLIFFORD – who would grow up to become FAIR ROSAMUND, the fabled mistress of Henry II. A Norman foundation, now mainly 16th-century, the church was restored by the Victorians, who gave it an unusual ARCADE OF OAK PILLARS. Set in a recess in the north wall of the chancel is the remarkably well-preserved oak effigy of a priest, possibly a monk from Clifford's long-gone Cluniac priory, his hands clasped in prayer and traces of red paint still visible in the folds of his robe. Dating from c.1280, this is THE OLDEST WOODEN EFFIGY OF A CLERIC IN ENGLAND.

Shobdon – St John the Evangelist. Here is ENGLAND'S ONLY ROCOCO CHURCH, known as the WEDGWOOD CHURCH owing to its fantastical white and pale blue rococo interior. It was built in 1752 for RICHARD BATEMAN, owner of Shobdon Court (long since demolished), who had the Norman church that was already there knocked down, retaining only the 13th-century tower and Norman font. Bateman was a friend of Horace Walpole and probably commissioned Richard Bentley, one of the architects of Walpole's Strawberry Hill extravaganza in Twickenham, to design St John's, although William Kent has been mentioned. Two doorways and the carved Norman chancel arch from the original church were rebuilt as a folly half a mile away, and are now sadly weathered.

Stoke Lacy – St Peter & St Paul. This Norman church was almost completely rebuilt by the rector's son, F.R. Kempson, in 1863. From 1871 to 1887 the rector was the REVEREND HENRY MORGAN, and he was followed by his son PREBENDARY HENRY MORGAN, who officiated at Stoke Lacy for 50 years from 1887 until 1937. In 1909, the Prebendary's son, HENRY F.S. MORGAN, unveiled to the parishioners of Stoke Lacy a prototype single-seat three-wheeled runabout that he had built for himself in the Rectory garage. This was THE FIRST EVER MORGAN CAR and 'HFS', as he became known, went on to found the famous MORGAN MOTOR COMPANY, which he ran until his death aged 77 in 1959. The company was then taken over by his son PETER MORGAN until shortly before he died in 2003. The Morgans are all buried in a family grave in the church-yard, and inside the church there are two small memorial windows showing Peter Morgan, the Morgan factory, and a selection of Morgan cars.

HERTFORDSHIRE

All Saints, King's Langley – cradle of the royal House of York

Furneux Pelham

St Mary's

An Earthly Plot

'Time Flies. Mind your Business'. So says the church clock, set on its 14th-century Perpendicular tower topped with a Hertfordshire spike, but it dissembles, for time actually stands still in this sleepy place of rose-covered cottages and sunken lanes. St Mary's stands proud upon a leafy rise above the undulating road and beckons you in to see its elegant 13th-century chancel, spacious nave and lovely 15th-century roof where gaily painted angels roost. They were restored in the 1960s by a local artist and some hold coats of arms, including that of the Norman de Furneux family who gave the village its name, while others hold musical instruments and bear names such as John, Paul, Ringo and George.

There are more bright angels in the windows of the south chapel, which was built in 1520 by Robert Newport, whose brass can be seen in the aisle. These angels are the work of WILLIAM MORRIS and are also seen playing musical instruments, a violin, a small pipe organ, a lute and a harp. The window dates from 1867 and is THE FIRST WINDOW IN WHICH MORRIS EVER USED THESE DESIGNS, which subsequently appeared elsewhere in places as far-flung as Tamworth, Tavistock, Putney and Boston, Massachusetts. There is another fine window here too, dating from 1874, which shows the Archangel Gabriel, designed by William Morris, in

one section, and the Virgin Mary with St Michael, by EDWARD BURNE-JONES, in the other two.

Furneux Pelham, peaceful though it may seem, has played its part in England's story, for the Elizabethan Furneux Pelham Hall was the home of LORD MONTEAGLE and is where, in 1605, he received a mysterious letter, ostensibly from his brother-in-law Francis Tresham, warning him to stay away from Parliament on 5 November. Monteagle showed the letter to James I's chief minister Robert Cecil, 1st Earl of Salisbury, and in so doing gave away the Gunpowder Plot.

King's Langley

All Saints

A Royal Plot

The momentous past of this historic village of kings is made real in the sturdy 13th-century church of All

Saints, set below the busy main road leading to London. Here, in the chapel at the end of the north aisle, not far from the site of the royal palace on the hill where he was born in 1341, lies EDMUND OF LANGLEY, fifth son of Edward III, brother of the Black Prince and John of Gaunt and founder of the royal House of York.

Edmund's great-great-grandfather HENRY III built a hunting lodge here in the 13th century, which was later transformed into a luxurious palace by Henry's son EDWARD I, whose Spanish wife ELEANOR OF CASTILE installed outlandish foreign refinements in it, such as carpets and baths. Their epicurean son EDWARD II greatly appreciated such things and spent much of his time here. In 1307 he rode out from Langley to attend the wedding of his niece MARGARET DE CLARE to his friend and favourite PIERS GAVESTON at Berkhamsted Castle.

The following year Edward founded a friary next to the palace in honour of his mother, which by the time of the Dissolution had grown into one of the richest in England, with a friary church to rival Westminster Abbey. In 1315, Piers Gaveston's body was brought to Langley, three years after his murder at Warwick, and buried there in great

reverence in front of a grieving Edward.

EDWARD III also stayed often at Langley and his wife, PHILIPPA OF HAINAULT, gave birth to their fifth son Edmund there in 1341, the occasion marked by a spectacular tournament. Edward III ruled his kingdom from Langley for two years during the Black Death in 1348–50, when it was unsafe to be in London.

After an eventful life Edmund of Langley was buried in the friary church in 1402, alongside his wife Isabella of Castile, who had died ten years earlier.

Edmund's nephew RICHARD II, son of the Black Prince, spent Christmases at Langley with his court, issuing proclamations from 'the Palace of Langley Regis'. In 1399, after he was murdered in Pontefract castle on the orders of his cousin HENRY BOLINGBROKE (Henry IV), Richard's body was brought to Langley for a furtive burial. As one contemporary chronicler put it, 'The great ones were not there, neither was there any crowd of common people.' His body was removed to Westminster Abbey by a repentant Henry V in 1414.

When the friary was dissolved in 1539, the black Purbeck marble and alabaster tomb of Edmund of Langley and Isabella was extracted from the friary church and brought into the village church, where it now resides, still richly carved and adorned with colourful shields and set upon a floor of old tiles also salvaged from the friary. The grave of Edward II's tragic companion Piers Gaveston was lost, and his bones lie somewhere beneath the playing fields of the Rudolf Steiner School, which now occupies what is left of the friary buildings.

Old Hatfield

St Etheldreda's

A Divine Plot

Shielded from the distasteful bustle of new Hatfield Town by a railway line and the crooked timber cottages and handsome red-brick houses of Old Hatfield village, St Etheldreda's stands aloof on a hill at the gates of mighty Hatfield House, drawing up her skirts like some haughty ancient dowager. She tends to be ignored by the hoi polloi as they hurry past toward the excitements of the Big House, and this is a shame for she has much to show them.

The present church dates from the 13th century, while the tower was added in the 15th century by CARDINAL MORTON, Archbishop of Canterbury and Lord Chancellor to Henry VII, who built the Old Palace next door where Elizabeth I grew up.

Not long after this the 13th-century south chapel was enlarged and divided

from the chancel by an arcade to serve as a private chapel for the owners of nearby BROCKET HALL. The second SIR JOHN BROCKET (d.1598) lies there with his wife and mother-in-law, while nearby are monuments by Flemish Sculptor JOHN MICHAEL RYSBRACK to SIR JAMES READE (d.1701) and SIR JOHN READE (d. 1711), father and son, whose family came into Brocket Hall by the marriage of Thomas Reade to Sir John Brocket's daughter Mary. The hall eventually passed to the Lambs, and buried in the Lamb family vault beneath the pulpit is WILLIAM LAMB, VISCOUNT MELBOURNE (1779–1848), Prime Minister and mentor to the young Queen Victoria. Beside him lies his colourful wife LADY CAROLINE LAMB (1785–1828), who introduced the waltz into England at Brocket Hall when she wasn't startling the guests by leaping naked out of a giant soup tureen.

Another premier lies in the churchyard, ROBERT GASCOYNE CECIL, 3RD MARQUESS OF SALISBURY (1830–1903), three times Prime Minister and the last to serve from the Lords.

But the grandest tomb of all is found inside the church in the opulent SALISBURY CHAPEL to the north of the chancel. Here we have ROBERT CECIL, 1ST MARQUESS OF SALISBURY (1563–1612), the man who foiled the Gunpowder Plot, who built the palatial Hatfield House and who enlarged St Etheldreda's to serve as his mausoleum. His tomb is majestic. His white marble effigy lies upon a table of black marble born on the shoulders of four women representing the four Virtues of Justice, Fortitude, Temperance and

dear Prudence, who throws caution to the wind by appearing bare-breasted. Under the slab is a skeleton, a reminder that Death makes us all equal.

St Paul's Walden

All Saints

A Family Plot

The church stands in a bare hilltop churchyard with wide views across the manicured grounds of two fine houses. It is a handsome Perpendicular edifice with a heavily buttressed 14th-century

tower topped by a traditional Hertfordshire spike. Set in the south aisle window, east of the south door, is a lovely example of medieval glass, a beautifully coloured, early 14th-century portrait of the Virgin Mary in a green and brown robe, carrying the Christ child, dressed in red, on her left arm and holding a spray of flowers in her right hand. It is a remarkable treasure.

Another notable feature is the elaborate turquoise interior of the chancel, designed and built in 1727 by Edward

GILBERT, owner of ST PAUL'S WALDEN BURY, a grand house standing half a mile away at the end of an avenue of trees. Gilbert's daughter married the wealthy Durham coal merchant George Bowes, and their daughter Mary Eleanor married John Lyon, 9th Earl of Strathmore, great-grandfather of ELIZABETH BOWES-LYON, mother of Queen Elizabeth II.

A wall tablet records the fact that Queen Elizabeth the Queen Mother was born in St Paul's Walden Bury in 1900 and baptised in the church on 23 September that year. She visited her childhood home at least once every year until she died in 2002 and is remembered by a tall memorial column in the churchyard.

Well, I never **knew this** *about*

HERTFORDSHIRE CHURCHES

Essendon – St Mary the Virgin. On 3 September 1916, St Mary's was badly damaged by a bomb dropped from a German Zeppelin, becoming only THE SECOND CHURCH IN ENGLAND EVER TO BE BOMBED FROM THE AIR. (The first was St Mary's, Snettisham, in Norfolk.) Inside is ONE OF ENGLAND'S ONLY TWO BLACK BASALT WEDGWOOD FONTS, donated by Mary Whitbread in 1778. The other is in Cardington church in Bedfordshire (*see* page 2)

Little Hormead – St Mary's. Set against a wall inside this delightful, small, early Norman church, which stands in a quiet churchyard overlooking fields, is a huge, solid wooden door covered in glorious swirling ironwork fashioned into foliage, birds and a sinuous dragon. It is over 1,000 years old and one of the oldest, best-preserved and most precious treasures from Norman England that we have. Also to be seen here are the simple scalloped doorway in which the door once hung, a beautiful, plain Norman chancel arch and a crude carving on the wall of a

grinning face in 15th-century head-dress, possibly the work of a pilgrim passing through on his way to Walsingham.

Shenleybury – St Botolph's. This little flint church, shielded from the busy main road by trees, sits one mile north of the hilltop village of Shenley. It was built in 1424 with a bequest from Maud, Countess of Salisbury, whose home Salisbury Hall lies a short way away across the fields. In 1753 the tower and chancel had to be pulled down after a fire, leaving just the nave and south aisle. The church was made redundant in 1972 after the parish boundaries changed and is now privately owned. It is possible, however, to get permission to view the two graves of interest in the churchyard here.

The tombstone of NICHOLAS HAWKSMOOR (1661–1736), the architect responsible for the towers of Westminster Abbey, Easton Neston in Northamptonshire, six London churches and two Oxford colleges, can be found under a yew tree. He lived at Porters, a large house about one mile to the west. Over by the wall is the simple gravestone of racing driver GRAHAM HILL (1929–75), twice World Champion and the only man ever to have won motor racing's Triple Crown – the Le Mans 24 Hours, the Indianapolis 500 and the Formula One World Championship. He lived with his family in a big house on Green Street in Shenley and was killed, ironically, in an air crash, while attempting to land at nearby Elstree airfield in foggy conditions.

Widford – St John the Baptist. The colourful east window of St John's is a memorial to JOHN ELIOT, 'APOSTLE TO THE INDIANS', who was baptised in the church in 1604. He emigrated to Boston in America in 1631 and taught himself the language and customs of the local Indians so that he could preach the Gospel to them in their own language. His translation of the Book of Psalms into the native language, published in 1640, WAS THE FIRST BOOK EVER PRINTED IN AMERICA. In 1663 his translation of the Bible into the Algonquian language became THE FIRST BIBLE EVER PRINTED IN AMERICA. Eliot spent the rest of his life establishing settlements for the Indians and ministering to the newly arrived slaves from Africa, and is THE FIRST MAN KNOWN TO HAVE RAISED HIS VOICE IN PROTEST AGAINST SLAVERY.

HUNTINGDONSHIRE

St Kyneburgha, Castor – the only church in England dedicated to St Kyneburgha

Barnack

St John the Baptist

Saxon Treasures and England's Earliest Spire

BARNACK is famous for its stone, known as BARNACK RAG, which was first utilised for building by the Romans, and was later used in many local churches and medieval abbeys, such as Crowland, Ramsey, Bury St Edmunds, Peterborough and Ely, the last two now cathedrals. When the Fenland abbeys were demolished at the Dissolution of the Monasteries, some of the Barnack stone was salvaged for building the colleges of Cambridge University. The quarry, which lies to the south of the village, was worked out by Tudor times and is now a nature reserve.

Barnack's superb church is built, appropriately, of Barnack stone and is noted for its LATE SAXON TOWER,

NORMAN BELFRY AND EARLY GOTHIC
SPIRE, all of which combine to make
a uniquely handsome ensemble. The
Saxons contributed the two lower
stages of the tower, which date from
1000 to 1020. On the south face there
is a crude Saxon sundial above a
window and a rudimentary Saxon
doorway into the tower. The west face
has a typical Saxon triangular headed
window and another doorway high up
in the wall, similar to that at Deerhurst
in Gloucestershire (*see* page 103), which
originally led to an outside gallery.
There are also various sculptures
including bird carvings and rope-work
set in window openings.

The Norman belfry stage is supported
with octagonal pinnacled buttresses,
while the short spire above it dates from
around 1200 and is regarded as THE
EARLIEST CHURCH SPIRE IN ENGLAND.

The entrance to the church is through
a simple Norman doorway of three
arches and carved capitals, sheltered by
an impressively high-pitched and stone-
vaulted Gothic porch with blind
arcading to the walls.

The Saxon tower arch inside is huge,
each end resting on a pile of rectangular
stone slabs, resembling a stack of photo-
graph albums. This distinctive arrangement is UNIQUE TO BARNACK. The
ancient stone bench on the west wall
served as a magistrate's seat when the
tower was used as a place to administer
justice.

The high, slender arcades are late
Norman, while the large and elaborate
font is probably Norman with Gothic
touches. The early 14th-century
Decorated east window sports an
unusual style of tracery.

Barnack's special glory can be found
on the wall of the north aisle, a quite
superb carving of CHRIST IN MAJESTY
that is reckoned to be over 1,000 years
old but looks almost new, and is ONE
OF THE FINEST AND BEST-PRESERVED
SAXON SCULPTURES IN EXISTENCE.

Buried in the Whetstone family vault in Barnack churchyard is GEORGE
GASCOIGNE (1535–77), a writer, poet and playwright of the early
Elizabethan age, who influenced the work of William Shakespeare and
others and was one of the principal architects of English literature. While
studying at Gray's Inn he presented the FIRST DRAMATIC COMEDY EVER
PRODUCED IN ENGLISH PROSE, *The Supposes*, translated from Ariosto –
which was used by Shakespeare as a source for *The Taming of the Shrew* –
and *Jocasta*, ONLY THE SECOND GREEK TRAGEDY PERFORMED IN BRITAIN
AND THE FIRST IN BLANK VERSE. Gascoigne introduced the sonnet to
English poetry, devised and performed the masques at the Earl of
Leicester's famous entertainment for Elizabeth I at Kenilworth Castle, and
was the first to extol Elizabeth in verse as a Virgin Queen, married to her
people. He then embarked on a new career as the FIRST ENGLISH WAR
CORRESPONDENT, writing an account of the sack of Antwerp by the
Spaniards in 1576, but died the following year while staying with his
friend and fellow writer George Whetstone at Walcot Hall in Barnack.

Fenstanton

St Peter & St Paul

'Ye Sons of Elegance, who truly taste
The Simple charms that
genuine Art supplies,
Come from the sylvan
Scene His Genius grac'd,
And offer here your tributary Sighs'

So reads the epitaph on the memorial
to England's foremost landscape artist
LANCELOT 'CAPABILITY' BROWN (1715–
83), to be found on the north side of
the chancel of Fenstanton's magnificent
church. In 1767 Brown was allegedly
given the 17th-century manor house at
Fenstanton by the Earl of Northampton
as a thank-you for designing the gardens
at Castle Ashby, and it remained in his
family for four generations. Capability's
grandson Thomas served as rector here
from 1789 to 1829, and Capability and
his wife are buried outside in the

Born in Northumberland, LANCELOT 'CAPABILITY' BROWN learned his trade as a landscape gardener under William Kent, and eventually married Kent's daughter. He set up his own business and quickly became highly sought after. Known for his catchphrase, on being shown around a new property, 'this site has great capabilities,' his aim was to 'perfect nature' with smooth, undulating lawns leading the eye away from the house towards hills and lakes and clumps of trees, creating a very 'English' view. He laid out some 170 gardens, including those at Petworth, Althorp, Burghley and Longleat, with the grounds at Blenheim Palace being regarded as his masterpiece. When asked to go to work on a property in Ireland, Brown declined, saying, 'I haven't finished England yet!'

churchyard (*see* panel, page 135). Fenstanton's 14th-century octagonal church spire dominates the village and the surrounding fenland. The church has a notable DECORATED CHANCEL, which is bigger than the nave and was built in the 14th century by a wealthy rector, William de Longthorne. The magnificent east window, with its delicate tracery and seven tall lancets, is 17 feet (5 m) across and THE BIGGEST PARISH CHURCH WINDOW IN HUNTINGDONSHIRE OR CAMBRIDGESHIRE.

In 1981 the John Howland Society donated a treble bell to the church, in memory of their ancestor JOHN HOWLAND, who was born in Fenstanton and sailed to America in the *Mayflower* in 1620. His parents are buried in the churchyard and among his descendants

are film actor Humphrey Bogart, Phillips Brooks, Bishop of Massachusetts, who wrote the words to the Christmas carol 'Oh Little Town of Bethlehem', the poet Henry Longfellow, and three U.S. Presidents, Franklin D. Roosevelt, George Bush and George W. Bush.

John's brothers Henry and Arthur followed him to America not long afterwards and their descendants include Presidents Richard Nixon and Gerald Ford. Arthur Howland was also an ancestor of Winston Churchill.

Kimbolton

St Andrew's

A Cradle of the New World

Kimbolton's handsome Georgian high street takes several sharp turns as it defers to the village church of St Andrew's with its striking 14th-century broach spire, a little too grand and lofty, perhaps, for its own tower. Mind you, this 13th-century rebuilding of a Norman church has much to be lofty about, for it houses a noble array of monuments and stained-glass windows in tribute to the mighty MONTAGU FAMILY, EARLS AND DUKES OF MANCHESTER, and owners of next-door Kimbolton Castle from 1615 until 1950.

In the south aisle, for example, there is a stained-glass window created in 1901 by the American artist LOUIS COMFORT TIFFANY, depicting the twin daughters of the 8th Duke of Manchester and his Cuban wife Consuelo Yznaga, THE ONLY TIFFANY WINDOW TO BE FOUND IN AN ENGLISH CHURCH.

Nearby is the tomb of HENRY MONTAGU, 1ST EARL OF MANCHESTER, who bought Kimbolton Castle in 1615 and who provides one of the many significant links this modest Huntingdonshire village has with America.

Kimbolton and America

*Henry VIII's first wife, CATHERINE OF ARAGON, was held prisoner in Kimbolton Castle for the last four years of her life. She died there in 1536 and is buried in nearby Peterborough Cathedral. Catherine of Aragon's mother was Queen Isabella of Spain, who sponsored Christopher Columbus's discovery of America in 1492.

*The owners of Kimbolton Castle at the time of Catherine of Aragon's incarceration there were the Wingfield family, one of whom, EDWARD WINGFIELD, is buried in the church. He was THE FIRST PRESIDENT OF JAMESTOWN, VIRGINIA, THE FIRST SUCCESSFUL ENGLISH SETTLEMENT IN AMERICA.

*The next owner of Kimbolton Castle, HENRY MONTAGU, 1ST EARL OF MANCHESTER, was the judge who, in 1618, sentenced to death Sir Walter Raleigh, the founder of Virginia, THE FIRST ENGLISH COLONY IN AMERICA.

St Andrew's Kimbolton

Little Gidding

St John the Evangelist

'Here, the intersection
of the timeless moment
Is England and nowhere.
Never and always . . .
. . . So while the light fails
On a winter's afternoon,
in a secluded chapel
History is now and England'
T.S. ELIOT, 'Little Gidding'

So overwhelmed was the poet T.S. Eliot when he visited Little Gidding in the spring of 1936, the hedgerows white with Queen Anne's Lace and mayflower, that he was moved to write the final part of his poetical reflections the *Four Quartets*, and to name it 'Little Gidding'.

There is nothing at Little Gidding except a farmhouse and a chapel, hidden in a grove of trees in the fields west of the Great North Road, lost in a deep peace and solitude. Here, in 1626, came NICHOLAS FERRAR and his family, refugees from the plague in London, and here they founded THE ONLY CHURCH OF ENGLAND RELIGIOUS COMMUNITY TO BE CREATED BETWEEN THE DISSOLUTION OF THE MONASTERIES IN 1541 AND THE OXFORD MOVEMENT OF THE 1830S.

NICHOLAS FERRAR (1592–1637) was a merchant and director of the Virginia Company, sponsors of the first American colonies, and when the company eventually failed he turned his thoughts to a more spiritual calling. He was ordained a deacon and set out to find a quiet place where he could found a devout community. The derelict manor

them on to a manuscript. When CHARLES I came to visit, he was so taken with the *Harmonies* he asked Ferrar to create one for his own son, the future Charles II. This gorgeously bound copy is now in the British Museum.

Charles I came to Little Gidding three times, the last time in 1646 to find refuge in the manor house the night after his defeat at the Battle of Naseby, even though Ferrar was by then long dead and buried in a tablet tomb outside the west door of the chapel.

Ferrar's community ended with the death of his brother John in 1657. The manor house, which was badly damaged by Cromwell's troops, was demolished in the 1850s and replaced by the red-brick farmhouse we see on the site today. The red-brick chapel was restored in 1714 and given a new Baroque west front with a bellcote. It was further restored in 1848, and renovated again in the 1920s. Inside, the layout is as it was in Ferrar's time, with wood panelling and two single rows of stalls facing each other across the aisle. The windows and chandelier were the gift of William Hopkinson, who brought Little Gidding in 1848. The simple wooden altar in the sanctuary is where Nicholas Ferrar and his king knelt together in prayer, the brass eagle lectern is the 17th-century original, while the chapel's greatest treasure is NICHOLAS FERRAR'S OWN LOCALLY MADE BRASS FONT which can now be seen in the next-door farmhouse, Ferrar House.

house of Little Gidding, deserted since the Black Death in 1350, and the chapel, which was being used as a barn, were perfect.

The community was formed of Ferrar's mother, his brother John and sister Susanna and their extended families, about 30 people in all. They restored the house and chapel, held services twice a day, taught and assisted the local poor, and lived their lives to the rhythms of Cranmer's *Book of Common Prayer*. They also wrote and bound books, including *Harmonies*, a blending of the four Gospels in chronological order, which Ferrar composed by getting his nieces to cut out the passages as he directed and then pasting

Well, I never knew this about

HUNTINGDONSHIRE CHURCHES

Alwalton – St Andrew's. Buried in the Norman church here are the ashes of HENRY ROYCE (1863–1933), one half of Rolls-Royce, the makers of the 'best cars in the world'. Royce was born in Alwalton and was the engineering genius behind Rolls-Royce, with the flamboyant Charles Rolls providing the money and marketing flair. At Rolls-Royce car factories the cars are known as 'Royces', rather than 'Rolls' or 'Rollers'.

Castor – St Kyneburgha's. This magnificent Norman church, built on the site of a Roman palace that was the second largest building in Roman Britain, is THE ONLY CHURCH IN ENGLAND DEDICATED TO ST KYNEBURGHA, a daughter of the pagan King Penda of Mercia. She founded a Saxon abbey here, stones of which are built into the walls of the present church. The tower, decorated with two tiers of blind arches, is one of THE BEST NORMAN TOWERS IN ENGLAND. The spire was added in 1350. Above the south porch is a carving of

Christ that dates from the days of King Alfred, while on a capital of the chancel arch is a Norman carving of St Kyneburgha being chased by two thugs. There is a 15th-century angel roof and, in the north aisle, a vivid 14th-century wall painting of the Martyrdom of St Catherine, showing the wheel on which the Emperor Maximus tried to break her. THIS PAINTING IS UNIQUE IN ALSO SHOWING THE EXECUTION OF THE EMPEROR'S PHILOSOPHERS WHOM CATHERINE HAS CONVERTED.

Great Paxton – Holy Trinity. Hiding amongst the trees and sandwiched between the village and the A1, this reclusive old church was once an important Minster. It was built around 1020 as a large cruciform church, rare for the Saxons, and is THE ONLY SAXON CHURCH IN ENGLAND TO SURVIVE COMPLETE WITH ARCADES, AISLES, CLERESTORY AND

CROSSING. There is little evidence of grandeur from the outside except for the two round-arched clerestory windows, but inside two bays of the magnificent Saxon arcade survive, supported on clustered pillars and with the deeply splayed Saxon clerestory windows above. The church brochure claims that the north crossing arch is THE HIGHEST UNSUPPORTED SAXON ARCH IN EUROPE. The priory church at Stow in Lincolnshire may dispute that, but the arch here is indeed wondrously tall.

KENT

The conical detached wooden bell tower of St Augustine's, Brookland, is unique in England

Barfreston

St Nicholas

A Symphony in Stone

You have to work hard to find BARFRESTON, just a pub and a smattering of cottages lost in a deep dimple of lush Kent countryside, but perseverance brings its rewards, in this case one of England's most dazzling jewels.

Approached from the east up a winding lane, Barfreston's Norman church strikes a fine pose above the road, its gorgeous, heavy-browed round window gazing proudly into the middle distance.

This east face, a hint of things to come, is in three stages: two basic blind arches that look a bit like bandy legs, then a line of blind arcading that incorporates three lancet windows, a corbel table, and finally the glorious wheel window, deeply recessed and surrounded with carved animals and foliage. The

eight spokes of the wheel are being swallowed, or regurgitated, whichever you please, by some rather fearsome faces with lots of teeth. There are niches either side, one sporting a knight on horseback, the other containing something indistinguishable, and some more worn carvings including what looks like a bat hanging upside down.

As you enter the churchyard further up the lane the church is revealed in its full splendour. It is an enchanting little two-cell building, no more than 50 feet (15 m) in length and not unlike an elaborate toy music box. One's first instinct is to slot the chancel back into the nave and take the whole thing home for the mantelpiece. There is no bell tower, SO THE CHURCH BELL HANGS IN A YEW TREE AT THE WEST END OF THE CHURCHYARD, A UNIQUE ARRANGEMENT. The lower parts of the church walls are constructed of flint for a strong base, the upper parts of softer Caen stone, good for carving. A corbel table runs around three sides of the church under the eaves, as does arcading, some of it blind, some decorated, some with windows in.

In front of you is BARFRESTON'S SUPERLATIVE GALLERY OF NORMAN CARVINGS, THE SOUTH DOORWAY. The tympanum shows CHRIST IN MAJESTY surrounded by angels and mythical creatures, mermaids, a griffin and a sphinx, and also two crowned heads, one male and one female, no doubt HENRY II AND ELEANOR OF AQUITAINE, monarchs at the time. Above this is the robed and mitred figure of a bishop. This seems likely to be ARCHBISHOP THOMAS À BECKET, murdered in Canterbury Cathedral in 1170, since Barfreston is adjacent to the route taken by pilgrims heading for his shrine at Canterbury. If it is, then it is THE OLDEST CARVED REPRESENTATION OF BECKET ANYWHERE.

The three arches above the tympanum are alive with action figures – a bowman, a bent old man with a stick, musicians with various instruments including a bear playing a harp, a chap filling a wine-skin from a barrel, a mason, dancers, pilgrims, someone riding a dog. The outer arch shows signs of the Zodiac along with Labours of the Months, scenes of rural activity associated with each month of the year. It is only possible to highlight a few examples of the wonderful carvings, as there are so many, all teeming with humour and variety, and hours of fun can be had discovering all the different illustrations and trying to work them out.

It is difficult to leave this exuberant doorway, but the interior of the church, although less rumbustious, does not disappoint. The view east to the wheel window and triple lancet framed in the triple chancel arch is gorgeous. The high middle arch is decorated with zigzags and dog tooth carvings and rests on twisted shafts. It is flanked by blind arches on either side where there would originally have been altars. String courses carved with animals and birds run round the walls above and below the windows. Everywhere there is something beautiful to look at.

Why is this wonderful church with all its exquisite carvings here? It is thought that while the church itself was built towards the end of the 11th century, the majority of the carvings were done around 1180, maybe by masons practising their craft before moving on to Canterbury Cathedral, or maybe by craftsmen just having fun,

away from the stern eye of the cathedral authorities.

Whatever the reason, those Norman carvers bequeathed us a church to relish and remember.

Brabourne

St Mary's

Oldest in Wood and Glass

Set in beautiful countryside beneath the North Downs, St Mary's is a large Norman church built on Saxon foundations. The nave, although Norman-built in around 1140, is of lofty Saxon dimensions and ends in a huge, high rounded chancel arch, rich in carvings, particularly the capitals.

The church can lay claim to some impressive Norman treasures. In the tower is a wooden staircase of 30 steps dating from 1150 and cut from oak trees that were growing in King Alfred's time, perhaps THE OLDEST WOODEN STAIRCASE IN ENGLAND.

- RELIC - GLASS -

On the north-east side of the chancel is a Norman window still with its original Norman stained glass, dating from around 1090. Most of England's older stained glass was smashed or removed by Henry VIII or Oliver Cromwell's Puritans, and this window of lovely muted colours is a remarkable survival, THE OLDEST COMPLETE STAINED-GLASS WINDOW IN ITS ORIGINAL POSITION IN BRITAIN.

Land of the Scots

On the south side of the chancel is a rare HEART SHRINE, a beautiful piece of sculpture showing a plain shield (which would originally have been painted) set beneath a Decorated arch. In the back is a recess designed to hold the silver or ivory casket containing someone's heart. It is thought that this shrine, which dates from 1300, may have been made for THE ORIGINAL 'SWEETHEART', JOHN BALLIOL, founder of Balliol College, Oxford, and father of John Balliol, King of Scotland. After Balliol died in 1268 his wife Devorgilla carried her husband's 'sweet heart' around with her in a silver casket until her own death in 1290, when she was buried along with the casket in New Abbey, or more popularly 'Sweetheart Abbey', in Kirkcudbrightshire, Scotland.

Eighteen generations of Balliol's descendants, appropriately called SCOT, lie buried beneath the chancel. The family lived near Brabourne at Scot's Hall in Smeeth from the 14th century until the end of the 18th century, and it was said that there was a time when you could ride for 50 miles from Scot's Hall to London and never leave Scot's land.

Magic

Set in the north wall of the chancel of St Mary's is an Easter Sepulchre (*see* Patrington, Yorkshire, page 314). This was once the tomb of SIR JOHN SCOTTE (d.1485), Comptroller of the Household of Edward IV, while the altar is actually a Scot tomb as well, covered in the family shields going all the way back to 1290. The tomb dates from 1600 and was created in memory of REGINALD SCOT, author in 1584 of *The Discoverie of Witchcraft*, an expose of the magic tricks used by witches, and considered to be THE FIRST EVER BOOK ON CONJURING. Reginald Scot is hence regarded as the FATHER OF THE MAGIC CIRCLE.

Brookland

St Augustine's

A Unique Candle Snuffer

I remember being driven past the church at Brookland as a boy, when the world was young, and the vision of this astonishing building on Romney Marsh has remained with me ever since. During the intervening years I have searched in vain for somewhere similar, but St Augustine is unique – there is simply no other English church like it.

What immediately catches the eye is the EXTRAORDINARY AND UNIQUE

FREESTANDING CONICAL WOODEN BELL TOWER. It has been variously described as looking like an old lady in crinoline, a space rocket and a Christmas tree. My favourite description is in the church guide, which likens it to a candle snuffer.

The story goes that the tower detached itself from the main church in astonishment when an old confirmed bachelor turned up to marry a local crone of great antiquity and debatable charms. In fact the bell tower was built separately because the marshy foundations of the main church were unable to bear the extra weight.

The first tower, put up at the same time as the rest of the church in about 1260, was just an open wooden frame slung with a single bell. A peal of bells was then installed in the 15th century and the cover put on, originally weatherboarded, and later shingled in 1936 and again in 1990, with 11,000 shingles and 35,000 bronze nails. The interesting weathervane on top of the bell tower is shaped like a dragon, while inside is a forest of criss-crossing medieval timbers, which legend says were taken from ships wrecked in the marsh.

With all this attention being paid to the belfry, it is easy to forget there is a church here as well, and a mighty fine church it is, long and low with two eastern gables. The porch doors are as eccentric as the bell tower: stable doors below, wild west saloon door shutters on top. Next to the porch is a quaint miniature clock tower with battlements.

Tithes

Inside all is light and elegance, a low ceiling with battered wooden cross beams and two graceful arcades of Gothic arches, leaning markedly and, in keeping with Brookland's penchant for quirkiness, not symmetrical, with six bays on the north side and seven on the south side. There are box pews and a double-decker pulpit, a vivid 13th-century wall painting showing the martyrdom of Thomas à Becket on the south chapel wall, and some fragments of medieval stained glass in a lovely Decorated window in the north aisle.

Since Romney Marsh was given over mainly to sheep, there wasn't a big enough harvest to warrant a tithe barn, and so a corner at the back of the church was used as a tithe room, where we can still see the scales used for weighing the corn, the cup for measuring the wine and the brass-yard for the cloth.

Best Lead Font

Last but certainly not least is BROOKLAND'S GLORIOUS FONT, universally acknowledged as THE FINEST OF ALL OF ENGLAND'S 30 SURVIVING LEAD FONTS. It dates from around 1200 and is ringed with two tiers of arcading, the top arches filled by the signs of the Zodiac, and below each sign a depiction of the labours and activities associated with the time of year that it represents. It amounts to a FASCINATING AND UNIQUE CALENDAR OF RURAL LIFE and a quite superb piece of Norman craftsmanship.

Brookland undoubtedly possesses one of England's most interesting and unusual country churches and should not be missed.

Cobham

St Mary Magdalene

World's Finest Collection of Brasses

Cobham is one of Kent's sweetest villages, a tiny piece of Olde England ignored by motorists hurrying past on the A2 on their way to France. There is an ancient half-timbered inn, the Leather Bottle, frequented by Dickens and featured in *The Pickwick Papers*, a fine Elizabethan hall and park, where Dickens took his last walk, and a 13th-century church containing THE LARGEST AND FINEST COLLECTION OF MEDIEVAL BRASSES IN THE WORLD. There are 19 in all, covering some 200 years, most of them of the Cobham family, who built the present church.

The oldest brass was laid down in 1320 and is to LADY JOAN COBHAM (d.1298). This is THE SECOND OLDEST BRASS OF A LADY IN ENGLAND and THE OLDEST UNDER A CANOPY. The inscription, which tells us, in rhyming Norman French, 'whoever prays for her soul shall have 40 days pardon', is THE OLDEST SURVIVING INSCRIPTION IN ENGLAND. The brass of RAUF DE COBHAM (d.1402) shows just his top half holding the inscription plate and is UNIQUE IN ENGLAND.

In front of the altar is one of ENGLAND'S FINEST ALABASTER CHEST TOMBS, that of the 9th Lord Cobham who died in 1558. His effigy lies on top next to that of his wife Anne, while all around, kneeling in prayer, are their ten sons and four daughters. One of the sons seems about to get up, in readiness, perhaps, to take his father's place.

Tudeley

All Saints

Chagall

There are 13 Chagall windows in Britain. One of them is in Chichester Cathedral and the other 12 are in All Saints, Tudeley, THE ONLY CHURCH IN THE WORLD TO HAVE ALL ITS WINDOWS DESIGNED AND PAINTED BY RUSSIAN-BORN ARTIST MARC CHAGALL.

But for a tragic accident All Saints would have remained a modest, unremarkable village church, similar to thousands of other churches across England, much loved by its congregation but scarcely known outside. Today it receives visitors from all over the world.

In 1963 SARAH VENETIA, 21-year-old daughter of SIR HENRY AND LADY D'AVIGDOR-GOLDSMID of Somerhill House near Tudeley, died in a boating accident off the Kent coast. Her parents commissioned Chagall, a favourite of Sarah's, to design a new east window for their local church of All Saints, in her memory.

The window, CHAGALL'S FIRST WORK IN ENGLAND, was duly installed in 1967, and at the unveiling Chagall and the d'Avigdor-Goldsmids were so delighted with the result it was agreed that Chagall would create windows for the whole church. Seven more were dedicated in 1974 and the final four put in place in 1985, by which time Chagall was 98. He died later that year, his work at Tudeley done.

And what work it is. As you enter the church you are submerged in a watery world of deep blues and dappled gold. The first instinct is to hold your breath, the second is to gasp in wonder.

All eyes are drawn to the blue east window, the MEMORIAL WINDOW, where a young girl is seen adrift in a surging azure sea, while friends and family watch from the shore and weep. The girl is raised from the deeps and puts a foot on the ladder to where 'Christ, the young man, the one whose presence draws young people', waits with an angel to welcome the girl into the comfort of Heaven. Almost central to the window is a young girl on a red horse – 'Horses are for happiness,' said Chagall. The window is never still.

The morning sun filtering through this gorgeous window casts a blue, flickering radiance on to the stones of the chancel floor, which slowly melds with pools of gold as the sun moves through the day and the light percolates through the yellow windows in the south wall. It is a magical experience.

Well, I never knew this about
KENT CHURCHES

Capel-le-Ferne – St Mary's. One of England's farmyard churches, St Mary's sits atop the downs above Folkestone and looks across the sea to France, from whence came the Norman builders who built this lonely little church 900 years ago. There is one small Norman window left in the nave, with foliage painted in the recess, a rare delight. The CELEBRATED TRIPLE CHANCEL ARCH comes from the 14th century and has three pointed arches resting on octagonal piers with, high above it in the screen wall, a Norman round-headed opening into which the rood cross once extended, silhouetted against the light from the east window. THIS FORMATION OF TRIPLE ARCH WITH ROOD OPENING ABOVE IS UNIQUE IN AN ENGLISH CHURCH.

Chilham – St Mary's. Chilham is Kent's most perfect show village, a lovely square of half timber and brick with a Jacobean

Castle at one end and a 15th-century church behind the White Horse Inn at the other. The towers of Canterbury Cathedral can be seen from the top of the church tower, 68 feet (21 m) high. St Mary's is thought to be THE LAST RESTING PLACE OF THE FIRST ARCHBISHOP OF CANTERBURY, ST AUGUSTINE. His shrine was brought here in 1538 to escape the desecration of his abbey in Canterbury at the Dissolution of the Monasteries. It disappeared in 1541, either spirited away to a safer place, or destroyed by jealous folk from Canterbury Cathedral who resented a place of pilgrimage to rival theirs; no one knows. There are also some fine monuments in the church to past owners of Chilham Castle, including one by FRANCIS CHANTREY and another to two young boys, ARTHUR AND EDMUND HARVEY, whose family owned the castle for 50 years until 1918. At their feet are a SHUTTLECOCK AND BAT, THE ONLY EXAMPLE OF CHILDREN'S TOYS ON ANY ENGLISH CHURCH MONUMENT.

Mereworth – St Lawrence's. ONE OF ENGLAND'S FEW CLASSICAL COUNTRY CHURCHES, St Lawrence's might be more at home in New England than in the Garden of England. The spire is immensely tall while the body of the church looks a bit like a handsome barn, and the result is spectacular if a little startling. It was built by an unknown architect in the 1740s, for JOHN FANE, 7TH EARL OF WESTMORLAND, half a mile

from the old village church, which was knocked down to make way for the Earl's splendid new Palladian Mereworth Castle. Inside the church are pillars painted to look like marble and a barrel-vaulted ceiling made of plaster with details painted with *trompe-l'oeil*. On the south side of the churchyard is the grave of REAR ADMIRAL CHARLES DAVIS LUCAS (1834–1914), THE FIRST PERSON TO BE AWARDED A VICTORIA CROSS. He won it in 1854 during the Crimean War when, as a midshipman on HMS *Hecla* during a naval battle in the Baltic, he picked up a live shell from the deck in his bare hands and threw it overboard, saving the lives of countless shipmates.

LANCASHIRE

*Old St Leonard, Langho – one of the rare English churches built
during the short reign of Mary I, 1553–1558*

Heysham

St Peter's

Ancient Tombs

Heysham today conjures up images of
nuclear power stations and ferry ports
but there is, happily, an old Heysham
of creeper-covered stone cottages, tea-
shops and a narrow, pretty, winding
street, strewn with flowers, leading

down to a lovely church by the water's
edge. The view from the churchyard
across the wide sands of Morecambe
Bay to the Furness Hills is exhilarating,
particularly when those hills are tipped
with snow.

St Peter's Church is built low and
solid against the elements. There was a
Celtic wooden church here in the 7th
century, which was replaced by a stone
Saxon church, recorded on the site in
1080. This church, in which can be seen
a blocked-up doorway in the west wall,

was made new by the Normans, with the chancel added in the 14th century, the south aisle in the 15th century and the north aisle put there by the Victorians, all creating the picturesque ensemble we see now. The lovely, plain, rounded chancel arch, of early Norman design with mouldings representing cables or ropes, was reworked in the 15th century, using the Norman stones. The font is from the 15th century and the sloping windows are mostly filled with clear glass, so that worshippers and visitors alike may look out upon the grand view.

Just inside the south door is the church's greatest treasure, THE FINEST VIKING 'HOG-BACK' TOMBSTONE IN ENGLAND, decorated along the sides with carved figures of men and animals, illustrating the ancient Viking legends of Sigmund and Sigurd. A bear holds on at each end.

A niche in the wall of the south aisle contains a fragment of a SMALL METAL CHALICE, which was found with the remains of a body in a stone coffin, uncovered from under the chancel during the Victorian renovations. The coffin now lies outside in the church-yard. It is believed that the occupant

of the coffin was the Norman priest who oversaw the rebuilding of the Saxon church.

Also discovered during the renovations, and now in the churchyard, is one of the doorways from the original Saxon church, rebuilt stone by stone by a rector of the time, the REVEREND JOHN ROYDS. Near to the churchyard gate is the shaft of a 9th-century Saxon cross decorated on one side with a haloed Madonna and on the other side with a carving of a quaint gabled house, occupied by three people looking out at a figure swathed in bandages, as if risen from the grave. Lazarus perhaps?

On the headland above the church-yard stand the gaunt ruins of a small chapel, THE ONLY EXAMPLE OF A SINGLE-CELL SAXON CHAPEL LEFT IN ENGLAND. It is dedicated to ST PATRICK, for this headland is said to be WHERE THE SAINT

HIMSELF LANDED IN BRITAIN WHEN HE SAILED FROM IRELAND IN THE 5TH CENTURY.

A few steps away on the cliff-top are two remarkable sets of graves cut into the living rock, one group of six and a pair. They are shaped for a human head and body, with a socket at the head to hold a cross, and would have originally been covered by stone slabs. The bones in these stone coffins were found to be from the 10th or 11th century, but Neolithic artifacts were excavated from underneath them and Heysham is now regarded as THE FINEST NEOLITHIC SITE IN NORTHERN EUROPE.

Ribchester

St Wilfrid's

Cotton and Commuters

RIBCHESTER is a sleepy little place that has grown up on the site of the important 1st-century Roman fort of Bremetennacum. The River Ribble meanders past on its way from mysterious Pendle Hill, which lurks in the distance. 'It is written upon a wall in Rome; Ribchester was as rich as any town in Christendom,' wrote William Camden in 1586. Cotton once was king. Now commuters to Manchester and Blackburn rule.

The parish church of St Wilfrid's sits above the ruins of the 'principium' or headquarters of the Roman camp. It is a lovely example of a 13th-century Early English village church and features three tall, elegant lancet windows at the east end, which are typical of the period.

According to parish records the first known rector of Ribchester, one Drogo, was drowned while trying to ford the Ribble in 1246. Although it seems almost inconceivable that anyone could get into difficulties in the gentle stream that babbles by the village presently, when in spate the Ribble can suddenly turn violent and flood the meadows and the churchyard. Indeed the 17th-century sundial in the churchyard is mounted on a column at the top of a square base of six sandstone steps, to keep it from being washed away.

Hoghton Tower

Two chantry chapels were added to the church in the 14th century, both enclosed by fine oak screens. One is named for the HOGHTONS OF HOGHTON TOWER (where in 1617 James I knighted a loin of beef and created the 'Sir' Loin steak); the other is known as the DUTTON QUIRE and possesses a faded wall painting of St Christopher carrying the Holy Child, before which pilgrims about to ford the Ribble would pray for a safe crossing. This is THE ONLY SUCH IMAGE OF ST CHRISTOPHER IN LANCASHIRE AND THE BIGGEST IN ENGLAND. Some 300 victims of the Black Death are said to be buried beneath the floor of the Quire.

A panelled oak gallery was erected at the west end of the church in 1736, supported by two stone pillars that came from the Roman fort. Two similar columns can be found holding up the porch of Ribchester's White Bull Hotel.

The beautifully carved oak pulpit is Jacobean. It was installed in 1636 by the vicar Christopher Hindle, and bears his initials. Hindle, a staunch Royalist, was banished from his living during the Commonwealth but still turned up at the church to preach every Sunday. On one famous occasion a group of villagers who supported Parliament occupied the pulpit to prevent Hindle from speaking, so he just delivered his sermon from the pulpit steps. He was eventually defeated and forced to retire to Blackburn.

Stydd

St Saviour's

Threesome

Half a mile north-east of Ribchester, narrow Stydd Lane leads off to the tiny hamlet of STYDD, where you can find a trio of intriguing church buildings. First, on the left, is the ROMAN CATHOLIC CHURCH OF ST PETER & ST PAUL, built in 1789 to look like a barn so as to disguise its function as a church, at a time when Catholics were forbidden to have public places of worship. THIS IS ONE OF THE FEW SURVIVING PURPOSE-BUILT 'BARN CHURCHES' IN ENGLAND.

A little further on are the unique STYDD ALMSHOUSES, built in an odd kind of Dutch Baroque style in 1728 by the Shireburn family to house five poor people of the parish.

Stydd Almshouses

Beyond the almshouses, at the end of what has now become a farm track, is the enchanting little church of ST SAVIOUR'S, all that is left of a small community owned by the Knights of St John in the 13th century. The church, which has a simple rectangular plan with nave and small chancel but no tower, dates from the late Norman period, about 1190. There are two Norman windows in the north wall, and the doorway has a Norman arch with zigzag carvings. Inside there is a 16th-century carved octagonal font and a 17th-century oak pulpit with canopy, reached by some stone steps. A simple 17th-century oak screen separates the nave from the chancel, where there are some old stone coffins that could be those of the Knights. There is certainly an air of antiquity here, although this 900-year-old chapel is a youngster

compared to Roman Ribchester down the road.

Sefton

St Helen's

Tudor Splendour

The 'Queen of Lancashire' is how Arthur Mee describes St Helen's in Sefton. Its sheer size and majesty dominate the tiny hamlet at its feet and defy the advancing tendrils of suburban Liverpool, while the tall, elegant spire can be seen for miles around across the flat landscape.

St Helen's is thought to be MERSEYSIDE'S OLDEST BUILDING, although little remains of the original Norman chapel built here at the end of the 12th century by the

Molyneux family, owners of Sefton Hall, which stood long ago in moated splendour just across the road.

Apart from the tower and spire, completed in 1320, most of the church we see today was built in the reign of Henry VIII, and it houses perhaps THE FINEST TUDOR INTERIOR OF ANY COUNTRY CHURCH IN ENGLAND. Nave, aisles and chapels are filled almost to the fine timbered roof with gorgeous Tudor woodwork, rich, dark oak pews, pulpit, stalls, and seven superb screens. Rows of poppy-heads march down the

nave, while the ends of the pews are carved with birds and animals, flowers, a cock crowing at Peter's denial, a crown of thorns. Each pew sports a different letter of the alphabet, only x,y and z are missing. The ends of the choir stalls are alive with creatures, including a unicorn, winged monsters, a lion, a rabbit, and a hart wearing a crown.

There are special pews for everyone, the churchwardens, the mayor, and the 'corporation' (the local bowling club). The BLUNDELL PEW by the Lady Chapel and the SEFTON PEW south of the chancel are caged in with beautiful screens. The superlative rood screen, known as the 'glory of Sefton', is considered THE FINEST SCREEN IN THE NORTH OF ENGLAND. The trumpet stem pulpit and canopy is Jacobean, dated 1635, and sumptuously carved with foliage.

Molyneux memorials are everywhere, brass plaques, alabaster effigies, stone monuments. In a recess in the north chapel, there is a 13th-century effigy of Sefton's oldest inhabitant, Crusader

WILLIAM DE MOLYNEUX who died in 1289, and in the floor south of the chancel a brass of SIR WILLIAM MOLYNEUX (d.1548), who distinguished himself at the Battle of Flodden Field, with his own hands capturing two Scottish standards including that of the Earl of Huntly. An inscription tells of his deeds and the captured standards appear above his head.

Tunstall

St John the Baptist

*Stainless Knights and
Peerless Sisters*

THE CHURCH OF ST JOHN THE BAPTIST has Saxon origins and stands alone, well outside the village of Tunstall, having lost its Saxon village to the Norman invasion. It was made new by SIR THOMAS TUNSTAL of nearby Thurland Castle in 1415, the same year he was knighted by Henry V at the Battle of Agincourt. A subsequent Lord of Thurland Castle, Sir Thomas's great-grandson BRIAN TUNSTALL, died heroically at the Battle of Flodden Field in 1513 and was dubbed the STAINLESS KNIGHT, becoming THE MOST SENIOR ENGLISHMAN OF RANK TO DIE IN THAT BATTLE. He was immortalised by Sir Walter Raleigh in the poem 'The Stainless Knight and the Battle of Flodden Field'.

The church that Sir Thomas Tunstall built is a handsome place, with crenellated parapets above the aisles and a fine embattled tower boasting four carved angels above each of the belfry openings. Sir Thomas himself is buried inside, beneath a battered effigy in the Chapel of the Holy Trinity. A lion lies at his feet.

Embedded in the surround of a window in the north aisle is a ROMAN VOTIVE STONE or altar, inscribed with dedications to Hygeia, goddess of healing, and Aesculapius, god of medicine. It is possibly the work of a medical man from the nearby Roman camp at Over Burrow. The beautiful east window contains 15th-century Flemish glass donated in 1810 by Richard North, a later occupant of Thurland Castle.

But the feature of this wonderful church that will thrill every student of English literature is a small room above the south porch, reached by a ladder attached to the wall. Here, in this room, every Sunday, the BRONTË SISTERS, MARIA, ELIZABETH, CHARLOTTE, EMILY AND ANNE, would eat their lunch, having walked two miles from their boarding school at Cowan Bridge to attend Sunday School.

The CLERGY DAUGHTERS' SCHOOL at Cowan Bridge was founded in January 1824 by the vicar of Tunstall, THE REVEREND WILLIAM CARUS WILSON. Maria and Elizabeth Brontë were enrolled there in July that year, aged 10 and 9, Charlotte in August, aged 8, and Emily in November, aged 6. They hated it. Discipline was harsh, the girls were ill-treated and badly fed and they were teased and bullied by the older girls. Maria and Elizabeth both died of consumption not long after being brought home in 1825. Charlotte later gained some sort of revenge by portraying the school as the unpleasant Lowood in her novel *Jane Eyre*, with Rev. Wilson as the self-righteous head-master Mr Brocklehurst. Tunstall's

church became Brocklebridge church.

The walk from Cowan Bridge to the church at Tunstall is through the most gorgeous, uplifting countryside and today it is hard to imagine the misery the girls must have endured as they hurried along the lane, cold and hungry and homesick. For the modern church lover Tunstall is idyllic. For the Brontë sisters, Tunstall was a place where, to quote Reginald Heber, poet and Anglican Bishop of Calcutta, '. . . every prospect pleases, and only Man is vile'.

Well, I never knew this about
LANCASHIRE CHURCHES

Bleasdale – St Eadmer's. Bleasdale's remote 19th-century church, sitting alone in fields with the Bowland Fells in the background, is THE ONLY CHURCH IN ENGLAND DEDICATED TO ST EADMER, the Lindisfarne monk who discovered St Cuthbert's final burial place, now the site of Durham Cathedral.

Claughton – St Chad's. A small church built in 1815 incorporating materials from previous buildings of 1300 and 1602. In the bellcote on the west gable are two bells, one dated 1727, the other 1296. This older bell, ONE OF ONLY 60 BELLS IN ENGLAND THAT CAN BE DATED TO BEFORE 1300, was long considered to be THE OLDEST DATED BELL IN ENGLAND, until the discovery in 1972 of a bell on the church at Lissett in the East Riding of Yorkshire dated 1254. Claughton's bell is now THE SECOND OLDEST DATED BELL IN ENGLAND.

Heysham. The ROCK GRAVES AT HEYSHAM appear on the cover of the BEST OF BLACK SABBATH CD, a compilation album released in the year 2000.

Langho – Old Church of St Leonard.
The handsome little church beside the
Black Bull Inn at Old Langho, north
of Blackburn, was completed in 1557
and is ONE OF THE VERY FEW CHURCHES
IN ENGLAND THAT WAS BUILT DURING
THE SHORT REIGN OF MARY I, 1553–58.
Much of the fine stonework of the interior, including the font and piscina,
came from nearby Whalley Abbey,
demolished at the Dissolution of the
Monasteries. The church is noted for
its exceptional Jacobean bench ends,
which are carved with dates and initials.

**Pilling – Old St John the Baptist's
Church.** Built in 1717, this unassuming
old church is a superb example of an
UNSPOILED GEORGIAN CHURCH, and
has a quite gorgeous interior, with faded
wooden pews, box pews at the front
for the gentry and a two-stage pulpit.
There is a wood-fronted gallery along
the entire length of the north and west
walls, supported by slender Tuscan
columns, and the whole ensemble is
washed with pale marsh light streaming
in through large windows of clear glass.
The church owes its unaltered state to
being made redundant when a new and
larger church was opened 100 yards to
the north in 1887.

Rivington Church. The little Tudor
church at Rivington, on the edge of the
West Pennine Moors not far from
Bolton, is unusual in that it has NO
DEDICATION and is known simply as
Rivington Church. It was founded by
JAMES PILKINGTON (1520–76), the first
Protestant Bishop of Durham, who was
born in Rivington Hall, and has THE
ONLY DETACHED BELL TOWER IN
LANCASHIRE, built in 1542 to house a
large bell from Wigan church and now
used as a tool shed.

LEICESTERSHIRE

St Mary & St Hardulph, Breedon – home of the oldest angel in England

Bottesford

St Mary's

Who Do You Think You Are?

Here, in Leicestershire's most northerly village, capital of the Vale of Belvoir, is LEICESTERSHIRE'S TALLEST SPIRE, at 210 feet (64 m), and LEICESTERSHIRE'S BIGGEST VILLAGE CHURCH; indeed, one of THE BIGGEST VILLAGE CHURCHES IN ALL ENGLAND. It is known affectionately as the 'Lady of the Vale'.

The spire can be seen from all across the vale and is something of a landmark. During the Second World War it lay directly in the path of the Lancaster bombers taking off from RAF Bottesford, and a red light, operated by a switch on the church wall, was positioned at the top of the spire to alert the pilots. A number of these brave men who were killed during the war are buried in the churchyard.

In March 1945 the spire proved too tempting a target for a German pilot, who strafed the church with his guns before being chased away and shot down. Marks in the church stonework tell the story of when St Mary's, Bottesford, became THE LAST PLACE IN BRITAIN TO BE ATTACKED BY THE LUFTWAFFE.

The spire is also very visible from the Bull Inn in Market Street and would no doubt have drawn admiring glances from comic duo LAUREL AND HARDY,

who stayed at the inn over Christmas in 1952 while appearing at the Empire Theatre in Nottingham. Stan Laurel's sister Olgand owned the Bull at the time and even got the pair to help behind the bar.

It is more than likely that Laurel and Hardy visited the church, and when they did they would have walked up Market Street, turned right up Church Lane and entered the church-yard across a beautiful little two-arched 16th-century packhorse bridge over the River Devon, built by a rector of Bottesford called Dr Fleming. He almost drowned while trying to get to church when the river was in flood and had the bridge built in gratitude for being rescued.

The path from the bridge takes you through a tunnel of weeping willows and copper beeches, until the church is revealed in all its majesty, marching rows of Perpendicular windows and pinnacles dwarfed by the lofty tower and spire – most unusually the spire is 36 feet (11 m) taller than the tower and yet it all looks perfectly proportioned.

As you enter the church, take a look at the UNIQUE FONT at the west end – a 15th-century octagonal bowl standing on a Renaissance base of orna-mental table legs.

The nave is tall and bright, with red carpets and cushions, pews of golden wood, pale stone arcades bathed in light flooding in through the clerestory windows. Above the chancel arch are traces of a 15th-century Doom wall painting. South of the chancel arch is a carved wooden Jacobean wine-glass pulpit standing on a slim stem.

Remember Your Manners

But it is the chancel beyond that we have come to see. This is from the original Norman church built by Robert de Todeni, William the Conqueror's standard-bearer and builder of Belvoir Castle; but there is very little Norman work left to see, for this is now almost a mausoleum, filled with a breathtaking array of monuments of every style and taste in marble and alabaster and brass and stone and wood. EIGHT EARLS OF RUTLAND ARE BURIED HERE, from the 1st Earl to the 8th, an uninterrupted family timeline from the Reformation to the Restoration.

Moving east, we come to two wall monuments facing each other. On the south wall is the tomb of EDWARD, THE 3RD EARL (1548–87) one of the Commissioners who tried Mary Queen of Scots. Opposite, on the north wall, is the colourful tomb of JOHN, THE 4TH EARL (1559–88). He and his wife rest their heads on green and red cushions, at their feet are red-painted beasts, and their ten children kneel around them. At the east end of the monument is the tiny, poignant kneeling figure of a son who died in infancy.

Next, in the centre of the chancel, is the UNIQUE TOMB OF HENRY MANNERS, 2ND EARL OF RUTLAND (1526–63), who lies with his wife under what appears to be an ornate dining table with four bulbous, ornamented legs – in fact a representation of an Elizabethan Communion Table, with the mourners kneeling on top. HIS BREASTPLATE IS UNIQUE ALSO, IN THAT IT IS NOT THE USUAL ONE PIECE BUT RATHER MADE UP OF LAMINATED PLATES.

In front is the more traditional tomb of THOMAS, 1ST EARL OF RUTLAND (1492–1543), cupbearer to Henry VIII and Lord Chamberlain to Anne of Cleves. He assisted in the divorce of Henry VIII and Catherine of Aragon, put down the northern uprising against the Dissolution known as the Pilgrimage of Grace, and roughed up the Scots during the 'Rough Wooing'.

On the floor beside the tomb is a wonderfully well-preserved early 15th-century brass of a former rector of Bottesford, HENRY DE CODYNGTON, who died in 1404.

Flanking the 1st Earl to north and south are GEORGE, THE 7TH EARL (1580–1641) and JOHN, THE 8TH EARL (1604–79), both dressed in Roman togas, the latter's tomb sporting a rather alarming toothless, grinning skull. Both these monuments are the work of GRINLING GIBBONS.

Beyond the 8th Earl, against the north wall, is ROGER, THE 5TH EARL (1576–1612), who lies amongst rich colour and decoration one step above his wife Elizabeth, the only child of Sir Philip Sydney.

On the south wall is the immensely tall and celebrated 'witchcraft tomb' of FRANCIS, THE 6TH EARL OF RUTLAND (1578–1632), THE ONLY TOMB IN ENGLAND TO RECORD THE DEATH OF TWO HEIRS TO AN EARLDOM BY WITCH-CRAFT. The Earl lies between his two wives Frances and Cecilia, while kneeling at his feet are two boys holding skulls, his sons by Cecilia, who

France in 1421 aged 25. At his head is the small black marble figure of ROBERT DE ROOS, who in 1257 became Lord of Belvoir by marrying Isabel, last in the line of Robert de Todeni, builder of Belvoir Castle. Sir William's granddaughter Eleanor de Roos married George Manners, and their son Thomas Manners became the 1st Earl of Rutland.

Burton Lazars

St James's

Chitty Chitty Bang Bang

This little church with its funny-looking bell turret, topped with a mini spire, sits above the village on the crown of the hill, with wide views over Leicestershire and neighbouring Rutland. The body of the church is late

'dyed in their infancy by wicked practice and sorcerye'. Three servants at Belvoir, a mother and her two daughters, were accused of using witchcraft to murder the boys and were executed in 1618.

Finally, lying either side of the colourful east window are, on the south side, SIR WILLIAM DE ROOS (1368–1414) and, on the north side, JOHN DE ROOS, who died at the Battle of Bauge in

Norman, a reworking of an earlier Norman church built by Roger de Mowbray. In the mid 12th century he established England's foremost leper hospital here, the HOSPITAL OF ST MARY AND ST LAZARUS OF JERUSALEM, taking advantage of the area's natural spring water and hilltop breezes. The emblem of the ORDER OF ST LAZARUS was a red cross on a white background, the origin of today's RED CROSS.

Almost taller than the bell turret is a huge, pinnacled stone monument, 20 feet (6 m) high, that sits in the graveyard to the north of the church. Adorned with skulls and the figures of Time, Faith, Hope and Charity, and supported on four cannon-balls, it is the tombstone of WILLIAM SQUIRE (d.1781), a rich weaver. In his will he left funds so that he could be remembered by this splendid monument, with the remainder of his money going to the education of poor local children. By the time the memorial was finished there was no money left for the children.

Not far away, and enclosed by an ornate wrought-iron fence, is the family grave of COUNT ELLIOT ZBOROWSKI (1858–1903) AND HIS WIFE MARGARET, whose home was in nearby Melton Mowbray. Alongside them is their son COUNT LOUIS ZBOROWSKI (1895–1924), racing car driver and owner of the real CHITTY CHITTY BANG BANG, the car immortalised by Ian Fleming in his children's novel of that name.

Count Elliot Zborowski, whose background was Polish, was a wealthy landowner, while Margaret was an heiress to the Astor fortune. Both parents died by the time Louis was 16 and he reputedly became THE FOURTH RICHEST CHILD IN THE WORLD, owner of large chunks of Manhattan. He built his own cars, powered by aero engines and given the name Chitty Chitty Bang Bang on account of the noise they made, and then raced them himself, mainly at Brooklands in Surrey, which is where he was first spotted by a young Ian Fleming. Louis's father Elliot had died driving a Mercedes at a hill climb in France in 1903, when his cuff-links caught in the car's hand throttle. Count Louis himself also died at the wheel of a Mercedes, at Monza in 1924, when his car hit a tree during the Italian Grand Prix. He was wearing his father's cuff-links.

Gaddesby

St Luke's

Only a Horse

A graceful 13th-century broach spire guides us up narrow Church Lane to one of England's most joyous and unpretentious Decorated Gothic churches – not all of a piece, but with unexpected splashes of ebullience and splendour, such as the lavish carvings on the pinnacled and battlemented south-west face, with its lovely sculpted

frieze and stone canopies that seem to ripple like lace in a breeze above a rounded triangular window.

Inside, all is light and space, and the eye is drawn to the east end, not just by the tall Early English east window, but by the near life-size memorial to COLONEL EDWARD CHENEY of the Scots Greys (d.1845), which dominates the chancel. Cheney is captured rising from the saddle of one of the four horses that were killed from under him at the Battle of Waterloo in 1815. A bullet wound can be seen on the horse's chest and the animal's agonised death throes are etched in vivid detail. On the panel below, a Sergeant Ewart is shown in hand-to-hand combat with a French officer who is

attempting to recover one of Napoleon's eagle standards. The figures and the action are vital and almost alive.

The memorial was sculpted by Yorkshire-born artist JOSEPH GOTT in 1848 and originally stood in next-door Gaddesby Hall, which Cheney had inherited from his father-in-law John Ayre. It was moved into the church in 1917 after the hall and estate were sold.

Amazingly, this most lifelike and moving monument is THE ONLY MARBLE EQUESTRIAN STATUE IN ANY OF ENGLAND'S COUNTRY CHURCHES.

Twycross

St James's

England's Oldest Glass

The church, early 14th century with an austere 15th-century tower, stands somewhat stark upon a hillock on the edge of this red-brick village. Pleasant. Rural. A humble enough country

north of the chancel, along with more modest pews for the indoor and outdoor staff. The glass was rescued from the cathedral of Saint-Denis in Paris during the destruction that followed the French Revolution, and was brought to England, where it ended up in the collection of George III. His son William (later William IV) gave it to Earl Howe.

The oldest glass, which dates from 1145, is in a glorious roundel in the centre light, showing the PRESENTATION OF CHRIST IN THE TEMPLE, and is in superb condition, the colours of red and blue, green and gold, still vivid. The rest of the window has more wonderful antique glass, much of it from Sainte-Chapelle in Paris and dates from the mid 13th century. Particularly fine are two large panels in the centre light showing Christ being taken down from the Cross and Joshua's spies furtively smuggling grapes out of the Promised Land.

church, nothing out of the ordinary. But here, in the east window, you will find a remarkable treasure, THE OLDEST GLASS IN ENGLAND.

It was given to the church in 1840 by RICHARD CURZON, 1ST EARL HOWE, who lived at nearby GOPSALL HALL, and whose family box pew can still be found

Well, I never knew this about
LEICESTERSHIRE CHURCHES

Call Me Shirley

Breedon on the Hill – St Mary & St Hardulph. Here is one of England's more dramatically sited churches, high on a fortified Iron Age hilltop and teetering on the edge of an ancient quarry. It was founded as an abbey by the Saxons in the 7th century and later

dedicated to St Hardulph, who was a king of Northumbria and is buried at Breedon. The Saxon abbey became a Norman monastery, and then a parish church at the Dissolution.

Displayed on the walls inside are sections of a carved frieze from the Saxon church of about AD 800, THE LARGEST AND BEST PRESERVED COLLECTION OF

SAXON CARVINGS IN ENGLAND, if not Europe. Breedon's glory is the BREEDON ANGEL, an almost unspoiled full-length carving of an angel dressed in Byzantine robes and giving a Byzantine style blessing. A replica can be seen in the church while the original is kept locked in the tower, to be seen by invitation only. It is THE OLDEST REPRESENTATION OF AN ANGEL IN ENGLAND.

After the Dissolution, the manor of Breedon was bought from the Crown by the SHIRLEYS, a land-owning family who had come over with William the Conqueror, and in the north aisle stands the ornate SHIRLEY PEW, dated 1627, along with the impressive tombs of FRANCIS SHIRLEY (d.1571) AND HIS WIFE DOROTHY, JOHN SHIRLEY AND HIS WIFE, from 1585, and the huge columned monument of GEORGE SHIRLEY AND WIFE, erected in 1598. We come across the Shirleys again at Staunton Harold.

Quorn – St Bartholomew's. The village is known for THE OLDEST HUNT IN ENGLAND, established in 1696 and brought to Quorn in 1753 by HUGH MEYNELL. The Norman church, made of granite, rare in the Midlands, is known for the FARNHAM CHAPEL on its south side, ONE OF VERY FEW SURVIVING PRIVATE CHAPELS WITHIN A PARISH CHURCH. It was built in 1392 by JOHN FARNHAM and is separated from the main church by 16th-century plaster screens. Hanging on a wall in the chapel is a high-relief picture of a later John Farnham (d.1587) engaged in a musket fight, A VERY EARLY EXAMPLE OF A FRAMED HIGH-RELIEF PICTURE. Standing against the wall are some incised tomb slabs resembling brasses, THE ONLY SUCH INCISED TOMB SLABS IN ENGLAND.

Staunton Harold – Holy Trinity. Begun in 1653 as a private chapel to Staunton Harold Hall for SIR ROBERT SHIRLEY, this is THE ONLY CHURCH COMMENCED IN ENGLAND DURING THE COMMONWEALTH IN DEFIANCE OF OLIVER CROMWELL. (Holy Trinity in Berwick-upon-Tweed, completed in 1652, was built to a Cromwell-approved design.) Shirley paid for it with his life after being incarcerated in the Tower of London by Cromwell for spending lavish amounts of money on a church rather than on a new ship for the Navy. He died in the Tower three years later at the age of 27 and his body was returned to Staunton Harold for burial in his church.

Holy Trinity boasts a classic setting, on green lawns beside a stately Georgian house above a lake, and is virtually untouched, a precious example of a mid-17th-century church, inside and out. There is a profusion of woodwork inside, with box pews, oak panelling, and a glorious wooden screen and gallery at the west end supporting the organ, which was made for the church by Father Schmidt and is one of THE OLDEST CHURCH ORGANS OF ITS KIND IN ENGLAND TO HAVE SURVIVED IN ITS ORIGINAL CONDITION. The ceiling was painted in 1655 with scenes from the Creation, and there is a magnificent wrought-iron chancel screen created in 1711 by ROBERT BAKEWELL. Holy Trinity was gifted to the National Trust by the 12th Earl Ferrers in 1954.

LINCOLNSHIRE

Minster Church of St Mary, Stow – home to the tallest Saxon arches in Britain

Norton Disney

St Peter's

Disneyland

Once upon a time, in 1949, the man who made the name of Disney into one of the most celebrated names in the world came to Lincolnshire, in secret, to search among the tombs and monuments of this unassuming English country church by the River Witham to see what he could learn about the origins of his family and his famous name.

He found what we can still find today, a small village with a pub, a few houses and, at the end of the street, nestling among willows, a pretty church, with a 13th-century nave, a 14th-century chancel, a 15th-century tower, Elizabethan screen, Jacobean pulpit and pews – and an ancient chapel filled with DISNEYS of long ago.

He learned that the Disneys were a Norman family from the little village of Isigny, near Bayeux, who came over with William the Conqueror, fought at the Battle of Hastings and were given land in Lincolnshire, where they built themselves a Disney castle and lived happily ever after as lords of the manor until 1685, when William Disney took the wrong side in the Monmouth Rebellion against James II and was executed. The remaining members of the family fled, some to Ireland, from where later Disneys emigrated to America and dicovered a new kind of wealth and fame.

The earliest monument in the church at NORTON DISNEY to commemorate these folk of Isigny (d'Isigny) is set in an arched recess in the north chapel and dates from 1300. It is a stone figure of JOAN D'ISIGNY who, with her husband SIR WILLIAM D'ISIGNY, built the chapel. She is dressed as a nun, and her dog lies at her feet.

From 1350 comes a later JOAN DISNEY, her name now anglicised from d'Isigny. Hers is a SCULPTURED STONE EFFIGY OF UNIQUE DESIGN, unique to the Disneys that is, for there is a similar Disney tomb at nearby Kingerby (*see* page 170). Joan lies part covered by her coffin lid, which is carved in the shape of a cross, with just her head and shoulders peeping from the top and her slippered feet protruding below. The inscription, in Norman French begins 'ICI GIST JOAN QUI FUST LA FEMM MOUN GILLAN DISNI . . .' or 'Here lies Joan, who was the wife of Monsieur William Disney . . .' Monsieur William Disney lies on a ledge above her, clad in armour, his shield bearing the Disney crest of three heraldic lions.

Another Sir William Disney lies in the chancel, while occupying prime position on the floor of the chapel is HAUTACIA DISNEY, dressed in a long gown, lions at her head and feet, hands clasped in a fervent prayer that all the blood doesn't rush to her head, which is lower to the floor than her feet. This tomb dates from about 1399 and bears the inscription, 'Here lies Hautacia, daughter of William Disney, Lord of Norton'.

Most remarkable of all in the chapel is a SUPERB GENEALOGICAL BRASS dating from 1580. It is divided into five panels and shows two rows of half figures, WILLIAM DISNEY with his wife and nine children, four boys and five girls, kneeling in prayer and looking like they are announcing their names in speech bubbles shaped as scrolls, and an anxious-looking RICHARD DISNEY with a wife on either side. The brass, which is displayed in a hinged wooden frame so that you can see both sides, is what is known as a PALIMPSEST, in other words it has been turned over and used again. The original inscription on the reverse side is in Flemish and records the endowment of a mass in St Martin's Church at Middelburg in Holland in 1518. Amazingly, the final part of this actual inscription can be found on another palimpsest brass at West Lavington in Wiltshire.

Here, in deepest Lincolnshire, lies a cast of characters Walt Disney would have been proud to create himself.

Kingerby

St Peter's

A Magical Place

KINGERBY, a Disney stronghold of the 14th and 15th centuries, lies on the other side of Lincoln from Norton Disney. There is nothing there now but a 19th-century hall, built on the site of another Disney castle, and an exceptionally lovely old church, separated from each other by trees. Both sit in the middle of a prehistoric mound occupied by Stone Age men and Romans long before the Disneys came.

The church is just gorgeous, with a rugged, moss-covered tapering tower that has a continental look about it, a crooked 13th-century porch and a nave, chancel and aisle of different rooflines all covered with red tiles. If it wasn't for the wide, unmistakably Lincolnshire views all around, we could be in Spain.

The atmospheric interior appears at first sight to be empty, but there are treasures waiting to be found. High in the west wall is a circular opening that would once have let in light from the setting sun, a Saxon feature. There is a wonderful 17th-century wooden roof with moulded beams and a battered poor box on a stand, carved from a single piece of wood, with the inscription, 'This is God's treasury. Cast a mite into it. 1639'. The east window of the south aisle contains some exquisite and very rare 14th-century stained glass showing St Catherine with her wheel and St Cecilia, patroness of church music, with her organ.

Against the west wall of the south aisle are two crumbling effigies of knights of the 14th century, two Sir William Disneys, father and son. Sir William the elder was a companion of Edward II and died in 1316; his son died of the Black Death in 1349.

Standing against the wall in the chancel is a most unusual 14TH-CENTURY TOMB SLAB in the form of a carving in low relief of HENRY DISNEY, partly covered by a coffin lid decorated with shields and a cross, which he is grasping as you might a sword. His head and shoulders are visible at the top, while his feet protrude at the bottom. It would appear that THIS DESIGN IS UNIQUE TO THE DISNEYS, for the only other tomb like it anywhere is that of Joan Disney at Norton Disney (*see* page 168). Clearly, Walt was not the only Disney to have a creative imagination.

Sempringham

St Andrew's

A Saint, a Princess and a Poet

Alone on a hillock rising out of the Lincolnshire fens, at the end of a long winding farm track off a quiet B road, with not a farm or a cottage in sight, St Andrew's appears to be in the middle of nowhere, and yet 900 years ago this solitary church played a central part in England's medieval story, and still guards the memory of three remarkable characters, a saint, a princess and a poet.

If you can manage to find the church, the first thought that occurs is that the west tower is in the wrong place. This is because the Norman chancel and transept were demolished in 1788 leaving the central tower stranded at the east end, and it was another 100 years before the Victorians tacked on a rather half-hearted apse to try to put things right. The remaining Norman nave and arcade are magnificent, as is the south door, with three orders of carved arches. The Gothic crossing arches of the 15th-century Perpendicular tower are impressively tall.

Only English Order

The Norman church of St Andrew was built by JOCELIN DE SEMPRINGHAM in 1100 to replace a previous Saxon church, at the heart of what was then a thriving village. Jocelin's son GILBERT, born in 1083 with a 'repulsive physical deformity', was deemed unsuitable for a military

career, and after studying for the priesthood in France he returned to Sempringham as vicar. In 1131, after his father died, Gilbert used some of his inheritance to build a dormitory against the north wall of the church to provide accommodation for seven local women who wished to live a life of chastity and obedience. This was the beginning of THE GILBERTINE ORDER, THE ONLY MONASTIC ORDER EVER FOUNDED BY AN ENGLISH SAINT. The order was soon extended to include men, in separate lodgings, of course, and in 1139 Gilbert was granted land to the south of St Andrew's on which to build a priory. Over the next few years almost everyone in the local community joined the Order, leaving the village of Sempringham deserted.

Gilbert's piety and learning won him many important friends, including Henry II and his archbishop Thomas à Becket. In 1164 Becket sought refuge from Henry's wrath at Sempringham, before escaping to France with the Gilbert's help.

By the time Gilbert died in 1199 at the age of 106, there were 13 Gilbertine communities across England, and by the time of the Dissolution 350 years later there were 26. The only one of these still in use is St Mary's Old Malton in Yorkshire.

Gilbert was eventually buried somewhere in St Andrew's, no one knows exactly where, but there is a memorial to him outside on the south wall of the tower.

Last Princess

In early 1283 an infant child was brought to Sempringham to be hidden away from the eyes of the world for as long as she might live. Her name was PRINCESS GWENLLIAN, daughter and heir of the last Welsh-born Prince of Wales, Llywelyn ap Gruffudd, who had been killed in a skirmish with Edward I's men at Cilmery on the Welsh border in December the previous year. King Edward wanted to ensure that Gwenllian would not become a focus for rebellion, for not only was she heir to Llywelyn but her grandparents were Simon de Montfort and Henry III's sister Eleanor, Edward's aunt, which gave her a distant claim to the English throne. So Gwenllian was committed to the discreet care of the nuns at Sempringham, and there she lived out her life in prayer and in anonymity. Edward I's grandson Edward III came to see her at Sempringham in 1327 and granted her a pension for the rest of her life. She died ten years later in 1337 at the age of 54 and was buried near the walls of St Andrew's. Her grave has been lost, but a memorial stone of Welsh slate, erected by the Princess Gwenllian Society beneath a tree on the approach to the church, pays tribute to her as the LAST WELSH-BORN PRINCESS OF WALES.

First Poet

The priory at Sempringham was pulled down at the Dissolution of the Monasteries in 1538, and the stone used to build a manor house in its place. This in turn was abandoned and disappeared under the fields, leaving St Andrew's Church as the only survivor from the once flourishing monastic community. But Sempringham still had one more contribution to make. In the early 17th century Sempringham became a centre of the Puritan movement under the ministry of curate SAMUEL SKELTON, and when he decided to sail for America in

1628 to set up a church in Salem, Massachusetts, he persuaded some members of his Sempringham congregation to follow him to the New World. One of them was a young newlywed called ANNE BRADSTREET, who in 1650 would become THE FIRST PUBLISHED POET IN AMERICA.

Stow

Minster Church of St Mary

Mighty Saxon Church

This is THE MIGHTIEST OF ENGLAND'S SAXON CHURCHES and ONE OF THE OLDEST PARISH CHURCHES IN THE COUNTRY. The first church here was founded in the 7th century as the principal church of the diocese of Lindsey. This was burned down by the Danes of the Great Heathen Army in AD 870 and left in ruins, until Bishop Aelfnoth built it up again to serve as the mother church for the Lincoln half of his diocese of Dorchester. Aelfnoth's church also burned down, and in 1040 Bishop Eadnoth of Dorchester began a new church, part funded by Leofric, Earl of Mercia, and his wife Lady Godiva.

From this church come Stow's

magnificent crossing arches, the TALLEST
SAXON ARCHES IN BRITAIN, some 35 feet
(10.6 m) tall and 14 feet (4.3 m) wide. All
four arches are the same height and width,
an occurrence found in only one other
English church, St Mary the Virgin in
Norton, County Durham (*see* page 90).

At the base of one of the arches is a
delightful remnant from Aelfnoth's
church, a rough carving of a Viking
ship, probably scratched out by a
Scandinavian sailor in about 1000 and
THE OLDEST KNOWN DEPICTION OF A
VIKING SHIP FOUND IN ENGLAND.

After the Norman invasion Remigius,
the first Bishop of Lincoln, built the
nave as we see it today, but then decided
to move his see, and his cathedral, to

Lincoln, leaving the mighty minster at
Stow stranded in its tiny village. In
about 1130 Alexander, third Bishop of
Lincoln, replaced the Saxon chancel
with a majestic, richly carved new
chancel, complete with clerestory, ONE
OF THE LARGEST AND MOST RESPLENDENT
NORMAN CHANCELS IN ENGLAND. It
was sympathetically restored by J.L.
Pearson in about 1850.

In the 15th century a new central tower
was erected and four Gothic supporting
arches were inserted into the crossing
inside the existing round Saxon arches.
The effect as you gaze east down the
cavernous, echoing nave is extraordinary,
with the four Norman-style windows of
the chancel gleaming back at you like
some monstrous face through a cluster
of tall, uncoordinated arches.

Amongst the smaller treasures of this
truly epic church are a faded wall
painting from c.1210 in the north transept, showing ONE OF THE EARLIEST
KNOWN REPRESENTATIONS OF THOMAS
À BECKET (*see* Barfreston, Kent, page
141), and a beautiful Early English font
of 1200.

Well, I never knew this
about
LINCOLNSHIRE CHURCHES

Coningsby – St Michael's. Coningsby's
HUGE ONE-HANDED CLOCK can be seen
from miles away. Hardly surprising
since the gaily coloured clock face,
which is painted directly on to the

stonework of the tower, is 16½ feet
(5 m) across and the hand is almost 9
feet (2.7 m) long, making it THE
LARGEST SINGLE-HANDED CLOCK IN THE
WORLD. Clocks with no minute hand

were quite common before the middle of the 17th century but today are very rare. Another unusual feature of St Michael's 15th-century tower is that it straddles a public footpath, which passes underneath through two tall Gothic arches.

Heckington – St Andrew's. Here, in the centre of one of Lincolnshire's largest villages, stands one of England's most immaculate and untouched 14th-century Decorated churches. Owned by the monks of wealthy Bardsey Abbey, and built with money no object, St Andrew's was completed when church architecture in England was at its height and before the Black Death robbed England of its finest and most exuberant craftsmen. The chancel, which was the work of RICHARD DE POTESGRAVE, chaplain to Edwards II and III, has a spectacular east window of unsurpassed elegance and what most observers agree is THE BEST EASTER SEPULCHRE IN ENGLAND, a masterpiece of intricate carving as delicate as lace. On the opposite wall are the sedilia and piscina, equally extravagant and sump-tuous, and clearly the work of the same

skilled artisans. The three pieces together form what is widely acknowledged to be THE FINEST GROUPING OF DECORATED SCULPTURE IN ANY CHURCH IN ENGLAND.

Hough on the Hill – All Saints. Here we have a splendid Saxon tower, ONE OF ONLY FOUR SAXON TOWERS IN ENGLAND TO HAVE AN EXTERNAL STAIR-CASE TURRET. The top stage of the tower, added in the 15th century, is crowned with delicate pinnacles and looks somewhat puny and pretentious in comparison with its rugged Saxon base. There was once a priory in the field across the road from the church, founded by Henry I for Austin canons. King John sought refuge here in 1216, stripped of his jewels and his sanity after almost drowning in the Wash. Watched by the Saxon tower of All Saints he left here for Newark and a wretched, lonely death.

Scopwick – Church of the Holy Cross. This typically enchanting village church, much restored but retaining its simple, sturdy 13th-century tower, is one of very few English country churches dedicated to the Holy Cross. Buried in the extended churchyard is

PILOT OFFICER JOHN GILLESPIE MAGEE, son of an American father and an English mother, who died in a mid-air collision over Lincolnshire in 1941, while based at nearby RAF Digby. Shortly before he died he wrote, apparently on the back of an envelope, a short poem about his first flight in a Spitfire, called 'High Flight', which has since become regarded as THE BEST POEM EVER WRITTEN ABOUT FLYING. In 1986 President Ronald Reagan ended his tribute to the astronauts of the ill-fated Challenger Space Shuttle by quoting the first and last lines of Magee's poem. They had '. . . slipped the surly bonds of earth . . . to touch the face of God'.

NORFOLK

St Andrew's, East Lexham – Britain's oldest round tower, dating from AD 900

Binham Priory

Earliest English Decorated

'Very flat, Norfolk,' remarked Noël Coward and certainly, around Binham, the hills are modest, but they nonetheless create an idyllic backdrop to one of East Anglia's most atmospheric sites. The village keeps a wary distance from the grim grey walls of its intimidating parish church, garlanded as it is with jagged ruins, rising out of the purple heather like some huge beast. One can almost hear it roar.

Binham Priory was founded in 1091 by Peter des Valoines, a nephew of William the Conqueror, and was built up over the next 150 years. At the Dissolution it was all dismantled again, except for seven of the nave's nine bays, which were retained for use as the parish church. Apparently, what is left is about a sixth of the size of the original church, which makes one ponder – if this enormous edifice is merely one sixth, then what must the whole complex have been like?

We approach the church through a ruined gateway and are confronted by one of the most extraordinary sights in England, a magnificent if somewhat stark wall of red brick and stone, Gothic arcades and empty windows. It appears to be winking at you. The huge two-light window was bricked up without ceremony after it collapsed in 1809, while the two aisle windows either side are now open to the sky. But no matter how desolate or unpromising this 13th-century façade may be to the layman, it causes students of English church architecture to scream with rapture, for it marks THE DAWNING OF ENGLISH DECORATED GOTHIC ARCHITECTURE. The great west window shows THE EARLIEST EXAMPLE IN ENGLAND OF BAR TRACERY, an advanced form of delicate tracery developed in France in the early 13th century, primarily at Rheims Cathedral, that allowed for greater expanses of glass and hence heralded the big, tall, traceried windows so characteristic of later Decorated and Perpendicular Gothic architecture.

The evidence for this is that the west front at Binham is known to have been built by PRIOR RICHARD DE PARCO, who is also known to have left Binham in 1244, and therefore the west window must date from before 1244. The tracery in the Chapter House of Westminster Abbey, often thought to be the earliest tracery in England, was created in 1245.

Norfolk Norman

If you can tear yourself away from this wondrous façade, the sight that greets you on entering the 11th-century Norman nave is quite exhilarating: a vast, cavernous space with tier upon tier of round Norman arches marching up and away into the gloom. There are three tiers in fact, arcades, gallery and clerestory, all with arches and capitals and piers carved with zigzag and billet decoration.

Immediately in front of you in the central aisle is a 15TH-CENTURY OCTAGONAL FONT with illustrations of the seven sacraments carved on seven of the faces and the Baptism of Christ on the eighth. This type of SEVEN SACRAMENT FONT is found solely in East Anglia.

The only square feature anywhere in view is a Tudor window in the great wall at the east end, which was built after the Dissolution to cut off the parish church from the rest of the monastic buildings.

For lovers of Norman architecture, this has to be one of the finest views in Norfolk.

Houghton on the Hill

St Mary's

England's Earliest Anglo-Saxon Wall Paintings

In 1992 a group of ramblers came across a hidden clearing at the top of a thickly wooded hill a few miles south of Swaffham. There they found themselves standing in front of a tower, completely overgrown with ivy, just a glimpse of stone showing through to indicate that there was some sort of structure concealed underneath. They had, in fact, stumbled upon one of Norfolk's lost treasures, the Saxon-built early Norman church of ST MARY, HOUGHTON ON THE HILL. The village it once served was, by 1992, long gone. The churchyard was damaged by bombs dropped from a Zeppelin in the First World War. The small cottage and farmhouse mentioned by guidebooks of the 1930s were nowhere to be seen, just trees and brambles.

But this was no ordinary treasure the ramblers had uncovered. Since that extraordinary day, in an ongoing rescue mission led by BOB DAVEY, a churchwarden from nearby Pickenham, and his wife GLORIA, who made the discovery, the church has been cleared of vegetation, the roof and tower have been repaired and the building has been restored to a living building. In 1996, during the initial stages of restoration, a remarkable series of wall paintings were uncovered, THE FINEST SEQUENCE OF ANGLO-SAXON WALL PAINTINGS EVER FOUND.

The most significant of the paintings recovered so far can be found above the simple round chancel arch. This is

A DEPICTION OF THE TRINITY AS PART OF A DOOM OR LAST JUDGEMENT, A UNIQUE TREATMENT OF THE SUBJECT FOUND NOWHERE ELSE. On God's knee is a quatrefoil cross such as found in Anglo-Saxon manuscripts of the 11th century, and this dates the paintings to around 1090, meaning that these are THE EARLIEST WALL PAINTINGS EVER DISCOVERED IN ENGLAND and amongst the earliest in all of Europe.

Today the churchyard lawn is neatly mown, shrubs and flowers embellish the gravestones and a rejuvenated St Mary's is full of life and colour once more as it heads into its second millennium. This new chapter of its glorious story has only just begun.

Little Snoring

St Andrew's

It's All in the Name

There are more than 650 medieval churches in Norfolk, THE GREATEST CONCENTRATION OF MEDIEVAL CHURCHES IN THE WORLD. Of these, 124 HAVE ROUND TOWERS – MORE THAN ANY OTHER COUNTY IN BRITAIN. How,

then, does one decide which medieval, round-towered Norfolk church to write about? I had to choose LITTLE SNORING because how can you resist that name? Derived from a Saxon called Snear, apparently.

St Andrew's sits, like so many Norfolk churches, just outside the village on its own little hill, a landmark for miles around. As you approach from the village, the delightful, almost window-less, Norman round tower, which sports a quaint 18th-century conical cap with dormer windows, appears to be integrated with the rest of the church. It is only on arrival that one realises the tower is in fact detached, although a Norman arch on the eastern side tells us that it actually was once part of a different church, extending to the west. What happened to that church? No one seems to know – it is a mystery. The arch is now filled in but has a small door with a laughing face carved in stone on the wall above it, amused perhaps by our confusion.

The porch to the existing church almost crowds out the tower and shelters what must be a UNIQUE DOORWAY, consisting of THREE DIFFERENTLY STYLED ARCHES IN ONE, a crude Norman arch within a pointed zigzag arch surmounted by a rough horseshoe-shaped arch decorated with foliage. Since the rest of the existing church is mainly Gothic, this Norman doorway must presumably have come from the original church.

Inside, the church is plain and uncluttered, with few monuments or wall furnishings but an array of windows of every design and period from Norman to Tudor. A narrow, 13th-century Gothic arch leads through to the chancel, which is lit by a triple lancet and has an unusual piscina in the south-east corner supported by a cute miniature pillar. The font is Norman and carved with swirling patterns, while above the door is a RARE JAMES II HATCHMENT – rare, because James II ruled for just three years, from 1685 to 1688, at which point he was deposed in the Glorious Revolution.

Along the west wall are some large wooden boards recording the exploits of RAF airmen based at Little Snoring airfield during the Second World War, who used the church as a chapel.

There is nothing exceptional or momentous at Little Snoring, but it has an aura of tranquillity and permanence that is reassuring. It is an amiable place and one leaves feeling very much better for visiting.

West Walton

St Mary the Virgin

Feeling Detached

Here is a quite dazzling combination of ONE OF ENGLAND'S MOST MAGNIFICENT BELL TOWERS and ONE OF ENGLAND'S MOST LOVELY EARLY ENGLISH CHURCHES. The bell tower is unequivocally detached from the church, so detached that it is almost in the next county – we are in Norfolk's far west here, with Cambridgeshire lurking – and so majestic that it surely belongs to some Fenland cathedral rather than to the low, outwardly ordinary looking church slumped in the churchyard some 60 feet (18 m) to the north-west.

The tower was built in 1250 on the firmest patch of land in the vicinity, and perhaps they made it so grand simply because they could. The parapet and pinnacles at the top are 15th-century

Perpendicular, but the rest is early Gothic, three tiers of tall, slim arcading and narrow window openings resting four square on open arches, providing not only an elaborate lych-gate for the churchyard but a spacious shelter and meeting place for the village folk. The sturdy octagonal buttresses at each corner are AMONGST THE EARLIEST BUTTRESSES IN ENGLAND.

Unlike its sure-footed bell tower, the church itself almost floats on Fenland springs and has needed to be buttressed just about everywhere, although there are still numerous kinks and bulges in the fabric where things have shifted. On closer inspection the unprepossessing exterior is actually rather attractive, with some fine Gothic windows and a lovely line of arcading dotted with windows above the aisle roof.

The imposing porch is a touch over the top, a Gothic arch with dogtooth ornamentation surmounted by a stepped brick gable, with huge arcaded turrets on each side. The inner doorway is a mass of Gothic arches resting on capitals carved with foliage.

The interior is just beautiful. A dark brown 15th-century oak hammer-beam roof, supported by angels holding shields, looks down upon a nave lined with gleaming, elegant arcades of six bays each side, their arches resting on capitals carved with fluttering leaves above round pillars ringed with Purbeck marble columns. In the spandrels of the arches are roundels depicting the Tribes of Israel, 400 years old and in fine condition. The clerestory is a delightful mix of windows and blind arcades, some with traces of 13th-century wall paintings in a rich ochre.

The effect of this double layer of arcades, wondrous leaf carvings and clustered pillars is a shout of joy from the Early English masons and architects of the time, who were learning new ways of doing beautiful things, a celebration indeed of their developing craft and imagination. Alas, such undisciplined flowering of talent was brought to a premature end by the Black Death, and the Gothic architecture that followed, while undeniably handsome, is more restrained by the rules and mathematics of architecture.

Well, I never *knew this*
about
NORFOLK CHURCHES

Blakeney – St Nicholas. Standing on a rise 100 feet (30 m) above the marshes and the sea, with its splendid 15th-century Perpendicular tower rising a further 125 feet (38 m) into the sky, St Nicholas is halfway to being the highest point in Norfolk. No one seems to know what the SECOND, RATHER CURIOUS, OCTAG-ONAL TOWER tacked on to the east end of the chancel is for, although perhaps it was designed to make St Nicholas a distinctive landmark from the sea, clearly distinguishable from other churches along the coast. Inside, St Nicholas is famed for its RARE 13TH-CENTURY VAULTED CHANCEL, which is graced by

an east window that is ONE OF ONLY TWO MEDIEVAL SEVEN-LIGHT WINDOWS IN ENGLAND, the other being at Ockham, in Surrey (*see* page 273)

Booton – St Michael All Angels. Known as the 'Cathedral of the Fields', this extraordinary church, begun in 1875, sits over a mile away from its village in a corner of the manor-house garden. It is a feast of Victorian French Gothic with two high, slender west towers that look like waving crab claws. The inside is, appropriately enough, all about angels, with carved wooden angels holding up the hammer-beam roof and extremely pretty musical angels posing in the stained-glass

St Michael & All Angels, Booton

windows, all of them modelled on female acquaintances of rector and lord of the manor WHITWELL ELWIN, a descendant of John Rolfe and the Native American princess Pocahontas. He designed and built the church himself and paid for it with his wife's dowry. The carvings were done by a well-known local master carver called JAMES MINNS, whose carving of a bull's head can be seen on jars of COLMAN'S MUSTARD.

East Lexham – St Andrew's. Here we have THE OLDEST CHURCH TOWER IN ENGLAND. Dating from AD 900, it is a wonderfully rugged, round structure that seems to bulge in the middle before tapering off unevenly to a Victorian brick parapet. It has THREE ENTIRELY DIFFERENT BELFRY OPENINGS, two of them most unusual. The south-facing opening is traditional, twin arches on a central shaft, while the one facing north is also a twin opening, this time having a bulbous central shaft with strangely shaped capital and base. The third opening, facing east, is HEWN OUT OF A SINGLE SLAB OF STONE IN THE SHAPE OF A MALTESE CROSS, AND IS UNIQUE IN ENGLAND. The tower and its church, which is 11th century and later, sit on a pagan mound in a farmyard, and make a charming rustic picture.

Gunton – St Andrew's. Something a little different here. St Andrew's is THE ONLY COMPLETE CHURCH DESIGNED BY ROBERT ADAM IN BRITAIN and his only work in Norfolk. It stands in the grounds of Gunton Hall and was built in 1769 for the owner of the hall, SIR WILLIAM HARBORD, to replace a medieval church destroyed some years earlier. The style is Palladian and the church sports a vast portico supported on Doric columns that emerges with a slightly startling flourish from the trees. The interior is classical with a west gallery, panelling, a coved plasterwork ceiling and a frieze around the nave supported on wooden columns with elaborate gilded capitals.

Northamptonshire

All Saints, Earl's Barton, with England's loveliest Saxon tower

Brixworth

All Saints

Real Romanesque

This is THE LARGEST SURVIVING CHURCH OF SAXON ORIGINS IN BRITAIN. It sits majestically on a hill above the old houses of the village, its grandeur undiminished by the unthinking modern bungalow estates that are creeping ever nearer.

All Saints was founded in 680 by monks from Peterborough who set up a mission here to convert the heathen of Mercia. Its impressive size suggests that this was an important, possibly royal foundation, perhaps the legendary lost Saxon meeting place of CLOFESHO, where a series of synods were convened in the 8th and 9th centuries.

The church is certainly huge, and yet it was once even bigger, as wide as it is long, with aisles or chapels running

along either side of the nave. It is thought that this first church was damaged by the Vikings and the arches of the arcades leading through to those aisles were filled in with windows and bricks to form the outside walls of the present church.

While the building contains elements from many building periods, the architecture and form are overwhelmingly Saxon. The numerous Saxon arches, both inside and out, are constructed from rich red Roman tiles, neatly illustrating the origins of the word Romanesque. The lower part of the tower, with its tiny windows and minute blocked-up south door, formed the original two-tier porch of the 7th-century church, while the splendid external stair turret was added during the 10th century and is ONE OF ONLY FOUR EXTERNAL STAIR TURRETS IN BRITAIN. The upper portion of the tower and the spire were added in the 15th century.

Let's Walk

At the east end is a square medieval apse, a Victorian reconstruction of the 7th-century Saxon apse. Running round the outside of the apse is a SUNKEN AMBULATORY, from which pilgrims could view relics contained in recesses in the outside wall. THIS IS ONE OF ONLY THREE SO-CALLED RING CRYPTS LEFT IN BRITAIN.

You enter the church through a large Norman doorway inserted into a larger original Saxon doorway, which has a huge double arch of red tiles. Set into a niche beside the door is a Saxon carving of an eagle. Once you are inside, the impression is of light and space. The nave is lofty and uncluttered. The high west wall is a fine sight. A Saxon doorway leads through to an antechamber under the tower known as a narthex. Above this is a Saxon gallery arch and above that a three-light Saxon window, possibly refashioned by the Normans.

Looking down the nave, the red-tiled arches march eastwards towards a vast 14th-century chancel arch, while the original Saxon chancel arch is set in the east wall of the choir and leads through to the apse. Blocked-up Saxon doorways either side once gave access to the ambulatory.

Earl's Barton

All Saints

England's Loveliest Tower

Here, to my mind, is THE LOVELIEST TOWER IN ENGLAND. Half-timbered in

stone, it is almost pure Saxon to a height of 63 feet (19 m) and constitutes the most elaborate and joyous example of Saxon architectural decoration in the country. The tower was constructed in AD 970, and apart from the addition of the clock of 1650 and the battlements of 1450, which replaced a pyramidal roof, it has stood here essentially untouched for over 1,000 years. There are four levels of Saxon work, and the half-timbered effect is created by the stone pilasters that run up the walls of the tower from top to bottom. These are not merely for show but are formed from the outer edges of stone blocks inserted into the walls to help reinforce the structure.

The tower originally stood alone and contained the church on the ground floor. It was also a place of refuge, with the pointed windows in each face serving as observation points, while the doorway at the second level of the south face could only be reached by a ladder, which was pulled up in the event of an attack.

The ground-level doorway in the west face is made from vertical stone slabs, which run through the thickness of the walls, while the inner arch rests on horizontal slabs decorated with miniature arcading. THIS DECORATIVE ARCADING IS UNIQUE TO EARL'S BARTON.

At the fourth level of each face are glorious belfry openings made up of rugged, rough-hewn five-light arcades. These are common enough on Saxon church towers but Earls' Barton is THE ONLY SAXON TOWER IN THE WORLD TO HAVE BELFRY OPENINGS IN ALL FOUR FACES.

The rest of All Saints rather lives in the shadow of its tower, but the church can also boast of ONE OF THE FINEST NORMAN DOORWAYS IN NORTHAMPTONSHIRE, a gorgeous 15th-century screen, painted with birds and saints in 1935, and some very unusual Norman blind arcading with chevron-carved arches on the walls of the chancel.

Fotheringhay

St Mary All Saints

House of York

The pretty stone village of FOTHERINGHAY, set beside the River Nene, is the ancestral home of the illustrious ROYAL HOUSE OF YORK, and the stately church of ST MARY ALL SAINTS contains the resplendent tombs of some prominent members of that turbulent family. St Mary's, a church of extraordinary strength and beauty, resonates with history and dominates

the flat landscape for miles around, seeming to float above the water meadows in which it stands. The high walls appear to be made almost entirely of glass, while crowning the great square tower, in place of a spire, is a magnificent octagonal lantern, laced with pinnacles and topped with a weather-vane in the shape of the York emblem of a Falcon and Fetterlock. SUCH A TOWER IS UNIQUE IN NORTHAMPTONSHIRE.

The church was begun in 1415 when EDWARD, 2ND DUKE OF YORK, had Fotheringhay's Norman parish church rebuilt and enlarged to house a college established earlier in Fotheringhay Castle by his father EDMUND OF LANGLEY, FIFTH SON OF EDWARD III AND FOUNDER OF THE HOUSE OF YORK. Duke Edward was killed that same year at the Battle of Agincourt and was buried in the unfinished quire. His nephew RICHARD PLANTAGENET, 3RD DUKE OF YORK, had the nave completed

in 1434. The contract for the work states that William Horwood the mason would be paid £300 if the work was satisfactory, and if it was not he would be sent to prison.

The future KING RICHARD III, fourth son of the 3rd Duke of York, was born in Fotheringhay Castle in 1452 and baptised in the church.

In 1460 Richard, 3rd Duke of York, and his second son, 17-year-old Edmund, Earl of Rutland, were killed fighting the forces of the Lancastrian king Henry VI at the Battle of Wakefield, the first major battle of the Wars of the Roses. Their heads were stuck on pikes above York's Micklegate Bar with the message 'Let York overlook York', while their bodies were buried at Pontefract. Their corpses were rescued and brought home to Fotheringhay in 1476 by the Duke's eldest son, by then Edward IV, who led the funeral procession into the church and watched as his father and brother were laid to rest together in the same tomb in the quire. They were joined there 36 years later by the 3rd Duke's widow, CECILY NEVILLE.

These were the last of the Yorks to be buried at Fotheringhay, because in 1485 Richard III was killed at the Battle of Bosworth Field and the castle and church became the property of the victorious Tudors. At the Dissolution of the Monasteries the church was granted to the Duke of Northumberland, who dismantled most of the college buildings and the east end of the church including the quire leaving just the nave and tower for use as the parish church. This is the building we see today.

In 1566 Elizabeth I visited Fotheringhay and expressed her dismay at seeing the neglected tombs of her ancestors lying among the ruins of the quire. She ordered their remains to be exhumed and reburied in the parish church, where they now rest beneath two beautiful Elizabethan tombs either side of the altar, Edward, 2nd Duke of York, on the right, Richard, 3rd Duke of York, on the left. Richard's son Edmund, Earl of Rutland, who was buried with his father in the original tomb, is not mentioned on the new tomb although presumably, he was reburied here too.

The nave is spacious and bright, with light flooding in through the huge, clear Perpendicular windows of the nave and clerestory. The highlight of the furnishings is the SUPERB 15TH-CENTURY OAK WINE-GLASS PULPIT AND CANOPY, a gift from Edward IV. Gorgeously painted in red, green and gold, it brings a dash of colour and gaiety to the scene.

There is little of the original stained glass left, but in 1975 the Richard III Society donated a beautiful new window to St Mary's called the YORK WINDOW, which incorporates the arms of the various members of the York dynasty, including Richard III and his wife Anne Neville, in coloured glass, as well as the various York emblems, such as Richard III's White Boar, the Falcon and Fetterlock of York and the White Rose of York. On 2 October every year the Society fills the church with white roses to commemorate Richard III's birthday.

Grafton Regis

St Mary the Virgin

Royal Romance

Standing alone beside a handsome 17th-century stone house, this quietly beautiful little church looks like part of a Hollywood film set, a too perfect scene of Olde England. And its story could be from a Hollywood plot too, for it was here that a girl became a queen and the history of England was changed for ever.

The somewhat over-large tower of St Mary's Church was built in the early 15th

Mary Queen of Scots

A short walk across the fields from the church at Fotheringhay is the site of FOTHERINGHAY CASTLE, where MARY QUEEN OF SCOTS was brought in 1586 to be put on trial for treason. She was found guilty and executed on 8 February 1587 in the castle's great hall. It took three strokes of the axe to sever her head from her body, and afterwards her small dog GEDDON was found cowering under the folds of her gown, covered in his mistress's blood. Mary's body lay unburied in the castle for nearly six months before being taken away at night and buried in Peterborough Cathedral. When her son came to the throne as James I and VI, he had his mother's remains re-interred in Westminster Abbey.

In 1627 Charles I had the castle pulled down, full as it was of such unhappy memories for the Stuarts. There is nothing left of it save for a small mound in the middle of a field where the great hall stood. You can climb the mound and gaze at the River Nene winding its way placidly by, as Mary Queen of Scots would have done, and the Dukes of York before her. At certain times of year the fields are filled with QUEEN MARY'S TEARS, tall purple thistles descended from a patch planted here by the tragic Queen of Scots during her last days. Two hundred years after Mary died, a gold ring was found in the field. It was decorated with a lover's knot, which was entwined around the initials of Queen Mary and her second husband Lord Darnley.

century by SIR JOHN WOODVILLE, Sheriff of Northampton, who is buried inside in a stone altar tomb, his image incised on the alabaster top. In 1461 his great-grand-daughter ELIZABETH WOODVILLE, widowed with two young sons after her husband Sir John Grey was killed at St Albans during the Wars of the Roses, came home to Grafton and later went out to petition the King, Edward IV, when he came hunting nearby. They met under an oak tree, fell in love, and were married in secret in the Woodville family chapel in Grafton's Hermitage, a small but once important priory, on 1 May 1464. Elizabeth became Queen, then mother to the Princes in the Tower, and then grandmother to a line of kings when her daughter Elizabeth married Henry VII.

Elizabeth's grandson, Henry VIII, eventually came into possession of the manor house at Grafton and took Anne Boleyn there to woo her. They were such happy times that he awarded Grafton the suffix 'Regis' in gratitude.

The Woodvilles' manor house is no more, although some fragments can be found in the walls of the 17th-century house that stands beside the church now. The Hermitage where Edward and Elizabeth married and spent their honeymoon was demolished not long after the event, but the remains, which lie in a field just west of the village, have been excavated, and tiles bearing the crests of the Woodvilles and the House of York were uncovered. In 2000 Prince Charles, Prince of Wales, planted an oak tree beside the Hermitage to symbolically replace the 'Queens Oak' under which his ancestors met all those years ago.

Sir John Woodville, watching from his tomb in St Mary's Church, would have been proud.

Great Brington

St Mary the Virgin

From Here to Washington

This is a land of big skies and rolling open fields. Set upon a small hill on the edge of the village, with wide views across the parkland of ALTHORP HOUSE, ancestral home of the Spencer family, the church of St Mary the Virgin is pleasing but unostentatious – from the outside, anyway. Inside, it is a different story; for there, jostling for position in the Spencer Chapel, are the flamboyant monuments of 19 generations of Spencers, covering almost 500 years and making up one of the FINEST AND LARGEST COLLECTIONS OF MONUMENTS IN ANY ENGLISH CHURCH.

The earliest monument fills the arch between the chancel and the chapel and is that of SIR JOHN SPENCER, who died in 1522, and his wife Isabel Grant. They lie beneath a canopy, Sir John wearing a bright red cloak, and are watched over by a delightfully eccentric angel who clings to the underside. It was Sir John who purchased Althorp in 1508 and

then rebuilt the church and constructed the Spencer Chapel in 1514.

There are monuments here by many of the great sculptors including JASPER HOLLEMANS, JOSEPH NOLLEKENS, JOHN FLAXMAN and FRANCIS CHANTREY. All the Spencer women seem to exhibit a fine line in eccentric headgear, but perhaps the most bizarre of all the monuments is that by JOHN STONE of SIR EDWARD SPENCER, who died in 1656. He is seen rising from a funeral urn, fully clothed, his left hand resting on a bible stand.

One of the more elaborate monuments, the work of JASPER HOLLEMANS, is that of a later SIR JOHN SPENCER, who died in 1586, and his wife KATHERINE KITSON. Katherine's uncle by marriage was one JOHN WASHINGTON, an ancestor of George Washington, first President of the United States of America, and in this way the Spencers and the Washingtons are related by marriage.

In the floor of the chancel is the grave slab of 'Laurence Washington, sonne and heire of Robert Washington of Soulgrave in the Countie of Northamton'. He died here in 1616 and was the great-great-great-grandfather of George Washington. His slab bears the Washington coat of arms incorporating the stars and stripes that would form the basis of the American flag.

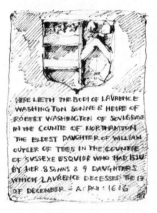

Other interesting features in the church are some wonderful 15th-century poppy-head bench ends, carved on one side only, and the colourful east window by EDWARD BURNE-JONES, which depicts the Adoration of the Lamb and was dedicated in 1912.

Well, I never knew this about
NORTHAMPTONSHIRE CHURCHES

Brigstock – St Andrew's. Here, not 20 miles from Brixworth, is another of ENGLAND'S FOUR EXTERNAL SAXON STAIR TURRETS, attached to a Saxon tower of the late 10th century. The tower and turret are massively solid and were built in a clearing in the middle of Rockingham Forest as a refuge from marauding Vikings for the Saxon woodsmen. The Saxon nave of the church also survives but was much refashioned by the Normans.

King's Sutton – St Peter & St Paul. Here is what Nikolaus Pevsner describes as 'one of the finest, if not the finest, spire in this county of spires'. Built in the late 14th century, it soars to a height of 198 feet (60 m) and provides a spectacular welcome to Northamptonshire for visitors from the south.

Woodnewton – St Mary's. Buried in the graveyard of this mainly 13th-century church are NICOLAI POLIAKOV (1900–74) and his wife VALENTINA. He was better known as COCO THE CLOWN, for many years the most famous clown in Britain. He only lived in the village for just over a year, but in that time managed to inspire the WOODNEWTON CLOWNFEST, a regular fund-raising event.

NORTHUMBERLAND

St Anne, Ancroft – a typical Northumberland border church with fortified 13th-century pele tower

Bamburgh

St Aidan's

Northern Lights

ST AIDAN'S CHURCH in Bamburgh occupies one of England's most important religious sites, and its story comes down to us from the very earliest days of English Christianity. The setting is spectacular, with the church standing in the middle of a wide, windswept graveyard high above the village, watched over by Bamburgh's mighty Norman castle, which stands on its lofty basalt bluff above the cold North Sea. In 1464, during the Wars of the Roses, this became THE FIRST ENGLISH CASTLE IN HISTORY TO SUCCUMB TO ARTILLERY FIRE, when the walls were brought down by Edward IV's cannon, and Henry VI was forced to flee.

Bamburgh was once the capital of the powerful Anglo-Saxon kingdom of Northumbria, and in 635 the newly crowned King Oswald, who had become a Christian while in exile in Scotland, asked Aidan, an Irish monk from St Columba's monastery on the Scottish island of Iona, to come south and set up a mission to convert the people of Northumbria to Christianity.

Aidan, today known as the 'Apostle of the North', began by founding a monastery on Lindisfarne, an island off the coast some miles to the north, and then set about building a place of worship at Bamburgh on the high ground across from Oswald's castle.

Seen from the road as you enter the village, the present church appears to have been somewhat randomly put together. There is a square tower at the western end, mostly 13th century, with a Victorian battlemented top, while the main body of the church is low and squat. Tacked on to the east end, seemingly as an afterthought, is an elaborate

chancel, laid out in 1230 on the exact site of St Aidan's original wooden church.

The interior of the church is light and airy. The nave seems taller from the inside and is held up by pointed arches resting on slender round pillars, while a high Gothic arch leads through to the chancel.

At 60 feet (18 m) in length, the magnificent chancel of St Aidan's is THE SECOND LONGEST CHANCEL OF ANY PARISH CHURCH IN ENGLAND. Behind the altar is a beautiful reredos of pale Caen stone with carved figures of St Aidan and St Oswald standing in niches above an array of northern saints.

On one side of the chancel a perpetual light shines on a simple shrine to St Aidan, marking the exact spot where he died in 651, leaning against the outside wall of his own church. The forked wooden beam against which he rested, the only remnant of Aidan's original building, can be seen above the font in the baptistry.

A Northern Knight

Set in a recess in the south wall is the worn figure of a recumbent knight lying cross-legged, dating from about 1320. He is referred to locally as SIR LANCELOT DU LAC, recalling the fact that Bamburgh Castle is thought to be the 'Joyous Gard' of Sir Thomas Malory's *Le Morte d'Arthur*, where Sir Lancelot came home to die.

So, when he was housled and eneled, and had all that a Christian man ought to have, he prayed the bishop

that his fellows might bear his body unto Joyous Gard.

'And now, I dare say,' said Sir Ector, 'that Sir Lancelot there thou liest . . .'

Cryptic

Beneath the chancel is a remarkable 13TH-CENTURY VAULTED CRYPT, which was rediscovered in 1837, having been lost for centuries. It is divided into two by a wall containing a small Saxon sundial and was probably built to exhibit relics associated with St Aidan. Also found when the crypt was reopened were five coffins lying on a stone shelf, containing the bones of various FORSTERS, a prominent Northumbrian family who provided 12 successive Governors of Bamburgh Castle over a period of some 400 years from the 12th century onwards.

A Northern Heroine

Off the nave, in the north aisle, is the effigy that everyone one comes to see, that of Northumberland's heroine, the lighthouse-keeper's daughter, GRACE DARLING. This effigy was originally under the canopy of her memorial in the churchyard outside but was replaced by a copy and brought into the church in 1885 when it began to weather badly. Nearby there is a stained-glass memorial window dedicated to her.

The distinctive memorial to Grace Darling outside in the churchyard was designed by Anthony Salvin and was placed so as to be visible to passing ships. The canopy had to be rebuilt

after a fierce storm in 1893, which sank 48 ships off England's east coast.

Grace herself lies in a family plot a little nearer to the church, alongside her parents and brothers and sisters, (*see* panel, page 197).

Bellingham

St Cuthbert's

Unique Stone Roof

This little church, set on a terrace overlooking the North Tyne river, and hidden away behind the half-timbered Black Bull hotel off the village square, is renowned for its astonishing BARREL-VAULTED STONE ROOF, UNIQUE IN ENGLAND. Built in the early 17th century, the roof is made of huge interlocking stone slabs supported by a series of rounded stone arches, and was designed to be fireproof – Bellingham lies close to the border with Scotland and more than once St Cuthbert's had been burned by raiders known as Border Reivers. Such is the weight of the roof that there are now 11 outside buttresses holding up the walls of the nave on both sides, put there in the 18th century.

The earliest part of the present church dates from 1180 but St Cuthbert himself is said to have consecrated the site some 500 years before, in about AD 663, when he visited the area and discovered the healing well that bubbles away in the lane next to the church. St Cuthbert s Well, or 'Cuddy's Well' as it is known, has never run dry and the water now flows through a Georgian conduit or pant. It is still used for baptisms and christenings today.

Bolam

St Andrew's

A Saxon Survivor

The church at Bolam is a classic example of a village church that has lost its village. There were once over 200 houses in Bolam, but as workers moved off the land and into the towns, the village dwindled and now St Andrew's stands in the middle of nowhere with just three small country

Grace Darling
(1815–42)

GRACE DARLING was the daughter of lighthouse-keeper William Darling and his wife Thomasina and lived with them in the LONGSTONE LIGHT-HOUSE, located about six miles offshore of Bamburgh, on the Farne Islands. On the night of 7 September 1838 there was a terrible storm and Grace was woken early by the commotion. Gazing out from her window she spotted the wreck of the paddle steamer *Forfarshire*, bound for Hull from Dundee, being pounded on the rocks about a mile away, and as the dawn grew lighter she was able to make out figures clinging to what was left of the vessel.

Conditions were far too bad for any hope of rescue from the mainland, so Grace roused her father and together they clambered into their tiny coble and rowed through the mountainous seas to the scene of the wreck. They managed to rescue five people from the rocks on that first attempt, including a woman who was holding on desperately to her two dead children. Grace's father then went back for the remaining four survivors. It was another three days before the storm abated and they could all be taken to the mainland.

The courageous rescue captured the imagination of Victorian England. Grace was pretty and slight and became one of the first 'celebrities', with her picture on the front pages of all the newspapers and reporters clamouring for her story. Endearingly modest, Grace shunned all the attention, and when she died tragically young of tuberculosis she attained almost saintlike status and was buried in Bamburgh before a huge crowd of mourners, with Queen Victoria personally sending her condolences and the Poet Laureate William Wordsworth penning a tribute to her.

Grace Darling's story is told in the Grace Darling Museum across the road from St Aidan's Church, Bamburgh.

houses for company. From the church-yard there is not a building in sight – just wide, glorious views of the Northumberland hills.

The church that Bolam left behind is a most handsome building with one of THE MOST HANDSOME SAXON TOWERS IN ENGLAND. Tall, square and completely un-buttressed, it has been gazing out across the Wansbeck valley for over 1,000 years.

The way into the church is through an exquisite small Norman doorway with carved dogtooth arches. The

crooked, pale stone interior is largely Norman and quite breathtakingly lovely. There is a tall, slightly uneven chancel arch and beautiful arcading to the south made up of slender round arches resting on RARE QUATREFOIL PIERS THAT ARE UNIQUE TO BOLAM. Also unusual are the sturdy stone altar rails.

At the east end of the south aisle there is a small chapel, which is full of interest. On the north wall is a low-relief carving of a shield and inscription, thought to be the de Bolam's coat of arms, while beneath lies a legless effigy of 14th-century knight SIR ROBERT DE REYMES, who died in 1324. He was from a Suffolk family who came north, acquired the half barony of Bolam in 1295 and built SHORTFLATT TOWER, a pele tower hidden in trees a little to the south-west of the church. He chose a turbulent time to move to the Borders and ended up fighting in the Scottish wars of that period, including at Stirling Bridge and Falkirk. The chapel where Sir Robert is buried is now known as the HEDLEY DENT CHAPEL after the family who have owned Shortflatt Tower since the 18th century.

In the south wall of the chapel is a relatively modern leaded window by LIONEL EVATTS that recalls the events of 1 May 1942, when a German Dornier 217 bomber dropped four bombs near to the church (they were aimed at a nearby railway), one of which crashed through the church wall and came to rest in the aisle. Fortunately it failed to explode and the only damage was the hole in the wall, now filled by the window. The bomber's pilot, WILLI SCHLUDECKER, returned to Bolam a few years ago to apologise, and wrote in the visitor's book, 'I am the pilot dropping my bombs 65 years ago . . . My age will be 87 in May. I am happy the church did not get destroyed.'

So are all the visitors who find their way to this lonely and beautiful ancient church.

Branxton

St Paul's

A Lost King's Last Resting Place

The view from the little church of St Paul at Branxton is windswept and magnificent, but forever tinged with melancholy. On 9 September 1513, on the bare hillside to the south, 15,000 men died during THE LARGEST BATTLE

EVER FOUGHT BETWEEN SCOTLAND AND
ENGLAND, THE BATTLE OF FLODDEN
FIELD. The victorious English army of
Henry VIII was led by the Earl of
Surrey, and the Scottish army by
Henry's brother-in-law James IV of
Scotland. Some 10,000 Scots perished,
including three Scottish bishops and 13
Scottish earls, and it is said that every
noble family in Scotland lost at least
one family member.

A tall memorial cross can be seen
from the churchyard, standing stark on
top of a hillock to the south-west and
marking the spot where KING JAMES IV
OF SCOTLAND BECAME THE LAST
MONARCH FROM THE BRITISH ISLES TO
DIE IN BATTLE. His mutilated body was
brought to lie in St Paul's Church overnight before being taken to Berwick-
on-Tweed and eventually to London.
Many of the dead were actually buried
in and around the churchyard. St Paul's
was rebuilt in 1849 but THE NARROW
CHANCEL ARCH FROM THE ORIGINAL
12TH-CENTURY CHURCH, BENEATH
WHICH THE DEAD KING'S BODY LAY, still
stands in place inside.

Bywell

St Andrew's and St Peter's

Double Delight

The only road to Bywell is a no-through
country lane off the main road from
Newcastle to Hexham. Go past the
great square bulk of BYWELL CASTLE,
built as a gatehouse in 1430 by Ralph
Neville, 2nd Earl of Westmorland, and

St Andrew's

used as a hiding place by Henry VI
after the Battle of Hexham in 1464.
Then veer left past the stone gateposts
of BYWELL HALL, designed in 1766 by
James Paine for William Fenwick and
now home to the Beaumonts, Viscounts
Allendale. When you can go no further
and all you can hear is the wind in the
trees and the bubbling of the Tyne,
there you will find two of England's
loveliest ancient churches, side by side
– Bywell is THE ONLY VILLAGE IN
ENGLAND TO BOAST TWO MEDIEVAL
CHURCHES, EACH WITH ITS OWN
CHURCHYARD.

Why there are two such churches
here is not known, but in AD 803 a
chap called Egbert was consecrated as
Bishop of Lindisfarne in the riverside
chapel at Bywell (now St Peter's
Church), and so Bywell was clearly a
place of some significance, a thriving
market town at the meeting place of
two important estates. The churches
later belonged to two different baro-
nies, BALLIOL and BOLBEC, and then
to two different monastic groups, at
which point they became known as

the WHITE CHURCH and the BLACK CHURCH after the colour of their monks' robes.

St Andrew's – the White Church

St Andrew's belonged to the White Canons of Blanchland and the church has THE FINEST SAXON TOWER IN NORTHUMBERLAND, with defensive walls 15 feet (4.6 m) thick. It is made from a particularly attractive sandstone of many hues and incorporates re-used Roman stones. The lower stages were constructed before AD 850, and the upper part, with its round-headed belfry windows, dates from about AD 1000. St Andrew's has NORTHUMBERLAND'S BEST COLLECTION OF 13TH-CENTURY GRAVESTONES, many carved with crosses, some set in the outside north wall, others set up on plinths inside. Also inside is the shaft of a 7th-century Viking cross set in a carved block of Roman stone. Another feature is the plain, eight-sided 12th-century font with a 17th-century oak cover.

St Peter's – the Black Church

St Peter's was the property of the monks of Durham, who wore black robes, and is in fact older than St Andrew's. The lower part of the north wall of the nave contains stones from an 8th-century church destroyed by the Danes in 794 and there are two Saxon windows in the wall above. The squat tower dates from the 13th century and has Norman foundations, while low down on the wall of the south aisle is a 12TH-CENTURY SCRATCH DIAL, very rare in the north of England. A stick or rod inserted into the hole casts a shadow on the various scratches, which represent the times of services and other significant moments in the day.

The interior of the church is bright and spacious with arcades of differing heights. A lower north arcade leads through to a chapel that was once used as a school, while the high south arcade consists of pointed arches resting on round pillars. Edward I gazes down from above the central pillar. He was king at the time this part of the church was built and visited during his expeditions north to fight the Scots. On the south side of the chancel are two lancet windows of Victorian glass, one in memory of vicar's wife GEORGIANA DWARRIS, who died in 1853 aged 28, and the other of a curate, her brother-in-law HENRY DWARRIS, who was drowned in the Tyne in 1855 at the age of 33.

The Tyne has long been an unpredictable neighbour to Bywell. In 1771 the river burst its banks and flooded the village, with ten houses lost and the newly built Bywell Hall engulfed in eight feet of water. Coffins were lifted out of the ground and swept away, along with cattle and people. The squire's horses were taken into St Peter's for safety and saved themselves from drowning by sinking their teeth into the tops of the pews. You can still see the teeth marks to this day.

Kirknewton

St Gregory's

Unique Chancel

St Gregory's sits at the heart of England's largest and least populated parish, surrounded by the green meadows of lovely Glendale and watched over by lofty YEAVERING BELL, site of Northumberland's biggest prehistoric camp. A church was first recorded here in the 12th century, but there are Saxon coffin lids incorporated into the Norman walls of the church, either from an earlier Saxon church or perhaps from AD GEFRIN, King Edwin of Northumbria's palace at the foot of Yeavering Bell.

This is one of only 35 churches in England dedicated to St Gregory, the pope who sent St Augustine to Kent to introduce Christianity into Anglo-Saxon England. In AD 601, Gregory dispatched a monk called Paulinus to join him, and in 625 Paulinus, who later became the first Bishop of York, came north to marry Princess Ethelburga, daughter of the first Christian Saxon king, Ethelbert of Kent, to King Edwin. They all stayed at Ad Gefrin, and Paulinus stayed on for more

than a month, baptising converts in the River Glen at a spot nearby marked with a stone column.

Inside the church, embedded in the wall to the left of the chancel arch, is a remarkable treasure, A CRUDE STONE SCULPTURE DEPICTING THE ADORATION OF THE MAGI. This was originally thought to be Norman, but today experts think it could be from much earlier, and hence much more precious, possibly brought here from the Saxon palace at Ad Gefrin. An oft-remarked feature of the sculpture is the fact that the Magi appear to be wearing kilts, which would make this THE WORLD'S EARLIEST KNOWN REPRESENTATION OF A KILT. However, if the stone came from Ad Gefrin, it could be that the sculptor was guided in his work by Paulinus, who was from Rome, and the Magi are in fact wearing Roman garb.

THE CHANCEL OF ST GREGORY'S IS UNIQUE IN ENGLAND. Kirknewton is only a few miles from the border with Scotland and evidently the church was frequently vandalised by border raids, so much so that in 1436 the vicar was licensed to hold services outside the church 'in any safe and decent place within the parish' for 'so long as the hostility of the Scots then existing should continue'. Later in the 15th century the chancel was fortified for defence, shortened, lowered and strengthened into a distinctive tunnel-like space, similar to the upturned keel of a boat, with thick, muscular stone walls curving inward from the floor to a plain pointed vault, just three feet (1 m) high. It is a wondrous sight.

Leaning against the wall of the equally low-vaulted south chapel is a grey medieval tombstone of 1458 incised with the figures of Andrew Burrell and his wife, from an old family of the parish.

In 1860 the nave of the church was renovated by John Dobson of Newcastle. The tower, which is constructed rather unsympathetically out of a different stone from the rest of the building, was added later in the 19th century. The architect decided quite wisely to remain anonymous.

Beside the tower, out in the churchyard, is the grave of Josephine Butler (1828–1906), a prominent Northumberland-born social reformer, feminist and courageous campaigner for women's rights, particularly those of prostitutes and their children.

Norham

St Cuthbert's

Fortress 'gainst the Scots

This is border country. There is nothing between England and Scotland here except for the glorious Tweed. St Cuthbert's is the nearest English

church to Scotland and, as such, bears the scars of conflict. It is an impressively rugged pile, every bit as intimidating as the castle on the hill made famous by J.M.W. Turner, not surprising since church and castle allegedly shared the same Norman architect. With its long flat roof and massive upright tower, the church resembles nothing so much as a stately oil tanker sailing down the Tweed, preceded by a green bow-wave of grass rippling through the gravestones.

Much has happened here. In the 7th century St Aidan crossed the Tweed here on his way from Iona to found his monastery on Lindisfarne. In AD 830 a church was built here and the dug-up bones of Ceolwulf of Northumbria, an 8th-century monarch and saint described by the Venerable Bede as 'the most glorious king', were re-buried underneath the porch. Gospatrick, 1st Earl of Northumberland, was also buried nearby. In AD 875 St Cuthbert's coffin and the Lindisfarne Gospels were brought to rest here on their roundabout journey to Durham.

Fragments of ornamental crosses and gravestones from the Saxon church were discovered in the foundations during 19th-century renovations, and these were collected together to form a tall pillar, which now stands inside under the tower.

The present church was begun in 1185, and along with the castle became a stronghold against the Scots for the Prince Bishops of Durham. In 1291 Edward I held a council in the church to arbitrate between claimants to the Scottish throne, choosing John Balliol. The following year Balliol returned to

Norham to swear an oath of allegiance to Edward.

The Norman church is best seen in the windows of the nave and the south arcade, with its strong round pillars and THE WIDEST NORMAN ARCHES OF ANY CHURCH IN ENGLAND. There is also good Norman work in the chancel arch and chancel, although the east bay was destroyed when Robert the Bruce fortified St Cuthbert's for use as his headquarters while besieging the castle in 1320. The stone effigy of a knight from this period, perhaps one of Bruce's, occupies a recess.

Although much restored in the 19th century, St Cuthbert's remains one of the best Northern examples of brute Norman power outside of Durham Cathedral.

Well, I never knew this about

NORTHUMBERLAND CHURCHES

Chillingham – St Peter's. A small, simple, stone-roofed Norman building in a shady churchyard on the edge of Chillingham Park, St Peter's contains what is often described as THE FINEST TOMB IN ENGLAND 'OUTSIDE A CATHEDRAL'. Framed beneath a pointed arch in the south chapel, the alabaster figures of SIR RALPH GREY AND HIS WIFE LADY ELIZABETH lie upon a sumptuous sandstone altar tomb as upon a resplendent four-poster bed. A lion lies at his feet, two little dogs at hers, while the sides

of the monument are carved with statues of saints and angels. There are still traces of the original reds and greens. The tomb dates from 1440 and is breathtaking. Sir Ralph, who was born in Chillingham Castle next door in 1406, was a crusader knight who in 1436 captured Roxburgh Castle from the King of Scots and held it against the entire Scottish army with just 81 men. He died in France in 1443. He would have known the famous CHILLINGHAM WHITE CATTLE, which who have roamed the park for over 800 years.

Ovingham – St Mary's. Here is THE BIGGEST SAXON TOWER ON TYNESIDE and a much admired 14th-century east window of three tall lancets. In the south porch is the gravestone of the artist THOMAS BEWICK (1753–1828), who was born across the Tyne in Cherryburn

House and is buried in St Mary's church-yard west of the tower. Bewick was one of Britain's finest wood engravers, whose work set the standard for book illustrations before the introduction of the photograph. He excelled in the study of animals and birds and illustrated, amongst other works, AESOP'S FABLES and the BOOK OF BRITISH BIRDS. His masterpiece was the CHILLINGHAM BULL, carved in 1789, an engraving of a bull from the famous herd of white cattle at Chillingham Park. The Bewick swan was named in his honour.

Warkworth – St Lawrence's. Set on a lovely shady lawn that runs down to the river, and looking up Warkworth's main street to the castle on the hill, St Lawrence's is a large Norman church with a very satisfying 14th-century spire, ONE OF ONLY TWO MEDIEVAL STONE SPIRES IN NORTHUMBERLAND. The nave, showing deep splayed Norman windows, is 90 feet (27 m) long, THE LONGEST

St Lawrence's, Warkworth

NAVE IN NORTHUMBERLAND, and the pure Norman chancel has a superb stone rib-vaulted roof in the style of Durham Cathedral.

On the morning of Sunday, 9 October 1715, General Forster of Bamburgh Castle arrived with an army of Northumbrian Jacobites and attended a service in St Lawrence's taken by the Old Pretender's chaplain. After the service Forster led the congregation into the market place and declared the Pretender as King James III, making Warkworth THE FIRST TOWN IN ENGLAND TO DECLARE FOR JAMES STUART. The prayer book used by the chaplain on that occasion can be seen in the vestry.

NOTTINGHAMSHIRE

St Wilfrid's, Scrooby, where William Brewster was baptised – the religious leader of the Pilgrim Fathers and the man who devised Thanksgiving

Blyth

St Mary & St Martin

Early Norman Glory

Blyth, which sits on the old Great North Road, is now bypassed, and its wide and lovely main street is lined with coaching inns, sturdy red-roofed houses and creeper-covered cottages. The church sits on the northern edge of the village and is beset by bungalows, which only go to accentuate the height and majesty of St Mary's 15th-century tower, a landmark 100 feet (30 m) high.

The bungalows occupy the site of the 18th-century Blyth Hall, demolished in 1972, while the church is all that is left of NOTTINGHAMSHIRE'S FIRST MONASTERY, a Benedictine priory founded in 1088 by Roger de Busli, who fought at Hastings with William the Conqueror. He based the design of his priory church at Blyth on the Abbey of

Jumièges in Normandy, constructed some 40 years before in 1048, and as a result Blyth, while not the country's oldest Norman building, provides THE OLDEST EXAMPLE OF THE PURE NORMAN ARCHITECTURAL STYLE IN ENGLAND. The original Norman work can be seen in all its lofty brutality and strength in the nave, with its round arches and hugely tall, double-height clerestory. It survived the Dissolution by becoming the parish church.

Blyth is breathtaking, its unabashed Norman ruggedness and splendour proclaiming Norman power and religious authority over the conquered Anglo-Saxons, who would never have seen anything so high or mighty before. It is absolutely gorgeous, if you like Norman work, and would have been even more gorgeous when painted and decorated as it originally was.

In 1180 the elaborate south porch was added, and 50 years after that the wooden roof was replaced by stone vaulting. At the beginning of the 14th century the south aisle was enlarged to accommodate the burgeoning congregation of Blyth, and in the early years of the 15th century a great wall was built at the crossing to separate the priory church in the east from the parish church in the west. At the same time the parish church was given its own bell tower at the west end, with a small but exquisite canopied west door.

Largest Wall Painting

The new east wall was then painted on the parish side with a massive DOOM, an illustration of the Last Judgement showing the dead rising out of their tombs and being directed by angels, either to heaven where they are greeted by Jesus and Mary, or to a vivid red hell where they are tortured by demons. This marvellous work faded over the years and was only rediscovered in 1885, finally being properly conserved and renovated in 1987. It is THE LARGEST MEDIEVAL WALL PAINTING IN ENGLAND.

The lower centre of the painting is blank, and this is probably where the tomb of EDWARD MELLISH, now in the north aisle, was originally sited against the wall. Mellish, who died in 1703, was responsible for pulling down the ruins of the old priory and rebuilding Blyth Hall. He also had installed in the church a wooden screen, gallery and family pew with pictures of saints on the panels. The two painted screens that survive are superb examples of 17th-century artwork.

Clumber

St Mary's

A Victorian Masterpiece

Here in the Dukeries (*see* panel) is one of England's most satisfying Victorian churches. Set in luxuriant parkland and shimmering above its own reflection in the lake, St Mary's was completed in 1889 for the 7th Duke of Newcastle in the grounds of his country house CLUMBER PARK. The house fell into ruin and was eventually demolished in 1938, but thankfully the spectacular church was deemed too beautiful to lose and

was rescued by the National Trust, who now look after it. The architect was G.F. BODLEY and he regarded St Mary's as his masterpiece. The spire, which is based on the spire of Patrington in Yorkshire's East Riding (*see* page 313) soars to 180 feet (55 m) and the high, echoing vaulted interior is richly endowed with carvings in stone and wood.

The outstanding glory of Clumber is the stained glass, almost all of it by the greatest of all the Victorian stained-glass designers, CHARLES KEMPE (*see* panel). CLUMBER BOASTS MORE OF HIS WORK THAN VIRTUALLY ANY OTHER ENGLISH CHURCH and stands as a fine memorial to a supremely talented Victorian artist.

THE DUKERIES is an area of Nottinghamshire south of Worksop that at one time contained four ducal estates in close proximity. They were CLUMBER HOUSE, principal seat of the Duke of Newcastle, demolished in 1932, THORESBY HALL, principal seat of the Duke of Kingston, now a hotel, WELBECK ABBEY, principal seat of the Duke of Portland and still owned by the family, and WORKSOP MANOR, a seat of the Duke of Norfolk, the surviving parts of which are now home to the Worksop Manor Stud.

CHARLES EAMER KEMPE (1837–1907) was born in Brighton, where previous generations of his family were responsible for developing Brighton's Kemptown area. He wanted to become a priest, but a bad stammer precluded him from preaching and so he made the decision that 'if he was not permitted to minister in the Sanctuary he would use his talents to adorn it'. His began his career studying ecclesiastical architecture with his friend George Frederick Bodley, and the two would go on to work together on many projects, such as at Clumber. The first recorded stained-glass window designed by Kempe is the Bishop Hooper Memorial window installed in Gloucester Cathedral in 1865. Over a period of 40 years Kempe's workshop created windows for thousands of England's churches. They can usually be identified by their prevailing yellow wash and by the appearance somewhere in the design of Kempe's trademark wheatsheaf.

Nottinghamshire has two churches showing particularly fine examples of Kempe's work: ST MARY'S, CLUMBER, and ST MARY MAGDALENE, HUCKNALL, which boasts 25 windows by Kempe. The east window here shows a portrait of the poet LORD BYRON, who is buried in the church, along with his daughter ADA LOVELACE, a famous mathematician who assisted Charles Babbage with programmes for his calculating machine and is hence regarded by many as THE WORLD'S FIRST COMPUTER PROGRAMMER (*see* pages 88 and 243–4).

Edwinstowe

St Mary's

Church in the Forest

EDWINSTOWE is named for THE SECOND CHRISTIAN ENGLISH KING, EDWIN OF NORTHUMBRIA (586–633), under whose reign Northumbria became the most powerful of the Saxon kingdoms, stretching from the Humber in the south to Edwin's Burgh, or Edinburgh in the north. Having been converted to Christianity by his wife Princess Ethelberga, daughter of King Ethelbert of Kent, the first Christian English king, Edwin marched south to do battle with

the greatest of the remaining pagan kings, King Penda of Mercia. They met at the Battle of Hatfield Chase, fought somewhere in Sherwood Forest, near Cuckney, in what is now Nottinghamshire, and Edwin was killed. His lifeless body was carried away from the scene by his supporters and buried in a clearing to conceal it from Penda. When they returned to transport Edwin off to his final resting place in Whitby Abbey, they raised a wooden chapel over the site, which became known as 'Edwin's Holy Place' or EDWINSTOWE.

In 1175 the wooden chapel was replaced by a stone church, one of many churches erected on the orders of Henry II as penance for the murder of Thomas à Becket, and it was in the doorway of this 'church in the forest' that ROBIN HOOD AND MAID MARIAN WERE SAID TO HAVE BEEN MARRIED.

St Mary's has been variously added to over the years. The north arcade is 13th-century, the south arcade is 14th-century, as is the font, while the

extremely fine broach spire was attached to the top of the bell tower in the 15th century and has since been repaired three times after being struck by lightning.

In the north aisle can be seen the FOREST MEASURE, a piece of string course used in the days of Edward I as a standard measure for calculating land rents.

In the chancel there is a UNIQUE DWARF PILLAR PISCINA, which is a basin set on a column where priests could wash their hands. Piscinas were usually wall mounted, and this one in St Mary's is THE ONLY KNOWN PILLAR PISCINA FROM THE 13TH CENTURY IN ANY ENGLISH CHURCH.

The oak altar rail is a memorial to a previous vicar of Edwinstowe, the REVEREND FRANK DAY-LEWIS, father of the Poet Laureate CECIL DAY-LEWIS and grandfather of the only actor to have won the Oscar for Best Actor three times, DANIEL DAY-LEWIS.

Buried in the churchyard to the west of the tower is another distinguished incumbent of St Mary's, the REVEREND EBENEZER COBHAM BREWER (1810–97), compiler of *Brewer's Dictionary of Phrase and Fable.*

Pilgrim Fathers

A number of Nottinghamshire churches are associated with the story of the Pilgrim Fathers, a group of religious separatists who emigrated to America on the *Mayflower* in 1620 and established the Plymouth colony, in what is now Massachusetts, one of the first

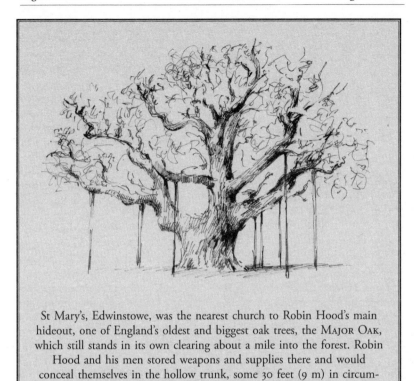

St Mary's, Edwinstowe, was the nearest church to Robin Hood's main hideout, one of England's oldest and biggest oak trees, the MAJOR OAK, which still stands in its own clearing about a mile into the forest. Robin Hood and his men stored weapons and supplies there and would conceal themselves in the hollow trunk, some 30 feet (9 m) in circumference, while plotting their next escapade.

successful colonies founded by the English in North America.

Babworth – All Saints

The dissenting sermons of Puritan minister RICHARD CLYFTON (1553–1616), given from the pulpit of All Saints where he was pastor from 1586 until he was deprived of the living in 1605, inspired two young men who would grow up to become leaders of the Pilgrim Fathers. They were WILLIAM BRADFORD, a farmer's son from

Austerfield in Yorkshire, who was 12 years old when he first walked to Babworth to 'enjoy Mr Richard Clyfton's illuminating ministry'. On the way he would pass by the home in Scrooby of WILLIAM BREWSTER and the two would walk to Babworth together, no doubt discussing their religious views. Brewster was the only university-educated Pilgrim Father, and when they reached Plymouth he became the colony's religious leader and initiated Thanksgiving for good harvests and for the colony's survival. He also acted as adviser to the much younger William Bradford, who became the colony's second and longest-serving governor.

All Saints sits on its own amongst trees in the landscaped grounds of Babworth Hall, laid out in the 18th century by Humphry Repton. The path that the two men took through the trees to Babworth has been preserved and can still be followed. The church itself dates mainly from the 15th century and remains much

as Bradford and Brewster would have known it. In 1951 THE CHALICE USED BY RICHARD CLYFTON FOR COMMUNION SERVICES was discovered amongst bones in a vault beneath the north aisle, where it had been buried for safe-keeping during the Civil War. It can be seen in the church today.

Scrooby – St Wilfrid's

A place of pilgrimage for Americans, St Wilfrid's, mostly 14th-century and with an unusual octagonal spire rising from a square tower, is where WILLIAM BREWSTER was baptised and his family worshipped. Amongst the 17th-century pews there is one known as 'Brewster's Pew'. When Richard Clyfton was removed from Babworth, the Separatist congregation from there began to meet at Brewster's home near the church, SCROOBY MANOR, most of which was demolished in 1636, with only a wing remaining as a farmhouse.

Well, I never knew this about
NOTTINGHAMSHIRE CHURCHES

East Leake – St Mary's. This elegant 14th-century Decorated church, which sits in a wide, well-tended churchyard in the middle of a busy village in the Wolds, is the proud possessor of THE WORLD'S LARGEST VAMPING HORN, OR SHAWM. It is made of wrought iron and measures 7½ feet (2.3 m) in length and

21 inches (53 c m) across the mouth. The vamping horn was a musical adaptation by SIR SAMUEL MORLAND (1625–95) of his own invention, the megaphone, and was used for accompanying the choir before the widespread introduction of the organ. The vamping horn at East Leake, ONE OF ONLY FOUR STILL IN

EXISTENCE, was also THE LAST KNOWN TO BE USED IN ENGLAND, in the 1850s.

Elston Chapel and Elston All Saints.
Where Blyth is Norman grandeur, Elston Chapel is Norman simplicity. Just a nave and a chancel, it stands in the middle of a field and has no adornments save for an arch with zigzag decoration over the door. Inside is a complete set of 18th-century Georgian furnishings, with box pews, a two-deck pulpit and a wooden gallery at the west end. It is a most soothing place. On the other side of the village stands the parish church of ALL SAINTS, where ERASMUS DARWIN, grandfather of Charles Darwin and founder with James Watt, Joseph Priestley and Josiah Wedgwood of the Lunar Society, was baptised in December 1731. He was born at Elston Hall, which belonged to the Darwins until the 1940s, and All Saints is full of Darwin memorials.

Hawton – All Saints. Here we find some of the BEST 14TH-CENTURY STONE-WORK IN ENGLAND, much of it the work of those craftsmen who gave us the famous 'Leaves of Southwell' around the door of the Chapter House at Southwell Minster. The chancel at Hawton was built for SIR ROBERT DE COMPTON in 1325 and includes sedilia with carved canopies, one of ENGLAND'S

LOVELIEST EASTER SEPULCHRES, and a magnificent east window considered to be amongst THE FINEST DECORATED WINDOWS IN ENGLAND.

Kingston on Soar – St Wilfrid's. Almost totally rebuilt in 1900, this attractive but unassuming church stands opposite the village green and hides a remarkable treasure. Between the restored chancel and side chapel stands A VIVIDLY DECO-RATED CANOPY FORMING AN ARCHWAY. Amongst the exquisite carvings of shields and vines there are some 200 tiny figures of babies in tubs, or tuns – a pun on the name of the man who built the monument in 1535, lord of the manor SIR ANTHONY BABINGTON. He intended the chancel to become a family burial place and for the canopy to cover his tomb, but his great-grandson, another Anthony Babington, was executed in 1586 for plotting with Mary Queen of Scots to overthrow Elizabeth I, and the Babington lands and titles were forfeit. There is a story that the younger Anthony Babington hid on top of the canopy in St Wilfrid's for several days before being captured. A sad tale to go with such an exuberant piece of sculpture.

Babington Monument

Littleborough – St Nicholas. This tiny Norman church, built for William the Conqueror himself in the latter part of the 11th century, looks across the Trent to Lincolnshire. LITTLEBOROUGH IS ONE OF ONLY FOUR ROMAN SITES IN NOTTINGHAMSHIRE and the walls of the church include Roman bricks and tiles from the Roman fort that stood here guarding a stone causeway across the river, at what was one of the most important crossings on the main road from Lincoln to York. The ferry that replaced the causeway plied its trade here for nearly 2,000 years before being abandoned at the start of the 20th century. With a nave that is just 24 feet (7.3 m) long and a chancel measuring just 12 feet (3.6 m) in length, the church of St Nicholas stakes a claim to be NOTTINGHAMSHIRE'S SMALLEST CHURCH. It has a charming Norman doorway at the west end and a sturdy Romanesque chancel arch resting on Saxon pillars inside. One of the bells in the bellcote on the west gable was reputedly cast between 1190 and 1200, making it THE OLDEST BELL IN NOTTINGHAMSHIRE and ONE OF THE OLDEST BELLS IN ENGLAND.

Oxfordshire

Dorchester Abbey – birthplace of a Christian England

Dorchester

Abbey of St Peter & St Paul

England's finest Jesse Window

The sleepy, straggling village of Dorchester is a colourful combination of old pink brick, half timber and thatch set amongst willows and water meadows, caught between the Thames and the Thame. Peaceful it may be, but history and drama ooze from every brick and stone, for this is one of the earliest and most important Christian centres in England. First an Iron Age settlement, next a walled Roman town (Dorocina), it then became a Saxon cathedral city.

In AD 635 a Benedictine monk named Birinus arrived on a mission from Pope Honorius I to convert the Saxons of Wessex to Christianity. Standing knee deep in the Thame, with the Christian King Oswald of

Northumbria looking on, Birinus solemnly baptised King Cynegils of Wessex, a direct ancestor of our present Queen, and welcomed him into the Christian church, so that the two kingdoms could combine as Christians to fight against the last pagan king, Penda of Mercia. It was here, in Dorchester, that England became a united Christian country.

A cathedral was built on the spot and Birinus became the first Bishop of Dorchester, with a diocese that ran from the Humber to the south coast, the biggest diocese in the land. Two hundred years later King Alfred transferred the Wessex part of the see to Winchester and later the Normans transferred the remaining Mercian portion to Lincoln, leaving Dorchester somewhat in limbo. In 1140 Dorchester was rebuilt as an Augustinian abbey, which soon became very wealthy from pilgrims who came to see the relics of St Birinus. In the 14th century some of these riches were put into enlarging and beautifying the church.

At the Dissolution of the Monasteries, while most of the monastic outbuildings were demolished, the abbey church was bought from Henry VIII by a local merchant, SIR RICHARD BEWFFORESTE, and given to the village to serve as the parish church, which it has remained ever since.

Lead Font

The first impression as you enter the church by the south porch is one of immense space, for here is a huge area almost devoid of furniture. This is the People's Chapel, added to the abbey church in 1340 for use as the parish church. By one of the columns of the graceful 14th-century arcade leading through to the nave is a superb NORMAN LEAD FONT, cast in about 1170 and gorgeously decorated with 11 of the apostles sitting under an extravagant arcade. Only Judas is missing. This is ONE OF ONLY 16 ROMANESQUE LEAD FONTS IN ENGLAND AND THE ONLY ONE IN A FORMER MONASTIC CHURCH THAT WASN'T DESTROYED AT THE DISSOLUTION.

On the east wall of the chapel there is a vivid 14th-century wall painting of a Crucifixion scene. Above it is an arched recess with traces of another Crucifixion scene. It must have been a spectacular blaze of red when complete.

Glorious Glass

Through the arcade is the 14th-century nave with its blank Norman north wall contrasting sharply with the graceful south arcade. The view to the east is drawn to the magnificent GREAT EAST WINDOW, which fills the whole east wall and contains both medieval and Victorian glass. The bulky central pillar, inserted for strength, somehow manages not to ruin the elegance of the window.

On the north side of the chancel is THE FINEST JESSE WINDOW IN ENGLAND, with the Tree of Jesse illustrated both in the glass and on the carved stone mullions. The family tree of Jesus Christ burgeons upwards from Jesse, who reclines on the sill beneath, the delicate boughs of the tree picked out in the tracery and exquisitely decorated with biblical figures who are mirrored in the window lights. The figures of Christ and the Virgin Mary at the top of the tree were damaged by Cromwell's troops. Nonetheless, this 14th-century window is one of the wonders of England.

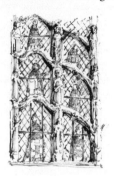

Against the south wall are three sedilia with high canopies, seats once reserved for the bishop and senior clergy. In the back of each seat there are small windows of 13th-century glass, amongst THE OLDEST STAINED GLASS IN ENGLAND.

Perhaps even older is the small roundel of glass set in the east window of the north chapel. This shows St Birinus, with bowed head, being blessed, while a companion looks on. It is dated *circa* 1225.

In the middle of the south aisle is the reconstructed shrine of St Birinus. His original shrine was lost at the Dissolution, but fragments were found in a doorway in 1870 and these have been incorporated into the new shrine.

Action Effigy

Nearer the altar is DORCHESTER'S FAMOUS 13TH-CENTURY 'ACTION EFFIGY' OF A KNIGHT, thought to be WILLIAM

VALANCE THE YOUNGER, who died in 1282. He is seen here in the act of drawing his sword and it is so lifelike that you can almost see him move. SIR HENRY MOORE was apparently inspired to take up sculpture after seeing this monument.

Ewelme

St Mary's

A Grand Old Lady

Ewelme is a hidden delight, lost in a fold on the western edge of the Chilterns. Signs point to the village from the main road but appear to lead nowhere. Suddenly the winding lane drops into an unseen valley and the bare fields turn into gardens. A pretty stream of watercress beds bubbles by. And there, dug into the side of the hill in brick and stone is a picture of medieval England – school, cloistered almshouses, stately church, bold and unchanged for almost 600 years.

The architect of all this beauty lies in St Mary's Church beneath ONE OF THE MOST CELEBRATED AND SUPERLATIVE MONUMENTS IN ALL OF ENGLAND. She is ALICE, DUCHESS OF SUFFOLK, grand-daughter of our first English author Geoffrey Chaucer.

The best way to enter the church is past the school, THE OLDEST STATE SCHOOL IN ENGLAND STILL IN ITS ORIGINAL BUILDINGS, and through an iron gate into the flower-filled square courtyard of the almshouses, designed for 13 poor men and still in use for their original purpose. From here there is a flight of steps up to a wooden door into the church.

St Mary's Church was built in about 1434, on the site of an earlier building, in the Perpendicular style of the day. Constructed in flint and stone, with brick in the embattled parapet, it closely resembles the church at Wingfield, in Suffolk, which was built some years earlier by the family of Alice's husband, WILLIAM DE LA POLE, 1ST DUKE OF SUFFOLK – he is buried there in the family plot. The East Anglian influence continues in Ewelme's interior, which is lofty and wide, with double aisles,

and filled with light from the clerestory windows. There is no chancel arch, the nave and chancel being divided by a RARE MEDIEVAL SCREEN OF WROUGHT-IRON BARS AND OAK PANELS, once highly coloured.

In front of the screen there is a plain, grey marble slab that marks the burial place of MICHAEL DE LA POLE, 3RD EARL OF SUFFOLK, older brother of Alice's husband William. He died at the Battle of Agincourt in 1415 and quite why he is buried here, when all the other de la Poles are buried at Wingfield in Suffolk is a mystery.

The cover for the medieval font is a marvellously ornate oak canopy of 1513, over 10 feet (3 m) tall, with a statue of St Michael at the top and a counterweight in the shape of a Tudor rose. It is watched over by a remarkable likeness of Edward III carved on the stone corbel of the arch above.

The chapel of St John the Baptist on the south side of the chancel is a magnificent example of Perpendicular craftsmanship. The ceiling of Spanish chestnut is square panelled, embossed with carved angels with spread wings and shields. The floor is laid with 15th-century red and yellow tiles, bearing the arms of the Chaucer, Burghersh and Roet families.

Chaucers in Splendour

Alice's parents, THOMAS AND MATILDA CHAUCER, appear in brass on the top of their fine chest tomb, which is encased in Purbeck marble and inlaid with brightly coloured shields. ALICE, DUCHESS OF SUFFOLK, LAST OF THE

CHAUCERS, sleeps nearby, in one of England's grandest tombs, set between the chapel and the chancel.

She lies full length in alabaster on the lid of the tomb, her head resting on a pillow born by four angels. Over her is a stone canopy carved with figures and adorned on each side with four tall pinnacles on which are perched wooden angels, almost touching the ceiling. They are amongst THE EARLIEST CARVED WOODEN ANGELS FOUND IN AN ENGLISH CHURCH. On her left arm Alice wears the Order of the Garter, a rare honour for a woman. Queen Victoria, before her coronation, sent her officials to Ewelme to learn the correct way for a woman to wear the Garter – the last woman to wear one before Victoria was Lady Margaret Beaufort, mother of Henry VII.

In the open space beneath the tomb is an emaciated figure covered by a shroud, a traditional medieval reminder

that we all face Death in the end. The cadaver gazes up at her own gorgeously frescoed roof, which can only be admired by those of us amongst the living who are prepared to lie down on the floor and twist the neck to see it.

It is the most extraordinary tomb for an extraordinary woman and we are fortunate that Cromwell's troops left the church and its monuments alone, along with the school and almshouses. The villagers say it is because the troops couldn't find the place, which even today seems a plausible explanation.

Buried outside in the churchyard, under a much less ostentatious gravestone, is JEROME K. JEROME (1859–1927), author of *Three Men in a Boat*, along with his beloved wife ETTIE.

Iffley

St Mary the Virgin

Perfectly Norman

Built in 1170, this is ONE OF THE FINEST NORMAN CHURCHES IN ENGLAND. It stands on a sloping lawn above the River Thames just downstream from Oxford, surrounded by houses of the old village, in an oasis of beauty and calm amongst the encroaching bustle of industrial Cowley.

Thanks to the fact that in the 14th and 15th centuries the lords of the manor of Iffley lived far away in Newbury, St Mary's was saved from redevelopment and has retained its original Norman form. There are four square or rectangular sections of

Alice, Duchess of Suffolk
(1404-1475)

Alice's grandfather, GEOFFREY CHAUCER, was married to PHILIPPA ROET, whose sister Katherine became the third wife of Edward III's son John of Gaunt, and in this way the Chaucers had some standing at court. Geoffrey and Phillipa's son THOMAS CHAUCER, five times Speaker of the House of Commons, acquired the manor of Ewelme through his marriage to MATILDA BURGHERSH, and Alice, their daughter, was largely brought up in the sumptuous manor house there. Edward III visited, as did John of Gaunt, who was Thomas Chaucer's godfather, and indeed was rumoured to be his real father. If true, then Alice had royal blood in her.

Alice was married at the age of 12 to Sir John Philip, who died barely a year later at the Siege of Harfleur in 1415. In 1424 she married Thomas Montagu, 4th Earl of Salisbury, but he died at the Siege of Orleans in 1428 before they could have children. Two years later in 1430 she married William de la Pole, then Earl of Suffolk, and over the next ten years, with her husband's help and expertise, Alice devoted much of her time and energy to the development of Ewelme as we see it today, with its fine church, brick school and almshouses.

The manor at Ewelme became a royal favourite. Alice and her husband were responsible for negotiating the marriage of Henry VI to Margaret of Anjou, and the royal bride stayed at Ewelme as a guest before her wedding. She returned, as a prisoner, after Henry was deposed by Edward IV. Henry VIII honeymooned here with Catherine Howard. Elizabeth I stayed as a girl and as a queen, and rode from here to see the Aldworth Giants 15 miles away in Berkshire (*see* page 11). Charles I's son Prince Rupert lived here for a while.

Today, there is nothing left of this gilded house save for a few bricks in the Georgian manor that has taken its place.

perfect proportions, baptistry, nave, tower and choir, all related by the Normans' favoured ratio of one to the square root of two. The single exception is an Early English chancel, added in about 1200.

Carvings

The WEST FRONT IS THE FINEST OF ANY NORMAN CHURCH IN ENGLAND and is laid out in a pattern UNIQUE IN ENGLAND. Three Norman windows sit above a round window, or oculus

(meaning Eye of God), restored to the original Norman design in 1838, and a doorway of beautifully carved arches, four rows of chevrons, two rows of beak-heads and a chain of symbols of the Zodiac.

The carvings of the south doorway are even better, having for a long time been protected by a porch. Here there are fighting beasts and battling Norman knights, flowers, green men and, on the left side of the inner arch, the mustachioed face of Henry II, king at the time, and still recognisable.

The belfry openings in the tower are all plain except for one on the south side, which boasts perhaps the finest of all the external carvings, with chevrons and an outer arch of almost perfect beak-heads.

Marble and Glass

On entering by the west door into the baptistry we see in front of us a huge, square, total-immersion font of Tournai marble set on four stone pillars. This is ONE OF ONLY SEVEN TOURNAI MARBLE FONTS IN ENGLAND (*see* East Meon, Hampshire, page 110).

The Norman window openings on each side of the font are filled with modern stained glass, the north window by Roger Wagner (2012) and the south window by John Piper (1995).

Looking east, the gaze is drawn to the two wonderful Romanesque tower arches decorated with layers of chevrons. They are perfect semicircles, and the height of the columns is identical to the distance between the capitals, ideal proportions that make the arches very pleasing to the eye. Each has two inset pillars of Tournai marble, THE EARLIEST

MARBLE PILLARS IN A PARISH CHURCH IN ENGLAND. They set a trend for such pillars in English churches, although subsequent builders tended to use marble from the Isle of Purbeck, which was cheaper and easier to get hold of.

The space under the tower between the two arches was the original chancel and has a roof ornamented with chevron ribs that meet at a charming central boss carved with a dragon and four cat heads. Nestling between the corner columns on the south side is a carving of a bird flapping its wings and settling on a nest. It is exquisite. Beyond the second tower arch the new early Gothic chancel looks very delicate after the robustness of the Norman work.

St Mary's, Iffley provides a perfect study of the art of Norman architecture and craftsmanship. Quite an education.

Well, I never knew this about
OXFORDSHIRE CHURCHES

Brightwell Baldwin – St Bartholomew's. Amongst the old tiles on the floor of the nave here is a brass inscribed to John the Smith who died in 1371. It is THE EARLIEST INSCRIPTION IN ENGLISH ON A BRASS ANYWHERE.

Caversfield – St Lawrence's. Removed from the bell cote here to inside the church is THE OLDEST INSCRIBED BELL IN ENGLAND, which dates from the early 13th century. The inscription tells us that '. . . Hugh Gargatt and Sibilla his wife had these bells erected'.

Clifton Hampden – St Michael and All Angels. Set in a glorious position on top of the sandy cliff that gives this riverside village its name, Clifton Hampden's 13th-century church was restored by Sir George Gilbert Scott in 1844. The building's great treasure is a crude but lively depiction of a boar hunt, carved by a Norman mason on a slab of stone that once formed the lintel of a doorway, and is now built into the north wall. Buried in the churchyard, on the south side, his grave marked by a small stone cross, is SERGEANT WILLIAM DYKES of the Grenadier Guards who, as a young soldier in Wellington's army in 1815, accidentally discharged his rifle, and in doing so, fired THE FIRST SHOT OF THE BATTLE OF WATERLOO.

Kidlington – St Mary the Virgin. Kidlington claims to be the second largest village in England, after Cranleigh in Surrey, while St Mary's boasts one of Oxfordshire's tallest spires, 170 feet (52 m) high and known as Our Lady's Needle. The choir stalls, still with their misericords, date from the mid 13th century and are thought to be THE OLDEST CHOIR STALLS IN A PARISH CHURCH IN ENGLAND.

Rutland

St Peter's, Tickencote, England's finest Norman chancel arch

Normanton

St Matthew's

A Rutland Landmark

Here is a church that appears to be walking on water. Surrounded by the lacustrine blue of Rutland Water, Britain's largest man-made lake, this Rutland landmark resembles a stately paddle steamer on the Mississippi – one

almost expects to see smoke emerging from the tower.

There was a church here, and a village, way back in the 13th century when this was dry land, but in the early 1700s the village was razed to the ground and the people moved to nearby Empingham in order to improve the view for the new owner of Normanton Hall, Lord Mayor of London and founder of the Bank of England, SIR GILBERT HEATHCOTE (1652–1733).

The church was allowed to stand as

a private chapel to the hall, and in 1764 the nave and chancel were rebuilt by Sir Gilbert's grandson, another Sir Gilbert, 3rd baronet. In 1826 the tower, which had survived from the 14th century, was replaced by the present Baroque structure, designed by Belgravia architect THOMAS CUNDY, based on the corner towers of St John's, Smith Square, in Westminster. Cundy also added the grand portico. In 1911 the Georgian nave and chancel were rebuilt to blend in with the tower.

In 1925 it was the turn of Normanton Hall to be pulled down, and the church was left standing somewhat forlornly on its own. In 1971, when the reservoir was being mooted, it was decided to demolish St Matthew's since it would be partly submerged by the new lake, but there was such an outcry that a plan was formulated to save it. The crypt was filled with concrete and rubble to secure the base, and the church was enclosed in concrete up to window level. The whole structure was then encircled by a wall of boulders, to act as a breakwater, and joined to the mainland by a causeway.

And some 250 years after Sir Gilbert Heathcote sent the good citizens of Normanton village packing, his memorial sculpture, by Flemish artist JOHN MICHAEL RYSBRACK, was removed from the wall of Normanton church and sent up the road to the church at Edith Weston. What goes around, comes around.

Normanton church now houses the Rutland Water Museum.

Stoke Dry

St Andrew's

What if . . . ?

Just a funny-looking church on a hillside with a couple of handsome stone houses for company – or so you might

think. But ST ANDREW'S, STOKE DRY, is a thrilling place for those who have a vivid imagination and a romantic view of history. For here there are mysteries that might just be true.

Above the north porch of the church there is a priest's room with an oriel window, built in Tudor times. This could be one of England's momentous places, for it is said that in this lovely tumbledown room, reached by a narrow, winding stairway, the course of English history was changed when SIR EVERARD DIGBY MET WITH ROBERT CATESBY AND OTHERS TO PLAN THE GUNPOWDER PLOT. It is plausible, for Stoke Dry was the main seat of the Digbys at the time, although nothing remains today of the home where Everard was born in 1578, except for some stones in the garden wall of the rectory.

Inside the church some splendid Digby tombs do survive, however. There is an alabaster monument to JAQUETTA DIGBY, wife of an Everard who died at the Battle of Towton in 1461, a table tomb in the chantry chapel with a headless effigy of an Everard who died here in Stoke Dry in 1540, and in the chancel is the grand tomb of our plotting Everard's grandparents, KENELME (d.1590) and ANNE DIGBY, with their 11 children, two of whom died in infancy and are here wrapped in swaddling clothes.

Some Interesting Headgear

Displayed on the walls of the chantry chapel are some POWERFUL 14TH-CENTURY WALL PAINTINGS SHOWING THE MARTYRDOM OF ST EDMUND, who is seen skewered to a tree by no fewer than 17 arrows, but is somehow still smiling. There are two archers shooting at him, and the one on the left is sporting a feathered head-dress remarkably similar to those worn by the Native American Indians in Hollywood westerns. Could it be that Europeans, or perhaps Vikings, had visited America long before

Columbus and brought back stories of such native warriors?

The other archer is wearing what looks like Norman headgear, while ST CHRISTOPHER, who is carrying the Baby Jesus and watching the scene with a rather austere expression on his face, appears to have a lampshade on his head, probably an exotic type of pilgrim's hat. NOWHERE ELSE IN ENGLAND IS THERE A PICTURE OF ST CHRISTOPHER IN SUCH A HAT. Indeed, nowhere else in England is there such a variety of medieval headgear on display.

Gunpowder Plot or not, American Indians or not, even the driest academic could not pour scorn on the glorious Norman columns of the chancel arch, decorated as they are with some of THE FINEST AND MOST VIGOROUS NORMAN CARVINGS IN ANY ENGLISH CHURCH. The most celebrated illustration in this rare picture gallery is of a grimly determined round-headed fellow pulling on a bell-rope, possibly THE EARLIEST PICTURE OF A BELL-RINGER IN ENGLAND. Below him is the Devil running away from the noise.

No one runs away from Stoke Dry in a hurry. It is a mesmerising place.

Teigh

Holy Trinity

Many Blessings

Could there be a more idyllic English setting? Gentle countryside, mellow stone walls, sheep, medieval church and Georgian rectory side by side. Certainly, when the BBC were looking for Jane Austen's England in which to film their 1995 adaptation of *Pride and Prejudice* they lighted upon Teigh as the perfect home for the unctuous Mr Collins.

From the outside, Holy Trinity Church looks medieval, but only the tower is 14th century; the rest was rebuilt in 1792 by George Richardson, a colleague of Robert Adam. The interior is pure Georgian and a complete delight, with box pews facing each other like the benches in the House of Commons chamber. The resemblance to Parliament is reinforced by the extraordinary pulpit, which sits above the west door and is flanked at a lower level on either side by reading desks, one for the parson and one for the clerk, not dissimilar to the layout of the Speaker's Chair in the Commons.

Tickencote

St Peter's

Best Norman Chancel Arch in England

Is this THE ONLY CHURCH IN ENGLAND WHERE THE CONGREGATION MUST TURN WEST TO HEAR THE SERMON AND THE READINGS? It would explain the arrangement of the pews, allowing worshippers to switch from facing east to west more easily. The parson uses a stairway in the tower to reach the pulpit and appears as if by magic. The illusion is made all the more vivid by the superb *trompe-l'oeil* leaded window behind the pulpit, with a lovely view of trees and sky.

The loveliness of this interior is completed by a beautifully carved Georgian mahogany font. An idyllic, even blessed place indeed.

Teigh is in fact many times blessed, for it is RUTLAND'S THANKFUL VILLAGE. A memorial plaque in the church informs us that the 11 men and two women of Teigh who went off to the Great War all returned safely.

Motorists speeding by on the A1 little realise what they are missing. Here, a short walk away from the main road along an avenue of trees, is an astonishing treasure, THE MOST ELABORATE AND BEAUTIFUL NORMAN CHANCEL ARCH IN ENGLAND. Made up of six orders, each having a different design, it displays every kind of Norman pattern and fills the width of the dividing wall from north to south. Weighed down by time and its own magnificence, it is slightly contorted, but when you enter the church and see it for the first time you cannot help but gasp.

Closer examination reveals that the first and innermost order is plain, the second is beak-heads, the third embattled. The fourth order alternates between foliage and grotesques and includes a muzzled bear, feline heads, various monsters and two crowned heads facing away from each other – since the arch dates from between 1130 and 1150 it seems likely they represent King Stephen and the Empress Maud, who were battling over the throne of England at the time. The fifth order is zigzag, while the sixth and outer order is of a UNIQUE FOLIAGE DESIGN FOUND NOWHERE ELSE IN ENGLAND.

Around the top of the arch is what is known as a billet hood-mould, which suggests that the arch was originally built as an outer doorway into a small chapel and that the nave was added later – thankfully protecting the arch from the weather.

Once you have feasted on this remarkable work of art, there is still more to see. The NORMAN VAULTING OF THE CHANCEL IS UNIQUE, having six divisions divided by enormous ribs carved with zigzags and meeting at a rare ornamented central boss, THE OLDEST BOSS IN ENGLAND. THIS SEXPAR-TITE OR SIX-CELL VAULTING IS FOUND IN NO OTHER NORMAN BUILDING IN ENGLAND and can only be found elsewhere in some Gothic vaulting in Canterbury Cathedral.

In a recess in the south wall of the chancel is ONE OF RUTLAND'S TWO WOODEN EFFIGIES, the other being at Ashwell (*see* below). It dates from the 14th century and depicts SIR ROLAND DANEYS (d.1362), lord of the manor, who fought for Edward III at the Battle of Crécy and represented Rutland at Edward's great parliament of 1352.

Back in the nave, by the south foot of the arch, there is a square 13th-century Norman font, carved along each side with arcading and at each corner sporting a quaint head. It complements the archway splendidly.

St Peter's was restored in 1792 in neo-Norman style, but we can be grateful that the chancel arch and the chancel vaulting were left untouched. The exterior decoration is a little over the top, although the restoration apparently kept to the original design, but a visit to this sweet corner of Norman England will never be forgotten.

Well, I never knew this about
RUTLAND CHURCHES

Ashwell – St Mary's. William Butterfield's only work in Rutland or Leicestershire, St Mary's is a modest, well-restored 13th-century church, sitting in the middle of a raised churchyard, on the northern edge of a quiet village in the gentle Rutland countryside. The narrow tower looks Victorian but is in fact 14th century. In the south chapel is ONE OF ENGLAND'S 90 OR SO WOODEN EFFIGIES, dated c.1320 and probably of SIR THOMAS TUCHET. There is also an incised stone slab commemorating JOHN VERNAM AND HIS WIFE ROSE, sadly

St Mary's, Ashwell

disfigured by 17th-century dated graffiti. Buried in the churchyard, to the south of the tower, is a former rector of Ashwell, the REVEREND JOHN ADAMS (1839–1903), THE FIRST CLERGYMAN TO WIN A VICTORIA CROSS. He received the award in 1879, when serving as chaplain in the British army in Afghanistan, for rescuing a number of 9th Lancers from drowning in a muddy watercourse while under enemy fire.

Burley – Holy Cross. Atop a pedestal in the south aisle of this 13th-century church is the most beautiful sculpted figure, by SIR FRANCIS CHANTREY, of LADY CHARLOTTE FINCH (1725–1813), governess to the children of George III and INVENTOR OF THE JIGSAW PUZZLE. As a means of teaching her royal pupils geography, Lady Charlotte devised a number of dissected maps, which she

drew by hand and used as visual aids. These jigsaws can be seen today at Kew Palace, where the children, including the future George IV and William IV, were brought up and had their lessons.

Although Lady Charlotte is buried at Ravenstone in Buckinghamshire, there is a memorial to her here because the house of BURLEY ON THE HILL, to which Holy Cross Church is attached by a covered walkway, was the ancestral

home of her husband WILLIAM FINCH and later of their son George, THE 4TH EARL OF NOTTINGHAM AND 9TH EARL OF WINCHILSEA, a founder of the MCC and Lord's Cricket Ground. The house had been built in the 1690s by Lady Charlotte's father-in-law, the 2nd Earl of Nottingham.

Market Overton – St Peter & St Paul.
Set in a lovely country churchyard high on a plateau, this unassuming church sits at a strategic viewpoint. The discovery last century of a hoard of Roman coins tells us that the Romans were here, while inside the church RUTLAND'S ONLY SAXON ARCH reveals the church tower to have Saxon origins. The extraordinary font is made from a hollowed-out Norman capital placed

upon an upturned Early English capital standing on a Roman base – a thousand years of history combined in one artifact. On the south wall of the church tower is a sundial given to the church by ISAAC NEWTON, whose mother came from Market Overton. Newton was inspired to experiment with time-keeping instruments after studying a primitive type of clock built by the Saxons, which was discovered in the churchyard here. Based on an Egyptian clepsydra, it was a bronze vessel shaped like a saucer and pierced with a hole. The time was measured by how long it took to fill up and sink when placed on water. Apparently, the Saxon clepsydra discovered in Market Overton took 62 minutes to sink – a pretty accurate measurement of one hour.

SHROPSHIRE

St Bartholomew's, Tong – the Westminster Abbey of the Midlands

Heath Chapel

Nothing Fancy

'Perfect. Small. Norman.' That is how Sir John Betjeman described Heath Chapel and he just about said it all, although he might perhaps have added 'hard to find', for the lanes are deep and winding, there are few signs and the church has no tower or spire to give it away. For more than 900 years Heath

Chapel has stood all by itself, dug into the soil of a far-flung field in the Shropshire hills north of Ludlow, and it is probably thanks to this solitude that it has escaped virtually untouched,

just a simple, unpretentious Norman church of nave and chancel, where the local farming community could worship, have their children christened, and pray for a good harvest.

There is little ornamentation, just some crescent hinges on the ironwork of the old oak door and rough chevron mouldings on the round arch above it. Inside, the chancel arch of two orders is plain but pleasing. The carved tub font is Norman, as are all the windows save for the one behind the pulpit, which was put there in the 17th century so that the priest could read his sermon. The wooden two-deck pulpit, box pews and squire's pew in the chancel are all Jacobean.

If you want to gaze upon honest Norman architecture and breathe in some real Norman dust, then somehow find your way to Heath Chapel, track down the key, which is either in the porch of the nearby farm or hanging on the back of the notice-board by the gate into the field, and sit down in one of the pews. Here is Norman England, pure and peaceful.

Pitchford

St Michael's

Wooden Wonders

Tucked away in trees at the end of a long avenue of limes, and somewhat overshadowed by Pitchford Hall, the exuberant black-and-white Elizabethan extravaganza beside which it stands, St Michael's is nonetheless unabashed, having been there for at least 300 years before the hall was even thought of. The church was built by Ralph de Pitchford in 1220, and consists of a simple nave and chancel topped with a small wooden belfry. Inside there are some delightful 17th-century box pews and four alabaster slabs to 16th-century Ottleys from the hall next door, complete with engravings of 50 Ottley children. But what really catches the eye is the huge, 7 ft (2.1 m) long WOODEN EFFIGY OF THE CRUSADER KNIGHT SIR JOHN DE PITCHFORD, who died in 1285 and is shown drawing his sword while a lion chews at the scabbard.

It was carved from a single piece of oak and is ONE OF ONLY THREE SUCH WOODEN EFFIGIES IN ENGLAND.

Perched in a lime tree just outside the churchyard is a 17th-century tree house, built in the same magpie style as Pitchford Hall and reputed to be THE OLDEST TREE HOUSE IN THE WORLD.

Tong

St Bartholomew's

Tong is tiny, an attractive mix of handsome red-brick mansions and pretty black-and-white cottages. St Bartholomew's Church, which dates mainly from 1410, sits grandly on a hillock on the edge of the village, and is much too large for such a small place. Festooned with pinnacles and battlements and sporting a central tower that morphs from square to octagonal to a short but rather cute spire, it could almost be a Disney castle or an Oxford college. But even such an extravagant exterior does not prepare you for the wonders within, a glorious timeline of Vernon monuments and tombs such as would grace a cathedral. Not without reason is St Bartholomew's known as

the 'WESTMINSTER ABBEY OF THE MIDLANDS'.

The Vernons lived at Haddon Hall in Derbyshire but married into the lordship of Tong and chose St Bartholomew's to be their burial place. The oldest tomb in the church sits beneath the north crossing arch and belongs to SIR FULKE PEMBRUGGE (1363–1409), Lord of Tong. He lies beside his wife LADY ISABEL, who founded the church in 1409. She was a lady at the court of Richard II and died in 1446.

Across from them, under the south crossing arch, is the superb tomb of Lady Isabel's son-in-law SIR RICHARD VERNON (1391–1451), who was Speaker of the House of Commons. His is considered to be ONE OF ENGLAND'S FINEST ALABASTER EFFIGIES.

To the west lies the altar tomb of Sir Richard's son SIR WILLIAM VERNON (1418–67), Knight Constable of England under Henry VI. It was his job to command the Army in the absence of the King.

Sir William's son SIR HENRY VERNON (1445–1515) lies in an archway that separates the south aisle from the chantry chapel. He was guardian to Henry VII's eldest son Prince Arthur, witnessed Arthur's marriage to Katherine of Aragon and was with them at Ludlow Castle when Arthur died there in 1502, setting in train the events that culminated in the Reformation.

Sir Henry was responsible for the building of the exquisite chantry chapel, known as the GOLDEN CHAPEL, in 1510. It has a spectacular fan-vaulted roof similar to that of Henry VII's chapel at Westminster Abbey, albeit on a smaller scale. High up on the west wall, set beneath a gilded canopy, is a bust of Sir Henry's youngest son, SIR ARTHUR VERNON (1482–1517), rector of Whitchurch. This is THE EARLIEST MEMORIAL OF ITS KIND IN ENGLAND.

Sir Henry's eldest son, RICHARD VERNON (1477–1517), is buried beneath a fine alabaster tomb set against the north-west crossing pier. He lies in effigy beside his wife MARGARET DYMOKE, whose father was Hereditary King's Champion to Richard III, Henry VII and Henry VIII and whose brother was Elizabeth I's Champion. At the west end of the tomb is a representation of their son SIR GEORGE VERNON, a cruel landowner known as the King of the Peak, who is buried in Derbyshire.

Nearby, in the south aisle, is the elaborate double-deck monument of Sir George's son-in-law SIR THOMAS STANLEY, second son of the Earl of Derby, who died in 1576. He lies on the top deck, with his wife Margaret, while their son SIR EDWARD STANLEY (1563–1632), the last of the Vernons to own Tong, resides below. The long epitaph, which appears at each end of the tomb, was written by WILLIAM SHAKESPEARE himself, in honour of his Stanley benefactors.

Apart from this glittering array of monuments St Bartholomew's can boast a unique treasure, THE ONLY MISERICORD IN ENGLAND THAT SHOWS A LILY CRUCIFIX, which is also THE ONLY LILY CRUCIFIX IN ENGLAND CARVED IN WOOD.

Outside in the churchyard is a rough grave that shifts from time to time and is a place of pilgrimage for visitors from all over the world, especially America. It is THE GRAVE OF LITTLE NELL, the heroine of Charles Dickens's novel *The Old Curiosity Shop*. Dickens's grandmother was a housekeeper at Tong Castle (demolished in 1954) and the author knew the village and the church well. In the book, Little Nell dies in a village in the Midlands, recognisable as Tong, and is buried in the churchyard, with her grandfather grieving at her graveside. *The Old Curiosity Shop* was a hugely popular novel, particularly in America, and visitors came in their droves to see the locations suggested therein. In 1910 the verger of St Bartholomew's recorded the death of Little Nell in the church records and dug a grave that he claimed was hers,

A LILY CRUCIFIX is a symbol combining a lily with the figure of the crucified Christ, the latter usually seen growing from the lily's stem. The lily represents the purity associated with the Annunciation, when the Angel Gabriel appeared to the Virgin Mary to tell her she would become the Mother of God, while the figure of Jesus illustrates the belief that the Crucifixion took place on the anniversary of the Annunciation. Thus the lily crucifix demonstrates the shared agony of Mary and Jesus. Such crucifixes are characteristic of the 14th and 15th centuries and are UNIQUE TO BRITAIN.

charging gullible visitors a shilling a time to see it. They still come to Tong to pay their respects to Little Nell.

Shropshire Black and White

Melverley – St Peter's

This utterly enchanting building is the oldest of Shropshire's two black-and-white churches and sits like a jewel on a bluff above the River Vyrnwy, looking across the Shropshire plain to Breidden Hill and Wales beyond. It was built in 1406, some years after Owain Glyndwr came out of Wales in rebellion against Henry IV and burned down the wooden chapel that stood here before, down on the river bank.

Everything about it is crooked, even if you haven't sampled the local ale at the Tontine pub, which guards the lane to the church. A crooked little belfry sits on a crooked roof, and a crooked porch covers a crooked door. Inside there is a crooked gallery reached by a crooked stair. All of it held together seemingly by faith, for there are no nails in St Peter's, just pegs.

The whole interior is vivid in dazzling white paint and brown timbers. A blunt screen of massive beams separates the nave and chancel. There is a Saxon font, old oak benches, a Jacobean pulpit and a lectern bearing a chained bible. This church is exuberant and fun. You cannot help but smile as you look around it. Even for non-believers, a visit to St Peter's is therapy.

Halston Hall Chapel

This is the less well-known of Shropshire's black-and-white churches, since it is a private chapel and can only be visited at certain times or by prior arrangement. Set amongst trees across the lake from Halston Hall, it is worth the effort. The half-timbered body of the church, constructed in the mid 16th century, nestles up against a stone tower of 1725, while inside is a delight, retaining the original 16th-century panelling and pews.

Buried in a vault beneath the chancel steps is 'MAD' JACK MYTTON, who inherited Halston Hall and a huge income in 1798 at the age of two and died aged 37 in a debtor's prison, having drunk six bottles of port and a glass of brandy every day, although probably not until he was a little older. Amongst his eccentricities were riding a bear into dinner while clothed in full hunting gear, dressing up as a highwayman and ambushing his departing guests, duck shooting naked on the frozen lake at night, attempting to jump a toll-gate in a horse and carriage, feeding his dogs on steak and champagne and nestling up in front of the fire with his favourite horse, Baronet. Now where is the harm in that?

Well, I never knew this
about

SHROPSHIRE CHURCHES

Three Towers

Llanyblodwel – St Michael the Archangel. Despite the Welsh name, Llanyblodwel is just in England, although on the Welsh side of Offa's Dyke. It has a famous black-and-white inn, a narrow bridge over the River Tanat and the most extraordinary church tower in Shropshire. Almost detached from its parent church, the rounded tower looks like a space craft on the launch pad and rises straight from the ground to the top of its cone-like spire without a parapet. St Michael's was ᴛʜᴇ ꜰɪʀsᴛ Nᴏʀᴍᴀɴ ᴄʜᴜʀᴄʜ ᴛᴏ ʙᴇ ʙᴜɪʟᴛ ᴡᴇsᴛ ᴏꜰ Oꜰꜰᴀ's Dʏᴋᴇ but was almost entirely rebuilt in the middle of the 18th century by the then rector Jᴏʜɴ Pᴀʀᴋᴇʀ, who modelled his extraordinary tower on that of Freiburg Cathedral in Germany.

Cardeston – St Michael's. A few miles to the east of Llanyblodwel there is another unusual 18th-century church tower that rises straight from the ground without a parapet, but at St Michael's the tower is square at the bottom, becoming octagonal and battlemented at the top.

Hodnet – St Luke's. This lovely church stands on high ground above a pretty village of black-and-white and red-brick cottages. There is a good Norman door and a chapel dedicated to the Heber-Percys, in which there is a medallion by Sɪʀ Fʀᴀɴᴄɪs Cʜᴀɴᴛʀᴇʏ of Bɪsʜᴏᴘ

HEBER OF CALCUTTA, who was rector here from 1807 to 1823 and wrote many of his famous hymns here, including 'Holy, Holy, Holy, Lord God Almighty'. His brother Richard, whose monument is in the chapel, was one of the founders of the Athenaeum Club in London. St Luke's has THE ONLY ENTIRELY OCTAGONAL CHURCH TOWER IN SHROPSHIRE.

Aston Eyre. Here is a small Norman church with no known dedication, built in 1132 as a chapel of ease for nearby Morville. It has a good Norman chancel arch, and the tympanum above the doorway, representing Christ's Entry into Jerusalem, is regarded as THE FINEST NORMAN SCULPTURE IN SHROPSHIRE. The carving is almost as sharp and clear as when it was first created and flows with a wonderfully vivid sense of movement.

Atcham – St Eata's. This is THE ONLY CHURCH IN ENGLAND DEDICATED TO ST EATA, who managed to combine being a disciple of St Aidan and a teacher of St Cuthbert with being the first Abbot of Melrose, in AD 651, and the second Bishop of Hexham, in 684. He died in 686.

Barrow – St Giles'. This lovely old church in a farmyard dates back to the 8th century and possesses THE ONLY SAXON CHANCEL IN SHROPSHIRE. There is a Saxon window, a Norman nave, three Norman windows and a part 11th-century Norman tower, capped in the 18th century.

Claverley – All Saints. Here is one of Shropshire's most picturesque villages, watched over by the tall, pinnacled, part Norman tower of All Saints. Above the arches and sturdy Norman pillars of the north arcade inside are SHROPSHIRE'S FINEST MEDIEVAL WALL PAINTINGS, a 12th-century gallery of jousting knights reminiscent of the Bayeux tapestry, and representing the battle between Virtues and Vices. In the churchyard is one of THE OLDEST YEW TREES IN BRITAIN, a hollow yew said to be 2,500 years old.

Minsterley – Holy Trinity. A RARE RED-BRICK CHURCH, and one of the few country churches to be constructed at the time of the Glorious Revolution in 1688, Holy Trinity, built for the Thynne

family of Longleat, has an extraordinary Baroque west front, with cherubs and a skull and crossbones carved in stone above the door. Inside can be seen a WORLD-FAMOUS COLLECTION OF MAIDEN'S GARLANDS, made of thin hoops of wood festooned with ribbons and paper flowers. These garlands, which date mainly from the 17th and 18th centuries, were carried at the funeral procession of a young girl who died unmarried and were then hung over her family's pew in the church in perpetuity.

SOMERSET

St Andrew's, Mells – a splendid Somerset Tower

Compton Martin

St Michael's

Norman Interior with Unique Pillar

St Michael's stands in an elevated churchyard above the village. A tall, 15th-century Perpendicular tower with outside stair turret and aisles with Decorated Gothic windows disguise what is essentially a 12th-century Norman church, one of only three or four in Somerset.

If the exterior is unremarkable, the interior is breathtaking. There is a lovely plain Norman font with a band of zigzags around the top of the bowl. Arcades of round Norman arches march eastwards on carved capitals and thick, round Norman pillars towards an extraordinary, misshapen chancel arch, resting on a distorted pier, both of which seem about to buckle under their own weight. Above the arch is a window, while above the north arcade is a rare Norman clerestory of three windows.

The low Norman chancel is a forest of competing arches with zigzag carving and a gorgeous stone vaulted roof. Above it is a dovecote or columbarium where the priest or lord of the manor kept his doves or pigeons, ONE OF ONLY TWO INTERNAL COLUMBARIUMS IN AN ENGLISH CHURCH, the other being at Elkstone, in Gloucestershire (*see* page 107). It was originally reached from outside by a door high up in the north wall. The door is still there but the steps leading up to it are gone.

But the most striking and curious feature of St Michael's is the easternmost pillar of the south arcade, which is carved in a SPIRALLING BARLEY SUGAR PATTERN reminiscent of the columns in Durham Cathedral. It is THE ONLY SUCH PILLAR FOUND IN AN ENGLISH COUNTRY CHURCH.

This is the sort of un-trumpeted English church that makes church crawling in England so satisfying. No outstanding treasures, no grand monuments, no expectations, just a beautiful place with a wealth of quirky features waiting to be discovered and enjoyed.

Culbone

St Beuno's

'But oh! that deep romantic chasm which slanted Down the green hill athwart a cedarn cover! A savage place! as holy and enchanted As e'er beneath a waning moon was haunted By woman wailing for her demon-lover!'
SAMUEL TAYLOR COLERIDGE, 'Kubla Khan'

The tiny church at Culbone really is in the country, the deep country. It may even be THE MOST ISOLATED PARISH CHURCH IN ENGLAND, for it sits 400 feet (122 m) above the sea tucked into a thickly wooded combe between Exmoor and the coast. You must either walk two miles along the zigzag path from Porlock Weir or abandon your car where the narrow lane ends at Silcombe Farm and clamber along a steep track down and down into the dark woods.

The walk through these ancient trees can be a bit eerie if the sea mist hangs low or the sea breeze rattles the oak leaves and whistles through the pines. The faint-hearted could be forgiven for turning back, for there appears to be nothing here save the noise of breaking waves, squirrels and unseen things rustling in the undergrowth. But persevere and you will soon be rewarded with the sound of a bubbling stream and a glimpse of an emerald green lawn. There it is, grey, quaint and lovable, nestling in a well-tended churchyard and seemingly bathed in sunlight whatever the weather, 35 feet (35.3 m) long and 12 feet (3.6 m) wide, with room for 33 people, THE SMALLEST COMPLETE MEDIEVAL CHURCH IN ENGLAND.

This has been a place of pagan worship for thousands of years and a place of Christian worship since the 6th century, when the Welsh saint BEUNO brought the Christian message to the south-west. The walls of the present church are 12th-century Norman, although the height of the nave indicates Saxon origins and there is a Saxon font and a small Saxon two-light window in the north wall of the sanctuary, cut from a single block of sandstone, which probably came from a Saxon church that stood here before. At the top of the pillar dividing the two lights is a worn carving of a smiling feline face.

The porch is 13th-century and the little spirelet was added in 1810.

Inside, both nave and chancel have a wagon roof, the screen and benches are 14th century and there is a fine Jacobean box pew for use by the squire of Ashley Combe House (*see* below). The atmosphere is timeless.

Through the centuries the church has served many different communities: hermits, charcoal burners, French prisoners and even, in the 16th century, a leper colony. Today it is mainly ramblers who visit, although services are held there fortnightly, when the church is always packed.

Poetry and Programmes

In the autumn of 1797 the poet SAMUEL TAYLOR COLERIDGE walked to Culbone from Porlock Weir and was inspired by the mystical atmosphere of the church to write his poem 'Kubla Khan'.

Google, Apple, Facebook – they all owe their existence and their inspiration to the enchantments of Culbone. Up on the hillside above the church are the ruins of an exotic Italianate mansion called ASHLEY COMBE, which was bought as a fairytale retreat by the EARL OF LOVELACE for his wife ADA LOVELACE, daughter of another poet, LORD BYRON. The gardens had terraces and staircases, tunnels and follies and grottoes, all carved out of these woods, some of which can still be explored in and around the church.

Ada took long walks in these gardens and woods with her friend the great mathematician CHARLES BABBAGE, inventor of the 'Analytical Engine', a calculating machine programmed by punch cards that is today regarded as the first computer. During these walks Ada and Chrles discussed uses for his amazing machine and programmes that might be created for it, and Ada came up with numerous ideas, being later credited as THE FIRST COMPUTER PROGRAMMER. In 1979 the US Department of Defense named a secret software programme, still in use today, ADA in her honour.

East Coker

St Michael's

The Poet and the Explorer

'In my beginning is my end. In my end is my beginning.' A corner of the 12th-century church of this idyllic village is given over to the memory of the poet T.S. ELIOT (1888–1965) whose ancestor, the Reverend Andrew Elyot, set out from here to go to the New World in 1669. The words above come from Eliot's poem 'East Coker', the second of his *Four Quartets*, and are inscribed on the wall plaque above where his ashes lie.

In the south aisle is a wall plaque in memory of another of East Coker's famous sons, WILLIAM DAMPIER (1651–1715), who was born in East Coker at nearby Hymerford House, now called Grove Farmhouse. Dampier was a buccaneering explorer and navigator, THE FIRST ENGLISHMAN TO LAND IN AUSTRALIA, in 1688, and THE FIRST PERSON TO CIRCUMNAVIGATE THE WORLD THREE TIMES. In 1709 Dampier piloted the ship that rescued Alexander Selkirk from the Juan Fernandez Islands in the South Pacific and brought him home to England. Selkirk's memoirs of his time as a castaway inspired Daniel Defoe's *Robinson Crusoe*. Dampier himself is mentioned in Jonathan Swift's *Gulliver's Travels* and was the inspiration for Coleridge's 'Rime of the Ancient Mariner'. His own book, *A Voyage Around the World*, published in 1691, contains the first known use in English writing of the words 'barbecue', 'avocado', 'chopsticks' and 'sub-species'.

St Michael's Church is unusual in that the tower is on the north-east corner.

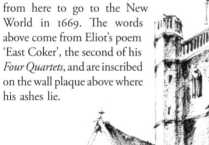

Mells

St Andrew's

Little Jack Horner
Sat in the corner,
Eating a Christmas pie;
He put in his thumb,
And pulled out a plum,
And said, 'What a good boy am I'

There can be few finer views of England than the glimpse over a golden garden wall of the majestic, pinnacled Somerset tower of St Andrew's standing proud beside the serried Elizabethan gables of Mells Manor.

The story goes that THOMAS HORNER, steward to Richard Whiting, the last Abbot of Glastonbury before it was dissolved in 1539, was sent to see Thomas Cromwell in London with the deeds to dozens of the abbey's manors, all hidden in a Christmas pie for safety. On the way Horner decided to dip into the pie and remove one of the 'plums' for his own delectation, and it turned out to be the manor of Mells. He duly took possession and his descendants have lived there ever since.

St Andrew's is approached along a medieval street laid out in the 15th century at the same time as the church was being rebuilt in Perpendicular Gothic. It brings you to the elaborate two-storey pinnacled south porch, which sweeps up to a high gable and a niche occupied by a modern statue (2002) of St Andrew as a fisherman with loaves and fishes at his feet. The porch has a fine fan-vaulted roof, as does the tower; otherwise the interior is pleasing but unremarkable except for a number of rather special memorials.

Memories of the Great War

Under the tower, on the south wall, is a memorial to RAYMOND ASQUITH (1878–1916), in the form of an inscription carved by ERIC GILL below a bronze wreath given by SIR EDWIN LUTYENS. Raymond, who was killed at the Somme, was the eldest son of Prime Minister H.H. Asquith and was married to KATHARINE HORNER. Katharine inherited Mells after her brother Edward was killed at Cambrai in 1917. Edward's memorial is in the Horner Chapel, on the north side of the chancel, a magnificent bronze statue of a horse and rider, THE FIRST EQUES-TRIAN STATUE EVER SCULPTED BY SIR ALFRED MUNNINGS. The plinth was designed by Lutyens.

During the run-up to the First World War the Horners and Asquiths entertained many of the artists of the day at Mells, such as the Pre-Raphaelite artist SIR EDWARD BURNE-JONES, sculptor and designer ERIC GILL, architect SIR EDWIN LUTYENS, who restored the manor house between 1902 and 1910, and the poet SIEGFRIED SASSOON, who is buried in the churchyard near the east wall. Buried nearby is LADY HELEN VIOLET BONHAM-CARTER, Prime Minister Asquith's daughter, along with her husband MAURICE BONHAM-CARTER, Asquith's Principal Private Secretary.

Mells Manor was inherited by Asquith's grandson Julian, 2nd Earl of Oxford and Asquith, the son of Raymond Asquith and Katharine Horner, and remains the private family home of the Asquiths today.

Orchardleigh

St Mary's

'There's a breathless hush in the close tonight
Ten to make and the match to win . . .
Play up! Play up! And play the game!'
HENRY NEWBOLT, 'Vitai Lampada'

There always seems to be a breathless hush around ENGLAND'S ONLY ISLAND CHURCH. Reached via a stone bridge across a moat, St Mary's sits on its own wooded island in the grounds of ORCHARDLEIGH HOUSE, which was built in 1856 for WILLIAM DUCKWORTH and is now a hotel. The church was built at the beginning of the 14th century and contains some rare 14th-century sculptures, a piscina and aumbry either side of the altar, 15th-century stained glass and a Norman font. It became an island church in 1800 when it was encircled by a moat on the orders of THOMAS CHAMPNEYS, the owner of the estate at the time.

In 1878 the building was extensively restored by SIR GEORGE GILBERT SCOTT. Services are held by candlelight since there is no electricity, and the church has become a popular venue for weddings.

A slate tablet records the burial here of the poet SIR HENRY NEWBOLT (1862–1938), most noted perhaps for his *Sea Songs*, from which comes the well-known poem 'Drake's Drum'.

> *'Drake he was a Devon man*
> *an' he ruled the Devon seas'*

Well, I never knew this about
SOMERSET CHURCHES

Chewton Mendip – St Mary Magdalene. Somerset is famous for its medieval church towers, and Chewton Mendip can boast the tallest and finest to be found on any of the county's country churches. Completed in 1541, it is 126 feet (38 m) high, THE FOURTH HIGHEST TOWER IN SOMERSET after Taunton, Wells and Glastonbury. The splendour is continued inside, with a superb fan vault forming the ceiling under the tower. Beside the altar is ONE OF ENGLAND'S THREE REMAINING 'FRID' STOOLS, where refugees from the law could once claim sanctuary. The others are at Hexham and Beverley. The church register goes back to AD 540 and is ONE OF THE OLDEST REGISTERS IN THE WORLD. The church bible is AN ORIGINAL FIRST EDITION KING JAMES BIBLE dated 1611, the year it was first published.

Oare – St Mary's. This picturesque little 15th-century church lies in a purple fold of Exmoor, not two miles

St Mary Magdalene, Chewton Mendip

from the sea. All around is wild and ruggedly beautiful, and redolent of the villainous Doones, for here is where LORNA DOONE married JOHN RIDD and here is the window, glazed now but empty then, through which CARVER DOONE fired his pistol at the bride,

St Mary's Oare

whom he wanted for himself. In this romantic place it is easy to forget that Lorna Doone was not a real person, but the heroine of a book, written in 1869 by R.D. BLACKMORE (1825–1900), whose grandfather was the rector here. People come from all over the world to picture the famous scene, but the church has other attractions, too. There are 18th-century box pews, a Norman font, and a UNIQUE 15TH-CENTURY PISCINA formed of a man's head held in two hands. There is also a memorial to NICHOLAS SNOW, who lived in the nearby manor house and often brought his friend the Prince of Wales, later Edward VII, to this church after they had been hunting on the moor.

Stoke St Gregory – St Gregory's. The church here is noted for its unusual octagonal central tower. Buried in the churchyard is HENRY WILFRED 'BUNNY' AUSTIN (1906–2000), Wimbledon finalist in 1932 and 1938, the last British player to reach the finals before Andy Murray in 2012 and THE FIRST TENNIS PLAYER TO WEAR SHORTS AT WIMBLEDON.

Weare – St Gregory's. This charming 15th-century church is noted for its fine Perpendicular tower and Norman font, dating from 1150. Buried in the churchyard is the late Queen Mother's favourite comedian FRANKIE HOWERD (1917–92), who lived in Wavering Down in the nearby village of Cross.

St Gregory's, Stoke St Gregory

STAFFORDSHIRE

St Andrew's, Clifton Campville – the tallest church in Staffordshire

Alstonefield

St Peter's

A Very Pretty Church

'As I'm an honest man, a very pretty church!' So said IZAAK WALTON (1593–1683) when he saw St Peter's Church for the first time, according to his angling friend CHARLES COTTON. Izaak Walton, who was born in

Stafford in 1593, is justly celebrated as the author of *The Compleat Angler*, a wistful story of three men on a fishing trip in Hertfordshire. Walton spent as much time as he could fishing on the River Dove, which runs through a famously beautiful dale below Alstonefield, and is overlooked from the churchyard.

Charles Cotton, Walton's fishing buddy, was born and lived at nearby Beresford Hall, now demolished, and inside the church, painted in radiant

light green, is the splendid COTTON PEW, made in about 1640 for Cotton's father Charles Cotton Senior. The imposing, two-deck pulpit that stands beside it against the chancel arch is dated 1637, and the elaborately decorated box pews in the nave, carved with flowers and foliage, are of a similar age.

While the Jacobean furnishings are outstanding, the church itself is simple and homely, with the structure showing elements of all the great church building periods – carved Saxon stones in the nave and porch, a sturdy Norman chancel arch, Decorated arcades and a Perpendicular tower.

In the churchyard there are two gravestones of particular interest, one to MARGARET BARCLAY who died in 1731 at the age of 107, and the other in memory of ANNE GREEN. Her circular headstone bears the date April 1518 and is THE OLDEST GRAVESTONE IN BRITAIN.

Clifton Campville

St Andrew's

Home Comforts

Here is one of the most grand but least known of England's country churches. The graceful spire soars above the low-lying meadows to a height of 189 feet (58 m), making this THE TALLEST CHURCH IN STAFFORDSHIRE. The brickwork at the tip of the spire is lighter in colour than the rest because the top broke off when struck by lightning during a violent storm in 1984 and had to be replaced.

The spire, and the tower from which it emerges, are 14th century, as is most of the church, although the north transverse contains a small 13th-century Early English vaulted chapel with a priest's chamber above it that was at one time used as a school-room. The chamber, which is reached by a spiral staircase, originally provided accommodation for a priest and still has its fireplace and open-drop latrine, ONE OF ONLY TWO SUCH MEDIEVAL LATRINES TO BE FOUND IN AN ENGLISH CHURCH.

In a recess in the south aisle there are the remnants of a wall painting from 1310 showing the Coronation of the Virgin Mary. In the middle of the Lady Chapel, which is surrounded by good 14th-century wooden screens, is the impressive Tudor tomb of SIR JOHN VERNON, a lawyer of Henry VIII's time who died in 1545. His alabaster effigy sleeps on top of the tomb alongside that of his wife Ellen.

Ingestre

St Mary the Virgin

Wren's Only Country Church

Standing in the august company of stately Ingestre Hall and its grand stables, amongst parkland landscaped by Capability Brown, this is one of the finest 17th-century churches in England and THE ONLY COUNTRY CHURCH EVER DESIGNED BY THE ARCHITECT OF ST PAUL'S CATHEDRAL, SIR CHRISTOPHER WREN. There is no direct proof that Wren was responsible for St Mary's because the papers relating to the church were lost in the fire that burned down Ingestre Hall in the 19th century. But the quality of the church speaks for itself, and WALTER CHETWYND, who owned the hall and had the church built in 1676 in memory of his wife who died in childbirth, was a friend of Wren at Oxford, and both were later fellows of the Royal Society. There is also an architectural drawing annotated by Wren and titled 'Mr Chetwynd's Tower' in a collection of Wren's drawings held in the Victoria and Albert Museum.

The exterior of the church is plain but the interior is lavish, with a lovely stucco ceiling typical of a Wren church, a rare treasure since so many similar plasterwork ceilings were destroyed during the Blitz. The pews are of Flanders oak, there is fine wooden panelling in the chancel, and the handsome wooden screen and carved pulpit and tester are the work of GRINLING GIBBONS, who so often worked with Wren in his London churches.

The church is filled with marble monuments of the Chetwynds and their relatives the Talbots. Some of them are gilded, which is quite unusual, and some are by SIR FRANCIS CHANTREY. They give St Mary's the air of a private family chapel, although when the church was consecrated in 1677 the Bishop very deliberately performed a christening, a marriage and a burial on that day, to make it clear that this was first and foremost a parish church.

A variety of interesting stained-glass windows, includes some 13th-century roundels in the side windows saved from the previous church and a vivid window by EDWARD BURNE-JONES showing a pelican trickling blood on to Adam and Eve.

Electric lighting was installed in St Mary's in 1886, making it one of THE FIRST CHURCHES OUTSIDE LONDON TO BE LIT WITH ELECTRICITY.

Tutbury

St Mary's Priory

Staffordshire's Oldest Building

Set by a fording place on the River Dove, Tutbury is an ancient village that has seen much history. Witness to it all

St Mary's Priory, Tutbury

is the priory church on the hill, begun in 1086 by Henry de Ferrers, who fought with William the Conqueror at the Battle of Hastings and was father of the 1st Earl of Derby. St Mary's is THE OLDEST BUILDING IN STAFFORDSHIRE STILL IN USE. It has long outlived the ruined castle behind it, where Henry IV grew up and Mary Queen of Scots was held before being taken off to Fotheringhay and execution. Of all her many gaols, she hated most of all the 'horrors of this medieval castle at Tutbury'.

Originally the church for the priory, St Mary's survived the Dissolution of the Monasteries because it was also used as the parish church. As you climb up to it from the village through the churchyard, the first sign that this might be a rather remarkable building is the NORMAN SOUTH DOOR, with its three orders of zigzag mouldings and carved capitals. The carved lintel above the door is Saxon and shows mounted men hunting a huge wild boar. But this is just an appetiser.

Walk round to the west end and there is THE GRANDEST NORMAN DOORWAY ON ANY COUNTRY CHURCH IN ENGLAND, seven deep, sculpted orders of magnificent carvings – birds, lions, human figures, beak-heads, ripples and zigzags. The second arch from the door, carved with griffins' beaks, is made of alabaster, mined locally. Created in 1160, it is THE EARLIEST EXAMPLE OF ALABASTER CARVING IN ENGLAND and THE ONLY EXAMPLE IN ENGLAND OF THE USE OF ALABASTER IN AN EXTERIOR ARCH. Being water soluble, alabaster does not usually survive for long outdoors, and is mainly used for monuments that are to remain inside, but somehow this alabaster arch has survived outside in almost pristine condition. Perhaps it is sheltered by the other arches around it. It is a unique feature of the most glorious doorway imaginable.

Inside, the nave, with its round arches and huge clustered Norman pillars, almost lives up to the doorway, but is embarrassed by the effete Gothic chancel arch and apse at the east end, both inserted by G.E. Street in the 1860s. To be fair, he did rescue the church from neglect. And we thank him for that.

Well, I never knew this
about
STAFFORDSHIRE CHURCHES

Ashley – St John the Baptist. Sitting on an ancient pagan mound in the middle of the village, this church looks medieval but is in fact a Victorian rebuild of 1860, with a 17th-century tower. The interior is overwhelming, bursting with fixtures and fittings of every kind, from brass chandeliers to a gilded oak reredos, while the monuments will simply take your breath away. Over the sanctuary arch is a RARE WEDGWOOD FUNERAL URN in memory of WILLIAM CHETWYND, whose wife introduced Wedgwood's pottery to the court of George III, and in the chapel on the south side of the church is a beautiful sculpture of THOMAS KINNERSLEY by FRANCIS CHANTREY. But pride of place must go to the enormously extravagant alabaster tomb of SIR GILBERT GERARD, who died in 1592 and is seen here lying in pomp next to his wife and her dog, with their eldest son Thomas watching over them from a kneeling position at their head. It is THE LARGEST ELIZABETHAN MONUMENT IN ANY CHURCH IN ENGLAND and if come across unexpectedly may cause the sensitive visitor to shie away in fright.

Hanbury – St Werburgh's. Set on a hill with black-and-white cottages at its gate, this church stands on the site of a nunnery founded in AD 680 by St Werburgh, the niece of King Ethelred of Mercia. She was buried here, but in 875 her bones were transferred to Chester to keep them safe from the Vikings. The present church is largely 13th-century Early English, with aisles rebuilt by the Victorians. There are a number of notable 17th-century tombs in the church, but the most precious treasure of St Werburgh's is in the south aisle, where SIR JOHN HANBURY can be found lying cross-legged and clad in armour with his sword and shield. He died in 1303 and his effigy is THE OLDEST KNOWN ALBASTER EFFIGY IN ENGLAND. On either side of the east window are small statues of Victoria and Albert – THE ONLY SUCH EFFIGIES ON ANY CHURCH IN ENGLAND.

Maer – St Peter's. The church, rebuilt in 1878 but retaining its tower of 1610, stands on a height overlooking the 17th-century Maer Hall, named after the mere in the park. In the 19th century Maer Hall was the home of the potter JOSIAH WEDGWOOD II, who is buried in the churchyard. Josiah's nephew, CHARLES DARWIN, proposed to Josiah's daughter EMMA WEDGWOOD, at Maer Hall, and they were married in St Peter's in 1839.

Rushton Spencer – St Lawrence's. Here is a delightfully quirky little church rightfully known as the 'Church in the Wilderness'. It sits on its own little hill at the end of a farm track off a narrow unmarked lane and enjoys wide views across Staffordshire and neighbouring Cheshire. Indeed, on

entering the church you might suppose you have strayed across the River Dane into Cheshire by mistake, for here is a charming timber church such as you might expect to find in Cheshire. In fact, St Lawrence's is THE ONLY TIMBER-FRAMED CHURCH IN STAFFORDSHIRE. And very lovely it is too. The original timber frame dates from the 13th century and was encased in stone in the 17th century.

SUFFOLK

St Peter & St Paul, Lavenham – 'the finest example of late Perpendicular in the world'

Boulge

St Michael's

*'Here with a Loaf of Bread
beneath the bough,
A Flask of Wine,
a Book of Verse – and Thou'*

Every year pink roses bloom over the grave of the gentle, eccentric intellectual who brought us these romantic lines.

The roses are grown from the rose bush that flowers by the grave of Omar Khayyam in Naishapur in Northern Iran, and were brought to England in 1893 by the artist William Simpson, for here, in this lonely country churchyard in deepest Suffolk, sleeps EDWARD FITZGERALD (1809–83), 'Old Fitz', the man who translated into English the fabulous *Rubaiyat of Omar Khayyam*. Not far away is the impressive stone FitzGerald Mausoleum, where the rest of his family lie. Apparently, Old Fitz didn't get on with them in life and didn't want to sleep with them in death.

The FitzGeralds virtually rebuilt the mainly 13th and 14th-century church of St Michael, which sits in what was once the parkland of the FitzGerald family home, BOULGE HALL, where Old Fitz grew up. The hall was demolished in 1955. There are no roads to the church, which is hidden in a ring of beech trees, just a grassy track and some hand-painted signs to indicate the way.

The interior of the church is quite dark, for all the windows are filled with a wonderful collection of Victorian stained glass, much of it dedicated to FitzGeralds, while the south side of the church is packed with tablets and monuments in their memory.

Underneath the Tudor tower there is a marble font, dated from around 1210, sitting on a round pillar of marble. The experts seem unsure if this is Tournai marble or Purbeck marble. Either way it is delightful.

'The Moving Finger writes: and, having writ, moves on' – and so must we, reluctantly, for this is a magical place.

Dennington

St Mary's

England's only Sciapod

The noble 14th-century tower of this amazing church stands tall and proud above the village green. Eighty feet (24 m) high, with walls five feet (1.5 m) thick, the soaring edifice guards a

building full of extraordinary treasures and thrilling surprises.

The view from the west end down the full 130 ft (40 m) length of the church to the glorious 14th-century Decorated east window takes in a wondrous array of woodwork, medieval benches and box pews, parclose screens, three-deck pulpit, wagon roof.

The bench ends of the 15th-century pews at the west end are breathtaking, supreme examples of medieval wood carving, and show beasts both real and imaginary, with angels, mermaids, dogs, THE ONLY MEDIEVAL DEPICTION OF A TORTOISE IN ENGLAND, what may be a giraffe and, most excitingly, THE ONLY REPRESENTATION IN THE WHOLE OF BRITAIN OF A SCIAPOD. A sciapod is a mythical creature from the North African desert that sleeps in the shade of its one huge foot, which it raises over its head like a parasol. The Dennington sciapod, intriguingly, appears to have *two* huge feet.

The east end of the nave is filled with box pews, the first two rows having hat pegs, always jolly useful. Either side of the chancel arch are two magnificent parclose screens enclosing north and

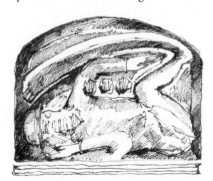

south chapels. Dating from 1450, they have both retained their lofts and much of their original colour and are considered amongst THE BEST MEDIEVAL SCREENS IN ENGLAND.

The south chapel contains the remarkably well-preserved tomb of SIR WILLIAM PHELIPS, LORD BARDOLPH (d.1441), friend of Henry V and hero of the Battle of Agincourt in 1415. He lies beside his wife, a gilded eagle at his feet, her feet resting on a winged griffin such as Harry Potter might have been proud to know. The superb artistry of their alabaster effigies, resplendent in blue and red and gold, is bathed in light from an adjacent window, and remains as lifelike as when it was fashioned over 500 years ago.

Incredibly, Dennington is not quite yet done with us – in the chancel, at the head of one of the window columns, is a most vivid carving of a Green Man, with piercing eyes and a sinister smile, peering out from a tangle of foliage, while hanging above the Communion table in the sanctuary is ONE OF ENGLAND'S ONLY FOUR SURVIVING MEDIEVAL PYX CANOPIES, where the Blessed Sacrament was preserved to represent Christ's eternal presence in the church.

East Bergholt

St Mary the Virgin

Wooden Bell Cage

This extraordinary church, one of the many in Suffolk built with the wealth from wool, stands at the highest point in the village and dominates the scene, although it appears somehow injured, like a judge without his wig. A huge construct at the west end, pierced by a passageway running under it, is the base for what was going to be the church's final glory, a massive Perpendicular tower. It was begun in 1525, but the local grandee and benefactor, Cardinal Wolsey, fell from grace in 1530 and the work stopped.

The following year, in place of the tower, a wooden bell cage with a tall, steeply pitched tile roof was erected in the churchyard to house the bells. It was meant to be temporary but is still there, the ONLY DETACHED MEDIEVAL WOODEN BELL CAGE IN ENGLAND. It houses five bells, the oldest dated 1450, which together form THE HEAVIEST PEAL OF FIVE IN THE WORLD. There are no ropes and pulleys and wheels – the bells

are hung with the open end facing up and rung directly by hand, a bit like a gong, which must be quite a task considering that one of the bells, the tenor bell, weighs well over a ton.

Bell tower

A Familiar Sight

The church that they did manage to construct before the money ran out is mainly 14th and 15th-century Perpendicular, with tall walls of glass and an embattled clerestory. If the south porch, with its priest's chamber above the entrance, seems familiar it is because it was the subject of one of the first

paintings exhibited by JOHN CONSTABLE, in 1810. He was born just down the road in a house, now gone, on East Bergholt's main street, and painted the church many times. There is a memorial window to him in the south aisle, and his parents, GOLDING and ANN, are buried in the north-east corner of the churchyard. Also buried there, near the east end of the Lady Chapel, is WILLY LOTT, whose cottage stars in a number of Constable's most famous paintings. Constable himself is buried with his wife Mary in Hampstead in London.

It is comforting to think that the view of this idyllic Suffolk church is not much changed from the days when Constable sat gazing at it while sucking the tip of his paintbrush.

Iken

St Botolph's

In the Land of St Botolph and Benjamin Britten

The *Anglo-Saxon Chronicle* tells us that 'Here, in 654 . . . Botwulf began to build the minster at Icanho.'

This makes Iken the oldest Christian site in Suffolk and Iken's church the original of some 70 churches around England dedicated to St Botolph, 'a man of unparalleled life and learning, and full of the grace of the Holy Spirit'. Botolph's Town, or Boston in Lincolnshire, and hence Boston in America, owe their origins to this windswept, marshy place.

The best way to appreciate the uniquely forsaken and isolated setting of the church is to approach it along the sinuous river path from Snape. St Botolph asked the local Saxon king for land in a 'waste and ownerless place' on which to build his monastery, and that is certainly what he got, for even today there is not much more to it than a muddy spit with the church and a couple of cottages on it. It is Suffolk at its most bleak, most wild and most alluring.

St Botolph was buried here in around AD 680 but 200 years or so later, due to constant Viking raids, which eventually destroyed the monastery, he was dug up from the ruins and removed to a place of safety. He finally came to rest, on the orders of King Canute, at Bury St Edmunds, although various relics were later distributed from there to other abbeys, such as Ely, Thorney and Westminster.

The church at Iken stands on the site of the old monastery, on a low hillock beside the Alde estuary, midway between Snape Maltings and Aldeburgh, its battlemented tower a landmark from them both. Benjamin Britten knew and loved Iken and made nearby Iken Hall the setting for his children's opera *The Little Sweep*.

The present building has been much restored after a fire in 1968 caused by sparks from a bonfire in the churchyard. The oldest part is the nave, which dates from c.1300 but has been rebuilt, and it has a fine newly thatched roof. The tower is 15th-century Suffolk-style while the chancel was added in 1862.

At the west end there is a lovely 15th-century font, with both the base and the bowl decorated in the Suffolk way with carvings of angels and evangelists. Next to the font, lying horizontally on a wooden stand, is the lower half of a 9th-century Saxon cross, found embedded in the tower wall during restorations. It is decorated with typical Saxon inter-lacing patterns and some sort of mythical beast or dragon, and was possibly erected as a memorial to St Botolph when his remains were taken away.

The inside of St Botolph's is quite sparse, with bare stone walls, red tiles on the floor and a few wooden pews, but it is a lovely place to sit and ponder, while the muddy waters gurgle by outside, just as they did for St Botolph all those years ago.

Wetheringsett

All Saints

Whicker's World

Here is a fine example of a typical 15th-century Perpendicular Suffolk church, flint and rubble, proud four-square tower with chequered buttresses and open belfry, and high, traceried clere-story windows. The bottom stage of the tower, where the bell-ringers operate, is open to the elements. Suffolk bell-ringers must be hardy types.

The church rather dominates the old pink-and-cream thatched cottages of the pretty village that clusters around it, but in a kindly, protective sort of way. The approach is across an attractive little wooden footbridge over the stream that runs along the main street. The south porch is solid and shelters a late 13th-century door. The tall nave arcades of the bright, spacious interior are prob-ably also late 13th century. The chancel is green.

The Seeds of Empire

In 1590 Wetheringsett welcomed a new rector, the Alan Whicker of his day, one RICHARD HAKLUYT (1522–1616), THE FIRST ENGLISH TRAVEL WRITER, who liked the place so much he stayed there for the remaining 26 years of his life.

It was in Wetheringsett that he wrote his ground-breaking tome *The Principal Navigations, Voyages and Discoveries of the English Nation*. Throughout the Elizabethan era, English explorers and adventurers sailed the oceans of the world extending the English horizon across the globe by discovering new lands and civilisations. Gilbert and Frobisher sailed west to look for the North West Passage, Grenville explored the South Seas, and Drake became the first Englishman and the second person to sail around the world. But until Haklyut came along, no one had thought to record these voyages so that others might learn from them.

Hakluyt, whose name is of Welsh origin, talked to all the great adventurers and explorers of the time, including Drake, Raleigh and Frobisher. He visited the ports and sea towns and sought out ship's captains as well as crewmen and sailors to hear their stories of strange lands and uncharted seas. In rich, ribald language he recounted not only their tales of bravery and ingenuity and wonder, but also their mistakes and disasters and disappointments. He kept the logs and charts they made, leaving an invaluable record for the traders, diplomats and merchants who would follow.

It was Hakluyt who persuaded Sir Walter Raleigh to establish a base in the New World from where he could search for the North West Passage, and it was Hakluyt who first suggested that these 'new found lands' could be colonised as trading places and outposts for the spread of the English way of life and language. He even came up with the name VIRGINIA for this virgin territory, in honour of Elizabeth I, the Virgin Queen. It was Hakluyt, rector of tiny Wetheringsett in Suffolk, who sowed the seeds of Empire in the minds of Englishmen.

Well, I never *knew this*
about
SUFFOLK CHURCHES

Blythburgh – Holy Trinity. This awe-inspiring 15th-century coastal church, 130 feet (40 m) long, with a spectacular clerestory of 36 windows, is known as the CATHEDRAL OF THE MARSHES and is considered by many to be SUFFOLK's MOST BEAUTIFUL BUILDING, quite a claim in a county so blessed with beauty. Visitors come from all over the world to see the glorious medieval

Holy Trinity, Blythburgh

wooden roof of the nave, decorated with angels that seem to flap their outstretched wings and fly along its length. They are peppered with shot, not as you might think from Cromwell's destroyers but from 18th-century parishioners shooting at jackdaws. The 15th-century bench ends, affixed to modern pews, graphically depict the Seven Deadly Sins and include Gluttony with his paunch, Sloth in bed, Avarice sitting on a pile of money and Pride dressed up like a peacock. The fronts of the choir stalls are decorated with 17th-century carvings of saints, while also in the chancel is ONE OF ENGLAND'S

FEW SURVIVING CLOCK JACKS, dated 1682. This Jack strikes a bell with his axe when services are about to begin.

Lavenham – St Peter & St Paul, and Long Melford – Holy Trinity. These two magnificent wool churches are famous across the world for their size and splendour.

LAVENHAM, described by the architect Augustus Pugin as 'the finest example of late Perpendicular in the world', has THE HIGHEST TOWER IN SUFFOLK, 141 feet (43 m) tall and unusual in that it has a parapet rather than battlements at the top. The tenor

Holy Trinity, Long Melford

bell that hangs in the tower was cast in 1625 and, it is claimed, has THE MOST BEAUTIFUL TONE OF ANY BELL IN THE WORLD.

LONG MELFORD'S nave is 153 feet (47 m) long, THE LONGEST OF ANY ENGLISH COUNTRY CHURCH. The Lady Chapel covers the entire eastern end of the church and has three gables and an ambulatory running around the inside. It is THE LARGEST LADY CHAPEL OF ANY COUNTRY CHURCH IN ENGLAND. The stained glass in one of the north windows shows a portrait of ELIZABETH TALBOT, DUCHESS OF NORFOLK, that is said to have inspired John Tenniel's drawing of the QUEEN OF HEARTS in the original illustrations for *Alice's Adventures in Wonderland*.

Ufford – The Assumption of Our Lady.

Here, in this stately 15th-century church set above the ford of the Saxon chief Uffa, is what is generally accepted to be THE MOST BEAUTIFUL FONT COVER IN THE WORLD. It dates from 1450, almost touches the roof and, at almost 20 feet (6 m), is THE TALLEST MEDIEVAL FONT COVER IN ENGLAND – the one at Southwold, 24 feet (7.3 m) tall, is a reconstruction. Made of beautifully carved and painted woodwork, a mass of open tracery and pinnacles, it is telescopic with the lower half sliding up over the higher part to leave the font clear. The tiny statuettes that filled its niches are mostly gone, but at the crown there is still a pelican pecking at its own breast to feed its chicks, a Catholic image of Christ feeding the Faithful with his own Body and Blood. When Cromwell's chief iconoclast William Dowsing visited Ufford he was so taken by the beauty of this font cover, describing it somewhat sardonically as 'glorious . . . like a pope's triple crown', that he left it undamaged.

SURREY

All Saints, Ockham, has one of only two seven-light east windows in a parish church in England

Albury

St Peter & St Paul

Go Forth and Multiply – or Maybe Not

This is one of Surrey's secret places, a Saxon church that sits above the Tilling-bourne in the grounds of Albury Park, laid out in the 1670s for Henry Howard, later 6th Duke of Norfolk, by the diarist and garden designer John Evelyn (*see* page 271). At first glance the most noticeable feature of the church exterior is the small 18th-century shingled cupola on top of the Norman tower, unique in Surrey.

One enters the church via the magnificent north door with long strap hinges, which dates from 1240 and is unlocked by a key over a foot (30 cm) long. The immediate impression is of space and light, for there is little or no furniture cluttering the empty

a dusty flagstone floor and a graceful arcade of three pointed arches. On the south wall opposite is a very well-preserved wall painting of St Christopher sporting a curly red beard, which dates from 1480, and a piscina set above a small pavement of 13th-century encaustic tiles. There are two marble slabs in the floor, one of c.1330 inscribed to William Weston, the other bearing the brass of John Weston, who died in 1440.

Saxon stonework can be seen in the north wall of the nave, and there are Saxon windows in the walls of the tower, which was built above the old

Saxon chancel by the Normans and is open almost to the roof. Painted in red on to the plaster of the north wall is a faint 12th-century consecration cross.

Buried beneath the new chancel beyond, which was added in the 13th century, is WILLIAM OUGHTRED (1573–1660), tutor to Sir Christopher Wren and rector of Albury for 50 years from 1610 until his death. He was a noted mathematician, inventor of the slide rule, and author of the definitive work on mathematics, *Clavis Mathematicae* (*The Key to Mathematics*) in which he first introduced the x symbol for multiplication and the :: symbol for proportion. An enthusiastic royalist, he apparently expired from sheer joy when he learned of the Restoration of Charles II to the throne. He is commemorated with a plaque on the east wall of the nave.

In complete contrast to the bare simplicity of the rest of the church is the lavishly decorated south transept, remodelled in the mid 19th century by AUGUSTUS PUGIN as a mortuary chapel

Albury Park

for banker Henry Drummond, owner of next-door Albury Park. The walls and ceiling of the chapel are richly painted in reds and blues and greens, the floor is tiled and the windows are filled with colourful 19th-century stained glass.

Enclosed within an iron fence in the churchyard is the grave of Sydenham Malthus, elder brother of the political economist Thomas Robert Malthus (1736–1834) who was the author of the controversial *An Essay on the Principle of Population*, in which he warns of the dangers of over-population. His ideas of competition for resources influenced Charles Darwin's Theory of Evolution and later the theories of John Maynard Keynes. Thomas Malthus was born at the Rookery in the nearby village of Westcott and lived in the Albury area for much of his early life.

Compton

St Nicholas

Seeing Double

Surrey's finest Norman church belongs to one of Surrey's prettiest villages, nestling beneath a narrow ridge of chalk known as the Hog's Back. The tower is 11th-century Saxon, with a 13th-century shingled Sussex broach spire, while the nave and chancel are 12th-century Romanesque, with a surviving Saxon chancel arch decorated with dogtooth by the Normans. The lovely, solid round pillars of the nave arcades are made of chalk and have huge, chunky square capitals, some scalloped and some carved with foliage.

Scratched on the inside of the chancel arch is some CRUDE GRAFFITI SHOWING THE FIGURE OF A NORMAN KNIGHT, comical but full of character. Since the church lies near the Pilgrim's Way, it may have been carved by a pilgrim on his way to Canterbury.

Beyond the chancel arch is one of Surrey's supreme treasures, THE ONLY DOUBLE SANCTUARY IN ENGLAND. The lower space has a beautiful stone vaulted roof behind a wide semi-circular Norman arch, which boasts much more sophisticated decoration than the chancel arch. The stained glass in the tiny Norman east window shows the Virgin and Child and is amongst THE OLDEST STAINED GLASS IN ENGLAND, dating from around 1210. The upper storey of the sanctuary, which may have been used as a chantry chapel, is protected by a simple oak balustrade carved from a single plank of wood. Made by the Normans in 1180, it is THE OLDEST PIECE OF DECORATIVE WOOD-WORK IN BRITAIN.

There is a small squint in the north wall of the chancel, which gave sight of the altar to a Saxon anchorite, and a Norman anchorite's cell on the south side of the chancel – Compton is THE ONLY CHURCH IN ENGLAND TO HAVE A CHANCEL SHOWING EVIDENCE OF TWO ANCHORITE CELLS.

Ockley

St Margaret's

Bells and Smells

Ockley sits on the Roman Stane Street that runs between London and Chichester and was the site of a major battle in AD 851 between King Ethelwulf of Wessex and the invading Danes, which ended in a victory for the Saxons. St Margaret's lies a little way off down a side road and has been here since 1291, although the present building dates mainly from the early 14th century. The tower was rebuilt in 1700 and contains THE OLDEST COMPLETE PEAL OF BELLS IN SURREY,

St Margaret's, Ockley

cast by the Whitechapel Bell Foundry and hung in 1701.

Ockley was the birthplace in 1616 of NICHOLAS CULPEPER, son of the rector and ONE OF THE FIRST ENGLISH HERB-ALISTS. He was the author of the best-ever-selling non-religious English text, *The English Physician with 369 Medicines made of English Herbs*, in which he advocates the use of herbs and natural medicines.

The rector here after Culpeper was the REVEREND HENRY WHITFIELD who, in 1639, left with 25 families from Ockley to found a Puritan settlement in the New World, at a place he named Guilford in what is now Connecticut. His home in Guilford was THE FIRST STONE HOUSE IN NEW ENGLAND and is now THE OLDEST SURVIVING BUILDING IN CONNECTICUT and houses a museum of early settlers.

The composer CHARLES VILLIERS STANFORD was married to JANE WETTON in St Margaret's in 1878.

Stoke D'Abernon

St Mary's

Oldest and Best in Brass

Almost impossibly in this busy, built-up part of the world, SURREY'S OLDEST CHURCH occupies a heavenly, peaceful spot, set in a secluded pocket of countryside beside the pretty River Mole in the grounds of a manor house, now a school. There are few signposts or hints to finding it and, even if you do, the church is likely to be locked, but persevere: it is open on weekend afternoons in summer and is well worth the annoyance.

The first church was built here in about AD 650 and incorporated materials from a Roman villa now buried beneath the lawns of the manor house – Roman brickwork can be seen in the walls of the chancel and the south nave. The original Saxon chancel arch, removed by the Victorians, also used Roman stones.

From its inception the church belonged to the Saxon landowner or thane at Stoke, and high in the south wall is a doorway, which once gave access to the thane's private gallery. St Mary's is THE EARLIEST CHURCH IN ENGLAND KNOWN TO HAVE HAD THIS ARRANGEMENT.

A pillar and two Transitional pointed arches survive from the north aisle that was added to the Saxon church in 1190, and on the pillar can be seen a faded painting of a crucifix, dating from the same period.

The chancel was rebuilt in the 13th century with a stone bench running around the walls and a fine stone vaulted roof. It is noticeably inclined a few degrees to the north of the nave, probably aligned to the direction of the sunrise at the time it was built. Part of a 13th-century painting of the Adoration of the Lamb survives on the wall to the right of the east window. Below it, on the south wall, is a CARVED OAK AUMBRY, OR CUPBOARD, UNIQUE IN AN ENGLISH CHURCH.

On the floor in front of the altar rails is THE FINEST MILITARY BRASS IN ANY CHURCH IN ENGLAND, 6½ feet (1.98 m) long and retaining the blue enamel on the shield. It is THE ONLY BRASS IN EXISTENCE TO SHOW A KNIGHT WITH A LANCE AND PENNON (a type of swallow-tailed flag carried by a knight on his lance in the days of Henry III), and is ONE OF THE THREE OLDEST BRASSES IN EUROPE. SIR JOHN D'ABERNON died in 1277 and his brass, which was originally dated to his death, was long considered the oldest brass of all, but it has more recently been dated to around 1320–5, contemporary with the brasses of SIR RODGER DE TRUMPINGTON (d.1289) at St Mary's, Trumpington, in Cambridge and SIR ROBERT DE BURES (d.1302) at All Saints, Acton, in Suffolk. It is hard to say which of these three is actually the oldest, but they can together be fairly described as the oldest brasses in Europe. The D'Abernon brass is huge. The brass to Sir John's son, Sir John D'Abernon the Younger, sits beside that of his father and dates from about 1327.

To the north of the chancel is the NORBURY CHAPEL, built by SIR JOHN NORBURY in commemoration of his part in the Battle of Bosworth Field in 1485. His funeral helm hangs on the wall and he is shown kneeling in a niche, oddly dressed in 17th-century garb. This is because the site of his original tomb is now occupied by a 13th-century rector, Richard le Petit, the first known rector of St Mary's. There are also two impressive Jacobean monuments to members of the Vincent family, who inherited Stoke Manor through marriage. Contained in a Roman casket encased in the east wall are the ashes of SIR EDWARD VINCENT, VISCOUNT D'ABERNON, His Majesty's Ambassador to Berlin from 1920 to 1926, who died in 1941 and was, after a run of 750 years, the last of the D'Abernons of Stoke D'Abernon.

Quite clearly this has always been a romantic place. In 1189 Stoke Manor hosted THE WORLD'S FIRST RECORDED HONEYMOON, that of William Marshal, Marshal of England and later Earl of Pembroke and Regent to Henry III, and Isabel de Clare, daughter of the Earl of Pembroke.

Wotton

St John the Evangelist

Diary of a Nature Lover

St John's sits in lonely splendour on top of its own knoll, down a short lane off the A25, with the wooded North Downs as a green and gold backdrop. The tall walls of the nave give away the fact that this was originally a Saxon church, of about 1050, rebuilt and enlarged by the Normans. The square, solid tower is the

most obvious survival from this 11th-century work. Further additions were made in the 13th century, including a Lady Chapel, later the EVELYN CHAPEL.

The 13th-century south doorway features a FASCINATING SET OF EIGHT SMALL STONE CARVED HEADS, believed to represent characters involved in King John's squabble with the Pope over the election of Stephen Langton as Archbishop of Canterbury. From the left they are the Papal Legate Cardinal Pandulf, a pilgrim, Queen Isabella, the Patron of the church, the Rector of Wotton, King John, Pope Innocent III and Stephen Langton. The carvings perhaps feed into the local legend that Stephen Langton was born in the nearby hamlet of Friday Street, where there is a pub named after him.

Inside, the Evelyn Chapel has a lovely oak screen of 1632, ONE OF THE OLDEST SCREENS IN SURREY. The chapel contains the fine Elizabethan and Jacobean monuments of three generations of the Evelyn family, who became lords of the manor in 1603 with the arrival of GEORGE EVELYN, who created the family fortune by introducing the manufacture of gunpowder into England from Flanders, establishing the first gunpowder mill at Long Ditton near Kingston.

George is seen kneeling between his two wives with their 25 children lined up beneath them. His son Richard kneels opposite his wife, with their five children below. The middle one of Richard's three sons is the diarist JOHN EVELYN, who is buried beneath a floor monument.

John Evelyn

JOHN EVELYN was born in Wotton House in 1620, was baptised in St John's, in a font that can still be seen inside the church, and was taught to read at the age of four in a room over the church porch. A staunch Royalist, he escaped the Civil War by travelling on the Continent, during which time he married MARY BROWNE, the daughter of the English ambassador in Paris. They returned to England in 1652 and settled at Sayes Court in Deptford, where Evelyn devoted his time to writing and to designing and laying out ONE OF THE FIRST FORMAL GARDENS IN ENGLAND, based on those he had visited in France and Italy. He went on to design a number of gardens, including those of his own family estate at Wotton in Surrey, where he created a famous grotto that still stands today, and at Albury, where he planted THE LONGEST AVENUE OF YEWS IN ENGLAND. His designs were hugely influential in the development of the formal English garden.

At the Restoration of Charles II Evelyn became much sought after at Court and was a founder member of the Royal Society. He discovered the wood-carver Grinling Gibbons working in a small cottage on the Sayes Court estate and introduced him to Christopher Wren.

In 1699 John inherited the Wotton estate from his brother and lived there until his death in 1706. He is celebrated for his diary, which, like that of Samuel Pepys, was not written for publication, but gives an important and discerning insight into 17th-century life in England, from 1641 until 1706, covering the Civil War, the Commonwealth, the Restoration, the Great Plague, the Great Fire of London and the Glorious Revolution.

CRABTREE AND EVELYN, maker of natural body-care products, is named in honour of John Evelyn as one of the first naturalists and conservationists.

Well, I never knew this about

SURREY CHURCHES

Abinger – St James. Abinger lies on the slopes of Leith Hill, the highest point in south east England, and St James is THE THIRD HIGHEST ANCIENT CHURCH IN SURREY, 584 feet (178 m) above sea level. Dating from the early 12th century, it was badly damaged twice in the 20th century, once by a flying bomb in 1944 and once by lightning during a storm in 1964. Not far from the church, in the fields behind Abinger Manor, is a Mesolithic pit dwelling excavated in 1950 by Dr L.S.B. Leakey. It is believed to be some 7,000 years old, THE EARLIEST HUMAN DWELLING PLACE FOUND IN ENGLAND, and makes St James the parish church of ENGLAND'S OLDEST VILLAGE.

Bletchingley – St Mary's. This fine Perpendicular church with its mighty Norman tower contains what is generally regarded as ENGLAND'S FINEST BAROQUE MONUMENT. The only signed piece of work by Richard Crutcher, it celebrates banker and Lord Mayor of London SIR ROBERT CLAYTON (d.1707) and his wife.

Burstow – St Bartholomew's. The church here has ONE OF ONLY TWO SHINGLED WOODEN TOWERS AND SPIRES IN SURREY, the other being on the other side of the county at St Peter's, Newdigate. Burstow's tower is

Clayton Monument

considered to be perhaps THE FINEST 15TH-CENTURY WOODEN CHURCH TOWER IN ENGLAND. From inside, the tower is a gorgeous forest of wood, timber and massive beams. Buried beneath the chancel is BRITAIN'S FIRST ASTRONOMER ROYAL, JOHN FLAMSTEED (1646–1719), who was rector here from 1684 until his death. Appointed by Charles II, Flamsteed founded the Royal Observatory at Greenwich (where the original observatory is named after him) and produced its first significant contribution to astronomy, a catalogue of over 3,000 stars. He was also THE FIRST MAN TO SPOT THE PLANET URANUS, although he thought it was a star.

Chaldon – St Peter & St Paul. Lost in trees on top of the Surrey Downs, in a delightful patch of unexpected countryside between Croydon and the M25, is a small village church that guards one of England's most remarkable and startling Norman treasures, the CHALDON DOOM. In the days when most Englishmen could neither read nor write, the Bible stories were told to them through pictures, and painted right across the west wall of Chaldon's church is perhaps the most dramatic and eloquent illustrated tutorial delivered to us by the Normans in the whole of England. Dating from c.1200, it shows the Ladder of Salvation linking Heaven and Hell, with tormented souls tumbling down it to be roasted and boiled in Hell, while others climb upwards to a Heaven filled with music and angels. The figures are grotesque but full of vitality, picked out in white against a vivid, blood-red background, and the effect is both powerful and chilling, exactly as it was designed to be.

Dunsfold – St Mary & All Saints. According to William Morris, St Mary & All Saints is 'the most beautiful country church in all England'. It lies above a stream in the Surrey equivalent of the middle of nowhere, about a mile

and a half from the village, and is perhaps THE BEST EXAMPLE IN ENGLAND OF A COMPLETE AND UNSPOILED 13TH-CENTURY VILLAGE CHURCH. Almost all of the building was put up between 1270 and 1290, although the bell cage is 15th century and there was some restoration in the 19th century. The pews, which are original and contemporary with the rest of the church, form THE OLDEST SET OF CHURCH PEWS IN ENGLAND and have UNIQUE BENCH ENDS, smoothly curved 'w' shapes ending in knobs with holes in them to carry candles.

Effingham – St Lawrence's. Buried in the churchyard of the much-restored 12th-century church of St Lawrence is BARNES WALLIS (1887–1979), inventor of the 'bouncing bombs' used in the Dambusters Raid to destroy dams in the Ruhr valley in Germany in 1943. Wallis, who lived in Effingham for 49 years, used the garden of his home, White Hill House, and Effingham's village pond to experiment with early versions of his bomb.

Ockham – All Saints. The most distinctive feature of this lovely church is the 13th-century seven-light east window, ONE OF ONLY TWO SEVEN-LIGHT EAST WINDOWS IN A PARISH CHURCH IN ENGLAND (*see* Blakeney, Norfolk, page 182). A smaller, modern-stained-glass window commemorates the philosopher WILLIAM OF OCKHAM (1285–1349) who was born in the village. He is celebrated as the author of OCKHAM'S RAZOR, which argues that the simplest answer is usually the right answer. Five hundred years after William, Ockham was the home of another original thinker, the first computer programmer ADA LOVELACE (*see* Culbone, Somerset, pages 243–4), who lived next door in Ockham Park, a red-brick Hawksmoor house which was rebuilt after a fire in 1948. Her husband's great-great-grandfather, the 1ST LORD KING (d.1734), Lord Chancellor of England, is buried inside the church beneath a splendid monument by the foremost sculptor of his day, JOHN MICHAEL RYSBRACK.

Warlingham – All Saints. Set into the south wall of this very pretty, low, red-roofed 13th-century church is a stained-glass window showing Archbishop Cranmer presenting the first English Prayer Book to Edward VI. In June 1549 Cranmer travelled to Warlingham from the Archbishop's Palace at Croydon to hear THE ENGLISH PRAYER BOOK THAT HE HAD COMPILED READ OUT FOR THE VERY FIRST TIME. On the window sill is a plaque commemorating THE VERY FIRST TELEVISED PARISH CHURCH SERVICE, which took place here in 1950 when the BBC broadcast Harvest Festival. Buried under a chest tomb in the churchyard is SIR JOSEPH SWAN (1828–1914), inventor of the incandescent electric light bulb, who lived in Warlingham for the last few years of his life.

SUSSEX

St Mary Magdalene, Rusper – a typical Sussex church, and the highest in West Sussex

Boxgrove

Priory Church of St Mary
& St Blaise

Norman Nave and Painted Vault

ONE OF THE EARLIEST OF ENGLAND'S GREAT NORMAN CHURCHES, BOXGROVE PRIORY was built in 1117, on the site of an earlier Saxon church. It was founded as a cell of the Benedictine abbey of Lessay in Normandy and began as a community of just three monks.

Scattered in the quiet fields all around are the ruins of the monastic buildings, torn down at the Dissolution. Left standing is the quire of the old priory, large, impressive and heavily buttressed, and now serving as a very grand parish church.

Inside is a heavenly blend of 12th-century Norman and 13th-century Transitional Norman, almost a timeline

of the gradual change from Norman to Gothic. The crossing arches are tall and slightly pointed and rest on huge clustered columns. THE OAK GALLERIES WITH WOODEN SCREENS AND CEILINGS THAT FILL THE TRANSEPTS ARE 15TH CENTURY AND ARE UNIQUE IN AN ENGLISH CHURCH.

The nave, which was originally the chancel, was rebuilt around 1220, and the huge round Norman arches of the arcades marching eastwards all encompass two pointed arches and rest on pillars of different designs – some round, some octagonal, some clustered, some of them early examples of the use of Purbeck marble. Towards the east end are three pillars formed of a central column surrounded by four smaller shafts, all of Purbeck marble. SUCH A DESIGN IS FOUND IN NO OTHER ENGLISH CHURCH, the only other examples being in the retro choir of Chichester Cathedral.

Vaulting

The rib vaulting above the nave is superb, with each vault extending over two pointed arches. This is THE EARLIEST EXAMPLE OF THIS TYPE OF DOUBLE BAY VAULTING IN ENGLAND and

gives the structure the necessary strength to cope with the tall clerestory.

The vaulting was painted by LAMBERT BERNARD OF CHICHESTER just before the Reformation in the 16th century for the priory's patron THOMAS WEST, 9TH LORD DE LA WARR of nearby Halnaker House. The patterns are of leaves and flowers, Tudor roses and the de la Warr crest and coat of arms.

The roof bosses are carved with faces and flowers. The second boss from the east end has EIGHT FACES WITH ONLY EIGHT EYES, EACH HEAD SHARING AN EYE WITH ITS NEIGHBOUR. THIS IS THE EARLIEST KNOWN EXAMPLE OF THIS DESIGN IN ENGLAND, later examples being found in Chichester and Canterbury Cathedrals.

The effect of the marvellous arcades, the varying pillars and the high, decorated rib vaulting, all bathed in light from the tall clerestory windows, is breathtakingly beautiful and explains why many consider Boxgrove to be THE FINEST CHURCH IN SUSSEX.

Renaissance Chantry

Perhaps the highlight of this extraordinary church is the glorious DE LA WARR CHANTRY, which stands behind the pulpit on the south side of the chancel and was built in 1532 for the Thomas West mentioned above. Entered through a gate of Sussex iron, it is made of Caen stone and covered with exquisite carvings from top to bottom, a SUPREME EXAMPLE OF RENAISSANCE GOTHIC ART. Many of the carvings are based on illustrations from a 15th-century French Book of Hours, including a king

Lewes Group

THE PRIORY OF ST PANCRAS IN LEWES, founded in 1081, was THE FIRST CLUNIAC HOUSE IN ENGLAND, an offshoot of the vast Benedictine monastery of Cluny in France founded in the 10th century and in its heyday the biggest Christian church in the world. The monks from Lewes travelled throughout Sussex, painting and decorating many of the small churches and chapels they came across in a style that became known as the Lewes School. The following churches are the four best surviving churches of the Lewes Group.

dodging Death by hiding behind a tree, and two young men clambering up another tree and dropping fruit into the outspread apron of a girl standing below. There are dragons and saints and heraldic shields and lots of those naked cherubs that were so popular in the Renaissance and are known as putti. Inside is a stunning vault painted in Wedgwood blue and white, with angels hanging upside down from the central pendant and lots more putti larking about. Poor Thomas never got to use his resplendent chantry, for he fell foul of Henry VIII and was forced to swap Boxgrove for a lesser property in Hampshire.

The grave of someone who did come to rest at Boxgrove can be found outside in the south-east corner of the churchyard. PILOT OFFICER WILLIAM FISKE lost his life in the Battle of Britain in 1940, THE FIRST AMERICAN AIRMAN TO DIE IN THE SECOND WORLD WAR.

Clayton – St John. This enchanting little church nestles under the South Downs below a famous pair of windmills called Jack and Jill and above a railway tunnel. The wall paintings, of c.1150, show souls progressing along the walls of the nave towards the Last Judgement of Christ, who sits in Majesty above the magnificent Saxon chancel arch of c.1040. Beside him, somewhat withdrawn, are the 12 Apostles, six either side, with St Peter and St Paul below receiving the Keys and Book of Heaven. The quality of these paintings, especially those over the arch, is remarkable, and they are described by Pevsner as 'unique in England for their extent, preservation and date'. Buried in the churchyard is NORMAN HARTNELL (1901–79), dressmaker to Queen Elizabeth II and Queen Elizabeth the Queen Mother.

Coombes Church. This little two-cell Saxon church is cut into the South Downs above Shoreham. It was mentioned in the Domesday Book and is thought to have been built in around 1040, although the chancel is 13th century. The frescoes were painted in about 1135 and include depictions of the Visitation, Christ in Majesty and St Peter receiving the Keys of Heaven.

On the underside of the chancel arch is a wonderfully humorous sketch of a man screaming in agony as he bears the weight of the arch on his shoulders. Entry to the churchyard is via a TAPSEL GATE, a type of wooden gate that rotates on a central pivot through 90 degrees and is UNIQUE TO SUSSEX.

Hardham – St Botolph's. This simple two-cell Norman church sits beside the Roman Stane Street in a hamlet on the marshy levels south of Pulborough and contains THE EARLIEST SET OF MEDIEVAL WALL PAINTINGS IN ENGLAND (a claim that may eventually be challenged by St Mary, Houghton on the Hill, in Norfolk, once the recently discovered wall paintings there have been full uncovered and restored – *see* pages 178–9).

The paintings in St Botolph's appear to have a narrative, starting on the chancel wall with an extraordinary vision of a naked Adam and Eve. Eve's hand is held behind her back ready to accept the forbidden fruit from a winged serpent. Across the arch Adam picks fruit from a tree

St Botolph's, Hardham

while Eve milks a cow. There are depictions of the Annunciation and the Visitation, scenes from Jesus' childhood, and at the west end of the north wall is St George riding a white horse, as he appeared to the crusaders at the Battle of Antioch in 1098. This is THE EARLIEST KNOWN PAINTING OF ST GEORGE IN ENGLAND.

In the tiny bellcote hangs BRITAIN'S OLDEST TOWER BELL, dating from before 1100.

Plumpton – St Michael's. This 12th-century Norman church sits in the shadow of the South Downs. It has a wonderfully basic square 13th-century tower with a huge buttress at each corner and a short, shingled broach spire. The wall paintings show Christ in the Heavenly City handing the Keys of Heaven to St Peter and the Book to St Paul, and what appears to be the Flight from Egypt. The church's special treasure is the painted recess of the Norman window in the south wall, a very rare feature.

Rusper

St Mary Magdalene

Nuns and Pianos

Standing at 406 feet (124 m) above the sea, Rusper church is THE HIGHEST CHURCH IN WEST SUSSEX and the second highest in all of Sussex after Crowborough. Records go back to the early 13th century, but there was probably a church here before that, associated with the Benedictine nunnery founded in Rusper by Reginald de Braose in about 1190.

The church was rebuilt in the 19th century, but the massive, fortress-like tower is the original 15th-century one. The view from the top is stupendous, encompassing the North and South Downs and much of the Weald. In 1975 a boy scout fell 70 feet (21 m) from the top of the tower but escaped with only a broken arm, his fall cushioned, it is said, by the prayers of the prioress and four nuns from the nunnery who are buried at the foot of the tower. A plaque on the tower wall commemorates their reburial here in the 19th century after the rebuilding of the church had disturbed the graves. Discovered buried amongst their bones was a rare and precious enamelled chalice, THE EARLIEST KNOWN EXAMPLE OF A DECORATED LIMOGES CHALICE IN WESTERN EUROPE. It is now in the British Museum.

Inside, set in the north wall of the chancel, is a brass showing JOHN DE KYNGSFOLDE AND HIS WIFE AGNES. Dated 1380, this is THE OLDEST BRASS OF A MARRIED COUPLE IN SUSSEX and THE LATEST KNOWN EXAMPLE OF AN INSCRIPTION IN NORMAN FRENCH RATHER THAN LATIN.

Throughout the church there are memorials to the BROADWOOD family of nearby Lyne House. It was the Broadwoods who had the church rebuilt in memory of their father John Broadwood, founder in 1783 of the piano manufacturer Broadwood & Sons. Amongst those known to have owned and played a Broadwood piano are Beethoven, Haydn, Liszt and Chopin.

On the west wall is an alabaster memorial to LUCY BROADWOOD (1858–1929), who was an enthusiastic collector of English folk songs and dances and founder member of the Folk Song Society. The BROADWOOD MORRIS MEN, established in 1972, were named in honour of Lucy, and every year on 1 May they place fresh flowers on her memorial and give a performance of morris dancing in the village.

Rusper church is not exceptional or filled with grand monuments and fittings, but it is a fine example of a living, much-loved village church, full of heritage and hidden delights, that remains at the heart of its community.

Worth

St Nicholas

Saxon Arches

Here, in what was a clearing in the great Forest of Anderida, which once covered 3,000 square miles of south-east England, is one of Britain's great Saxon churches, THE LARGEST SAXON CRUCIFORM CHURCH TO SURVIVE ON ITS ORIGINAL FOUNDATIONS IN ENGLAND.

One thousand years ago the forest here was so thick and impenetrable that when William the Conqueror's Norman agent arrived to assess the area for the Domesday Book, his Anglo-Saxon guide couldn't find the church. The agent shrugged and said, 'In that case, it can't be worth much.'

The modern setting is not, at first glance, very prepossessing. The church is squeezed between a modern housing estate on the edge of Crawley and the

M23, which reverberates in the background. A small side road leads back in time to a picturesque old Sussex cottage beside a delightful 16th-century lych-gate. The Ten Apostles, an avenue of lime trees, guide us to the church door.

The immediate impression is that there must be some mistake. This church is surely Victorian, not Saxon. And indeed, the tower, with its distinctive broached and shingled spire, is the work of the Victorian architect Anthony Salvin, who put it there in 1871. But once past this, the Saxon features begin to emerge. The lofty nave, the round-headed two-light windows, divided by stubby columns, high up in the walls, the long-and-short work at the corners, the stone pilaster strips and horizontal string course that run around the lovely curve of the apse. In fact, some 95 per cent of St Nicholas has been dated to the 10th century, between AD 950 and 980.

This is a huge church to build in the middle of nowhere, and it was probably connected to a monastic college of some sort, perhaps the abbey at Chertsey.

Prepare to gasp as you enter by the west door, for you will be confronted by THE MOST BEAUTIFUL SET OF ARCHES LEFT TO US BY THE SAXON WORLD. The chancel arch is immense, 22 feet (6.7 m) high and 14 feet (4.3 m) wide. Although not the tallest Saxon arch, which is at Stow in Lincolnshire, or the widest Saxon arch, which is at Wing in Buckinghamshire, this is THE EARLIEST, SIMPLEST AND LEAST SPOILED SAXON ARCH OF SIZE and is, to my mind, the loveliest and most pure. The plain, rugged, unadorned round stone arch rests on two square abaci on top of round columns such as you might find standing anywhere in Ancient Rome. This arch is a very early flowering of the Romanesque style later perfected by the Normans. The arches either side of the chancel arch are equally superb, just smaller. Together, the three are matchless.

The chancel arch sumptuously frames a semi-circular apse, which forms the LARGEST SAXON CHANCEL IN ENGLAND.

The three Saxon windows of the nave, two on the north side and one on the south side, make up THREE OF THE FOUR SURVIVING SAXON NAVE WINDOWS IN ENGLAND, the fourth being at Wing. They are positioned high up in the walls as a defensive measure, since the church would have acted as a refuge from raiders or bandits roaming the forest.

In the north and south walls are two very tall, narrow, triangular-headed doorways. The north doorway is completely blocked; the south one is occupied by a 14th-century door only half the height of the Saxon doorway. These doorways were known as

'KNIGHT'S DOORS', and were built to such a height so that a person of high standing could ride into the church on his horse, say his prayers before the altar and then ride out again without having to turn his mount.

Despite modern pews and modern lighting, Worth is redolent of Saxon England and still a sanctuary, a refuge from the modern world hurtling by outside.

The Sound of Music

Buried in the churchyard, not far from the west door, is ROBERT WHITEHEAD (1823–1905), INVENTOR OF THE TORPEDO, who lived at Paddock Hurst, a nearby country estate now occupied by Worth School. Whitehead developed his invention in Fiume, an Adriatic seaport then home to the Austrian navy, who were his first customers.

In 1912 Whitehead's granddaughter Frances was invited to christen one of the Austrian navy's new submarines, which was equipped with her grandfather's torpedoes. At the ceremony she was introduced to the submarine's commander, GEORG VON TRAPP, whom she later married. They had seven children before Frances died of scarlet fever in 1924. Von Trapp moved his family to Salzburg and hired an apprentice nun from Nonnberg Priory called MARIA to tutor the children. The story of their transformation into the Trapp Family Choir and their escape from Austria at the beginning of the Second World War provided the inspiration for the hugely popular musical and 1965 film *The Sound of Music*, starring Christopher Plummer as Baron von Trapp and Julie Andrews as Maria.

Well, I never knew this about
SUSSEX CHURCHES

Ovingdean – St Wulfran's. This is one of only two churches in England dedicated to the French missionary ST WULFRAN. Buried near the south porch is CHARLES KEMPE (1837–1907), one of the finest designers of stained glass of the Victorian era. His trademark, which appeared in all his windows, was a golden wheatsheaf. Also buried here is the inventor MAGNUS VOLK (1851–1937),

who in 1883 built BRITAIN'S FIRST ELECTRIC RAILWAY, which still runs along the seafront in Brighton.

Sompting – St Mary's. Sompting's church stands on a gentle rise above the village, from which it is cut off by the gruesome A27. Its proud possession is the unique Saxon tower, which is ENGLAND'S ONLY RHENISH HELM, a four-sided tower capped with a pyramidal roof, as found in the Rhineland. Built in stages between AD 960 and 1020, the tower has long-and-short work at the corners and pilaster strips running up the middle of each wall. The belfry windows have typical triangular-headed arches. Inside, on the north face of the tower, is the carved face of an early king, possibly Canute, who was king at the time and had a palace at nearby Bosham. The Saxon tower arch is half the width of the nave and rests on Corinthian columns carved with symbols of grapes and wheat. The nave is 12th-century Norman, built on the foundations of the Saxon nave. In 1184 the Knights Templar added north and south transepts, both with rib vaults and arches with foliated capitals. The south transept was built as a private chapel for the knights and was originally inaccessible from the church. It now serves as the baptistry and houses the 13th-century Norman font.

WARWICKSHIRE

St Peter's, Wootton Wawen – the oldest church in Warwickshire

Astley

St Mary's

Fit for Queens

From a distance St Mary's looks extraordinary: a long, wide, low church that has had all the air sucked out of it until rendered hunched and narrow. The cottages that surround it resemble retainers fussing over an elderly dowager.

High on the church tower is a Saxon sundial, indicating that there has been some sort of church on the site since Saxon times.

A chapel was recorded here in 1285 and then in 1343 SIR THOMAS ASTLEY of the adjacent ASTLEY CASTLE constructed what he called 'my fair and beautiful Collegiate church' here, a huge cathedral-sized building in the shape of a cross. Until the 16th century it had a lead spire, rising above the tower, and at its pinnacle a lantern

burned to guide the monks home through the forest.

This great church fell into disrepair at the Dissolution of the Monasteries, and in 1607 the new occupant of Astley Castle, RICHARD CHAMBERLAYNE, decided to create a new church from the ruin, rebuilding the tower, restoring the original Decorated chancel to serve as the nave and adding a small Gothic chancel on to the east end. The old east window can be seen, filled in, above the chancel arch inside, while some of its lovely 14th-century stained glass is scattered around in the other windows.

Adorning the nave are the STRIKING, 15TH-CENTURY, CANOPIED OAK CHOIR STALLS FROM THE COLLEGIATE CHURCH, still with their carved misericords and with the PAINTED FIGURES OF THE APOSTLES AND PROPHETS on their backs, a rare treasure.

Near the entrance door, behind iron railings, are three splendid effigies of relatives of the two future queens of England who lived at Astley. Nearest to the door is SIR EDWARD GREY (d.1457). Next to him is his daughter-in-law ELIZABETH TALBOT (d.1487) and on the far side is CECILY BONNEVILLE (d.1529), second wife of Sir Edward's grandson THOMAS GREY, 1ST MARQUESS OF DORSET. Thomas was the eldest son of Sir John Grey and Elizabeth Woodville.

Queen Elizabeth

SIR JOHN GREY brought his new bride ELIZABETH WOODVILLE home to Astley Castle in 1454. Daughter of Richard Woodville, Baron Rivers of Grafton in Northamptonshire, she was the beauty of her day. A few years later in 1461, Sir John died fighting for the Lancastrian cause in the Wars of the Roses at the Battle of St Albans and Elizabeth left Astley to return to her parents' home at Grafton with her two sons by Sir John, Thomas and Richard. The story of how she met and married Edward IV at Grafton, and thus became Queen of England, is told on pages 188–90.

Queen Jane

The next future queen to live at Astley Castle was LADY JANE GREY, who was Elizabeth Woodville's great-great-granddaughter twice over. Lady Jane's father, HENRY GREY, DUKE OF SUFFOLK, was Elizabeth's great-grandson through her first marriage to Sir John Grey, while Lady Jane's mother Frances was Elizabeth's great-granddaughter through Edward IV. Lady Jane spent her childhood between Bradgate in Leicestershire and Astley, and the room in Astley Castle where she studied, and from where she looked out at St Mary's church, has been rebuilt.

In 1553 Lady Jane married the Duke of Northumberland's son Lord Guildford Dudley. Her father, Henry Grey, and her new father-in-law the Duke, persuaded a dying Edward VI to make Lady Jane his successor, and she was proclaimed Queen on 10 July that year. Nine days later she was deposed by Edward's sister Mary. The following year Lady Jane was executed after her father Henry was implicated in the Wyatt Rebellion against Mary's proposed marriage to Philip of Spain. Henry fled back to Astley Castle and hid in an oak tree in the grounds for three days until he was betrayed to the Queen's men. The trunk of that oak tree still stands in Astley Park.

After this, Astley Castle went through several transformations from Tudor manor house to Gothick hall and then a hotel, but was gutted by fire in 1978 and now stands as a gaunt ruin above the church, in the care of English Heritage. The Landmark Trust have made a portion of the ruin habitable.

Queen of Literature

The parents of novelist GEORGE ELIOT were married in Astley church, and she was born nearby on the Arbury estate where her father was land agent. Eliot describes Astley church in her first published work, *Scenes of Clerical Life*, and based her Reverend Gilfil on the Reverend Bernard Gilpin, who was vicar of Astley when she lived there. Astley village becomes Knebley in the book.

Astley Castle

Berkswell

St John the Baptist

Norman Nave

Tucked away in leafy seclusion at the end of a lane off the village green, this stately 12th-century Norman church glows mellow pink. There is an unusual First World War memorial, like a small chapel, with open windows and a vaulted roof, by the gate into the churchyard. Three round-headed windows stand high in the chancel wall. The tower, sporting a huge clock, peeps over the top of the sloping roof. The half-timbered south porch resembles a cottage, inviting you in for tea and crumpets. In the cosy room above, the village schoolchildren once had their lessons.

You climb some steps to enter the church through a Norman doorway. The nave that greets you is tall and handsome, pale pink stone bathed in light streaming in through the clerestory windows. There are two wide Norman arches in the north arcade, while the south arcade has a gallery along its full length. There are some box pews at the back of the church and 15th-century wooden screens along the aisles.

The pulpit was made by the celebrated Yorkshire woodcarver ROBERT 'MOUSEMAN' THOMPSON and installed in 1926. It sports his trademark carved mouse, and since much of the other woodwork is also by Thompson there are a total of nine Thompson mice to be found in the church – looking for them all can be a pleasantly diverting pastime.

A noble Norman arch leads through to the unspoiled Norman chancel, lit by five lovely windows behind the altar. The beautiful Thompson choir stalls end in poppy-heads and depictions of six bishops with connections to Berkswell.

Norman Crypt

A door in the north aisle leads down under the chancel to Berkswell's masterpiece, a remarkably well-preserved 12TH-CENTURY NORMAN CRYPT TO RIVAL ANY IN ENGLAND. There are two rooms, divided by a thick Norman arch and lit by seven small windows. The first room is AN OCTAGONAL CHAMBER, UNIQUE IN ENGLAND, while the other room is rectangular with a stone altar at the east end. Both have gorgeous stone rib-vaulted roofs. On either side of the inner chamber small wooden doors block off the original in and out stairways that allowed the flow of pilgrims to pass through efficiently, indicating that the crypt was much visited. It is thought that this Norman crypt may have replaced an earlier Saxon crypt containing the relics of an 8th-century saint called Mildred, a much venerated Abbess of Minster in Thanet, Kent, who was related to the local king, Ethelbald of Mercia.

Like those at Repton and Lastingham, this crypt at Berkswell is one of England's peaceful places where, just for a moment, time really does take a break.

Wootton Wawen

St Peter's

A Feast of Features

Here, in the ancient Forest of Arden, set upon a hillock above a lovely black-and-white pub on a busy road leading to Birmingham, is the OLDEST CHURCH IN WARWICKSHIRE, home of the only significant Saxon work in the county. Not that the Saxon work is easy to spot,

for St Peter's is an eccentric and exhilarating gallimaufry of every different style and age and feature you could hope to find in a church, an A to Z of ecclesiastical paraphernalia. The view from the road could be of several churches – gabled, battlemented, Perpendicular, Decorated, Victorian.

We know there was a church here in Saxon times, for there is a charter from between AD 720 and 740 that still exists, in which Aethelbald, King of Mercia, grants Earl Aethelric land at Wudu Tun on which to build a minster. This wooden structure was burned to the ground by the Vikings, but around the end of the 10th century an Anglo-Danish landowner called Wagen began the present stone church. The lower part of the tower survives from this church and still forms the core of the building.

After the Norman Conquest the church and its lands were given to the ubiquitous Robert de Tosny, who fought with the Conqueror at Hastings. He gave it to his family abbey of Conches in Normandy, and the monks from there established a small priory next to the church and built the massive red-roofed early Gothic chapel that now forms the chancel.

Entering the church is a bit like going into one of those fairground mystery houses, echoing spaces with corridors and aisles leading off in all directions. Which church to enter first?

The nave is basically Norman, but much rebuilt and extended with the addition of a clerestory in the 15th century. At the east end of the nave there is a splendid 15th-century oak pulpit, delicately carved, two square parclose screens and an elaborate oak chancel screen set against the chancel arch.

The tower sits at the centre of the church on FOUR EXQUISITE SAXON ARCHES, with the altar in the open space beneath. Beyond are the chancel and Lady Chapel, with remnants of a 14th-century wall painting high on the

south wall and a variety of marble and alabaster tombs.

Nothing in this church is individually outstanding except, perhaps, the Saxon tower arches, but as a compendium of church treasures and memorabilia through the ages this collection in Wootton Wawen is unsurpassed. There is something special here for everyone.

Well, I never knew this about
WARWICKSHIRE CHURCHES

Berkswell – St John the Baptist. Buried in the churchyard here is MAUD WATSON (1864–1946), THE FIRST WIMBLEDON LADIES CHAMPION. She was the daughter of a former rector of Berkswell and lived next door to the church in the handsome Georgian rectory, now called The Well House. She was the winner of the very first ladies championship at Wimbledon in 1884.

Binton – St Peter's. A church has occupied this wooded hill, looking out across the Avon towards the blue distant Cotswolds, since 1286. The handsome church that stands there now was built in 1875, paid for by the Marchioness of Hertford of nearby Ragley Hall. From the churchyard, there are glimpses through the yew trees of the old parsonage where, in 1910, CAPTAIN ROBERT FALCON SCOTT, SCOTT OF THE ANTARCTIC, said farewell to his wife

KATHLEEN, daughter of Binton's rector, before setting out on his fateful voyage to the South Pole. Scott loved visiting Binton and walking by the river where William Shakespeare once walked. The beautiful pastel-coloured west window in the church, a masterpiece by CHARLES KEMPE (1915), is a memorial to Scott and his companions and tells the story of their expedition in four scenes. It is a poignant and inspiring piece of work.

Brailes – St George's. The magnificent bell tower of St George's church, which lords it over this delightful stone village in the south Warwickshire hills, stands 120 feet (37 m) high and houses THE THIRD HEAVIEST RING OF SIX BELLS IN THE WORLD. Only St Buryan in Cornwall and Queen Camel in Somerset have heavier peals.

Temple Grafton – St Andrew's. Just down the road from Binton, St Andrew's was built on the site of a Saxon church in 1875, the same year as Binton's church of St Peter. This is one of the places where WILLIAM SHAKESPEARE IS SAID TO HAVE MARRIED ANNE HATHAWAY in 1582. A licence issued by the Bishop of Worcester records the marriage of a Wm. Shaxpere to one Anne Whateley of Temple Grafton, with the name Whateley deemed to be a clerical error.

Whichford – St Michael's. Against the north wall of the chancel in this dignified, mainly 14th-century village church, is the tomb of JOHN MERTUN, rector of St Michael's from 1507 to 1537. The tomb is formed of a stone base with an incised alabaster tablet on top, showing Mertun in his robes. This rare carving is exceptional, amongst THE BEST INCISED ALABASTER CARVINGS IN THE BRITISH ISLES. Carved on the west side of the tomb, hard to find but worth looking for, is a pair of round glasses, THE EARLIEST KNOWN DEPICTION OF A PAIR OF SPECTACLES IN ENGLAND.

WILTSHIRE

Edington Priory – finest English architecture on the site of the battle where England was won

Edington

Priory Church of St Mary, St
Katherine & All Saints

Shades of Winchester

Edington's priory church, standing on
a tree-lined terrace below the northern
foothills of Salisbury Plain, is not so
much a country church as a country
cathedral, a sublime example of English

Gothic architecture. It was built in ten
years, between 1350 and 1360, when
Decorated was becoming Perpendicular,
and includes the best of both, particularly in its windows.

It is indeed fitting that this place
should possess such a fine illustration
of English artistry and craftsmanship,
for Edington is a cradle of the English
nation. Here, in AD 878, King Alfred
laid the foundations of England by
defeating the Great Heathen Army of
the Vikings under Guthrum at the

Battle of Ethandune. The Treaty of Wedmore that followed made Guthrum a Christian and sent him back to East Anglia, setting in motion the process of uniting the Anglo-Saxon kingdoms into one nation.

Edington Priory was founded by William of Edington, Bishop of Winchester, as a house for an order of Augustinian monks known as Bonhommes, or Bluefriars after the colour of their robes. If the church, particularly at the western end, resembles Winchester Cathedral then this is not coincidental, for William of Edington was responsible for Winchester's west front and began the remodelling of the cathedral's nave, which was completed by his successor William of Wykeham.

At the Dissolution of the Monasteries, the domestic parts of Edington priory were pulled down, although the outer walls of the priory grounds still stand to the north of the church, enclosing gardens and the remnants of the priory's fishponds. The priory church was given over to the parish.

Painted Glory

The tall, embattled south porch through which one enters is an unusual three-storey affair and has a vaulted ceiling.

Perhaps the most notable feature inside the church is the 17th-century plasterwork ceiling of the 75 ft (23 m) long nave, painted in the original pink and white and brilliantly lit by the tall windows of the clerestory. The plaster fan-vault ceiling of the tower crossing is also 17th century and also painted, with the ribs picked out in dark red.

Very effectively concealing the long chancel is a magnificent Tudor screen, with an intricately carved canopy and above it one of the very few rood-lofts left in England. An impressive wooden doorway leads under the loft and through the screen to the chancel.

Monumental Edington

The chancel has a white-painted plaster ceiling of 1789, eight canopied niches in the walls, two of them occupied, some 14th-century stained glass in the east window and a number of fine monuments. Against the south wall is the tomb of Sir Edward Lewis (d.1630). His effigy is revealed behind drawn-back curtains and rests slightly below that of his wife, Lady Anne Beauchamp, indicating that she was of higher social rank. Their children kneel in prayer below, and an angel, made of wood but painted to look like marble, floats above them holding a coronet.

To the north of the altar is a lovely memorial by Sir Francis Chantrey to Sir Simon Taylor, who died in 1815. He is shown as a handsome young man, on his deathbed and attended by two female mourners, who are perhaps

wondering how he got away. Sir Simon died unmarried.

Amongst the other interesting features of the priory church are a 15TH-CENTURY FONT, and an ALMOST COMPLETE SET OF CONSECRATION CROSSES, 12 inside and 11 outside, just one missing from the original 24. Consecration crosses mark the places where the bishop laid his hands when the church was consecrated.

Inglesham

St John the Baptist

Saved by Morris

This humble rustic church stands on a small pagan mound beside the River Thames with just swans and Inglesham House for company. There has been a church here since early Saxon days, and although most of the fabric of the present church is 13th century the interior is a most wonderful time capsule, containing furnishings and features that represent some 1,000 years of history, from Saxon to Jacobean. Even more remarkably, this magical place has been left untouched by over-enthusiastic Victorian restorers and remains inside almost exactly as it would have appeared to a 17th-century church-goer.

For this we have to thank WILLIAM MORRIS, pioneer of the Arts and Crafts Movement, who fell in love with St John's when he came across it during a day out on the river from his country home downstream at Kelmscott. The church was badly neglected and in need of repair, but Morris wanted to ensure that any restoration retained its unique medieval character. He supervised the work himself and Inglesham was fortunate in being ONE OF THE FIRST ENGLISH CHURCHES TO BE RESCUED BY THE SOCIETY FOR THE PROTECTION OF ANCIENT BUILDINGS (SPAB), which Morris and his friends had established in 1877.

From outside the building is rather plain, rectangular, with medieval windows, a 16th-century porch and a 13th-century bellcote with sundial.

Inside is a treasure trove. The octagonal font is 15th century. The Norman nave has two arcades of round pillars, the south with round arches, the slightly younger north arcade with transitional pointed arches. The capitals have stiff leaf carving. The nave and aisles are packed with the most lovely oak furnishings, 15th-century parclose screens carved with flowers in the aisles, 17th-century box pews and a pulpit with canopy.

Every wall is covered with wall

paintings, dating from the 13th to the 19th centuries. Some of the murals have been painted over up to seven times with the result that they can be difficult to decipher, although it is possible to make out a 14th-century Doom on the east wall of the north aisle, 15th-century angels above the chancel arch and a number of 18th and 19th-century texts, such as the Ten Commandments, Lord's Prayer and Creed.

The chancel is 13th century and has traces of a rare PAINTED STONE REREDOS on the east wall. On the floor is a Tournai marble slab of around 1300 with the outline of the brass of a knight. The altar rails are 18th century.

But the most precious jewel of all is to be found set into the wall of the south chapel, a simple but moving 11TH-CENTURY SAXON CARVING OF MOTHER AND CHILD. They are being blessed by the Hand of God, seen pointing down from Heaven. The carving had originally been on the

outside of the south wall and used as a scratch dial, but was brought inside the church in 1910. It is amongst the most beautiful, most powerful pieces of work in any English church.

Lacock

St Cyriac's

Picture Perfect

Lacock is the very essence of an English village: narrow, winding streets lined with medieval houses of golden stone, half-timbered fronts, gabled roofs and crooked porches, tithe barn, stately home. It is all so picture perfect that in 1995 the BBC chose Lacock to represent Meryton, Elizabeth Bennett's home town in *Pride and Prejudice*, and then returned in 2005 to film the village as Cranford. The cloisters of Lacock Abbey appeared as Hogwarts in a number of Harry Potter films.

Lacock's 15th-century church of St Cyriac in no way lets the side down. It is a majestically eccentric building of many disparate styles that head off in a variety of directions. There are high-pitched barn-like transepts, a stately Perpendicular aisle, embattled west porch, square tower, picturesque octagonal spire rebuilt in 1604 and, tacked on to the south side, what looks like the wing of a Jacobean manor house, in reality a priest's house known as the 'Cottage'. The whole edifice is alive with grinning gargoyles, including a man astride a crescent moon and a grotesque fellow smoking a pipe.

Inside, the church is full of interesting features, including an unusually shaped six-light window above the chancel arch, but the highlight is the Lady Chapel to the north of the chancel, built in 1430 by the Bonhams and the Crokes. It has a magnificent stellar vaulted roof with pendants, showing traces of the original colouring, and bosses carved with a wonderful variety of creatures, angels, bears, a woman in a skirt, a pug dog and even a snail, ONE OF ONLY TWO SNAILS ON A ROOF BOSS IN ENGLAND, the other being in Bury St Edmunds.

Against the north wall is the superb Renaissance-style tomb of SIR WILLIAM SHARINGTON (d.1553), who bought Lacock Abbey off the Crown after the Dissolution of the Monasteries. His daughter married a Talbot, and the abbey stayed in the Talbot family for 400 years until 1958 when it was bequeathed to the National Trust. The fine carvings on the tomb include

scorpions, the Sharington emblem, and a pair of remarkably detailed foliate Green Men seen in profile.

The chancel was re-designed in 1902 in memory of WILLIAM HENRY FOX TALBOT (1800–77), whose photo of

Lacock Abbey's oriel window, taken in 1835, is THE WORLD'S OLDEST PHOTO-GRAPH.

Lydiard Tregoze

St Mary's

Much to Admire

The delightful 15th-century church of St Mary is almost completely enveloped in the wings of the huge Palladian mansion that is Lydiard Park. Perhaps the two buildings huddle so close together because they are all that remain of the village of Lydiard Tregoze, which disappeared long ago. The great house, in a previous incarnation, was the home for more than five centuries of the mighty St John family, and the church is their mausoleum.

There is much to admire inside St Mary's. Box pews, a brightly coloured chancel screen and pulpit, both Jacobean, rich 15th-century stained glass in the windows of the aisles, 17th-century stained glass in the east window and some 15th-century wall paintings in the nave showing St Christopher, St Michael weighing souls, the Martyrdom of St Thomas à Becket and Jesus rising from the tomb. Most unusually, the porch is also painted, with the Head of Christ represented on the inside wall above the outer door.

So Good they Named him Twice

But what make this unassuming church one of England's most sumptuous

treasure-houses are the monuments of the St Johns. They occupy both the chancel and the St John Chapel to the south and were commissioned and laid out by the man who remodelled the church, and whose own spectacular tomb dominates the chapel, SIR JOHN ST JOHN (d.1648).

The St Johns were somewhat tenuously related to the royal family, by marriage if not by blood. Sir John St John's great-great-great-great-grandfather was the first husband of Margaret Beauchamp, whose daughter by her second marriage, Margaret Beaufort, was mother of Henry VII. Anyway, Sir John St John certainly rests royally enough, beneath a monument he himself designed in 1634, well before he died.

He lies in effigy between his two wives, surrounded by their 13 children. All the figures are sublimely carved from alabaster, so lifelike and so serene they could simply be sleeping. Sir John's first wife Anne in particular, her face framed in a lace bonnet, is heart-stoppingly beautiful. The three of them are covered by the most immense arched canopy, raised on eight pillars and rampant with pinnacles and sculptures of shields, of women and children and birds.

Above the door of the chapel Sir John's sister KATHERINE sits listening

studiously to her husband, SIR GILES MOMPESSON, who is reading from a book.

The oldest monument in the church is in the south aisle and commemorates Sir John's grandparents Nicholas and Elizabeth St John, who kneel together on tasselled cushions, beneath a gilded arch, dressed as Tudors in black and gold. The tomb was erected by their son, John's father, in 1592.

Against the north wall of the chancel is the jewel in Lydiard's sumptuous crown, A UNIQUE MONUMENT KNOWN AS THE GOLDEN CAVALIER. Two young attendants hold back the canopy curtains to reveal a gilded standing effigy of EDWARD ST JOHN, resplendent in battle dress, posing as if on a catwalk. Edward was Sir John's fourth, and obviously favourite son, who died in 1645 after being wounded in a cavalry charge fighting for Charles I at the second Battle of Newbury.

Sir John was a Royalist, and of his six sons, three died fighting for the Royalist cause, John at Newark, William at Cirencester and Edward at Newbury. The youngest two, Walter and Henry, fought for Parliament and survived.

On the chancel wall, beside the Golden Cavalier, is the ST JOHN TRIPTYCH, commissioned by Sir John in 1615 to commemorate his parents. They kneel on a sarcophagus while Sir John and his wife Anne stand deferentially to one side. The outer panels show the St John family tree, in incredible detail. The triptych is normally kept closed, but it is well worth agitating for someone in authority to open it up, for it is a dazzling piece.

In fact the whole church is dazzling, and home to some of the finest monuments of their kind in England. An unexpected delight.

Well, I never knew this about

WILTSHIRE CHURCHES

Clyffe Pypard – St Peter's. SIR NIKOLAUS PEVSNER (1902–83), architectural historian and author of the matchless county architectural guides known simply as 'Pevsners', is buried in the churchyard here along with his wife Lola. They lived in the village for many years. The mainly 15th-century church, situated in trees at the foot of a steep hill, is well worthy of such a distinguished resident. There is 16th-century Flemish stained glass in the windows of the north aisle, a fine 15th-century barrel roof, a canopied hexagonal oak pulpit dated 1629, gorgeously carved with flowers and birds, and a brightly painted and gilded 15th-century chancel screen that extends to cover the aisles. High up on the walls above the screen, two life-size chalk figures face each other across the chancel arch, JOHN GODDARD in armour and his wife ELIZABETH in Tudor dress. In the south aisle is a superb life-size white marble monument to THOMAS SPACKMAN (d.1786), a local carpenter who made good in London and left his fortune to the village. He is shown with a selection of his carpenter's tools.

East Knoyle – St Mary's. This would have been the first church that England's pre-eminent architect CHRISTOPHER WREN ever saw, for he was born in this

St Mary's, East Knoyle

pretty hillside village of thatch and stone, where his father DEAN CHRISTOPHER WREN was rector. The oldest part of St Mary's Church is the chancel, which is 12th century and has some Norman blind arcading on the north outside wall. The walls of the chancel inside are adorned with ornate, decorative plasterwork patterned with scrolls and texts, elaborate borders and quaint figures. We see cherubs, marigolds and Tudor roses and also biblical scenes, Jacob's ladder with angels climbing up to Heaven, Elijah being fed by ravens, the Ascension. All this was conceived and designed by Dean Wren, although the work was actually carried out by a local craftsman, ROBERT BROCKWAY. Did the young Christopher Wren think of these walls, perhaps along with the lovely 15th-century stone vaulted roof under the tower, when he was dreaming of his St Paul's Cathedral?

Sevenhampton – St James's. You might think that this modest Victorian church on a hillside but five miles from the beating heart of Swindon need not detain us long. But miss it at your peril, for here, beneath a gaunt obelisk in this quiet, unknown churchyard, lies the man who gave us the greatest spy of them all, Bond, James Bond. In his last years IAN FLEMING lived at next-door WARNEFORD PLACE, seen through the trees when the leaves are down, and he was buried here in 1964 after a heart attack. With him lie his wife Ann and their only son, Caspar.

WORCESTERSHIRE

Little Malvern Priory – England's smallest priory

Little Malvern Priory

Special to the Yorks

Nestling at the foot of the Malvern Hills, with Worcestershire and the Severn valley spread out spectacularly before it, the truncated and yet still very beautiful LITTLE MALVERN PRIORY is virtually all that is left of ENGLAND'S SMALLEST PRIORY, the Benedictine Priory of St Giles, founded as a daughter church of Worcester Cathedral in 1125.

The priory was never very wealthy or well managed, and by the 15th century most of the buildings were run down and dilapidated. In 1480 JOHN ALCOCK, BISHOP OF WORCESTER, had the church rebuilt and it is the chancel and crossing tower of his priory church that make up the building as it stands today. These elements were reprieved at the Dissolution of the Monasteries by being converted into use as a parish church, while the old nave and transepts were left to fall into ruin.

The tall and imposing old choir is now separated into nave and chancel by a 14TH-CENTURY WOODEN SCREEN, while there is an enjoyable CARVING OF TWO PIGS AT THE TROUGH on one of the bench ends that somehow escaped Henry VIII's wreckers. On the floor are some rare and delightful 14TH-CENTURY TILES from the famous kiln at Great Malvern Priory.

Roundels of modern coloured glass in the north window, the gift of the late MARIAN TOSELLO, a Friend of Little Malvern Priory, commemorate the poet WILLIAM LANGLAND (1322–1400), who was inspired by the view from Little Malvern to write his immortal 'Piers Plowman', one of the greatest poems of medieval English, about the life and times of an English peasant in the 14th century.

Very special indeed is John Alcock's great East Window, for although sadly incomplete it contains in stained glass ONE OF THE ONLY TWO SURVIVING REPRESENTATIONS OF EDWARD, PRINCE OF WALES, LATER EDWARD V. Also shown is Edward's mother Elizabeth Woodville, with three of her daughters,

Cecily, Anne and Catherine. Originally there were also portraits of Edward IV, his younger son Richard, Duke of York, and John Alcock himself. Apart from the 'Royal Window' in the north transept of Canterbury Cathedral, commissioned by Edward IV himself, this window in Little Malvern Priory is THE ONLY SURVIVING MONUMENTAL REPRESENTATION OF THESE IMPORTANT FIGURES FROM THE 15TH-CENTURY HOUSE OF YORK.

Little Malvern holds an important place in Yorkist history, for this was the 'poor religious house' where Margaret of Anjou, wife of the Lancastrian king Henry IV, was captured and held immediately after her defeat at the Battle of Tewkesbury fought nearby in 1471.

The church stands right next door to the meandering 15th-century black-and-white LITTLE MALVERN COURT, which grew out of the priory's domestic buildings and incorporates a surviving round tower from the original 12th-century complex. It is still lived in by the Berington family, who purchased the priory and its lands at the Dissolution of the Monasteries.

JOHN ALCOCK (1430–1500), as well as being Bishop of Worcester, and later Ely, was one of the great figures of late 15th-century England. A confidant of Edward IV, he was appointed tutor to the King's oldest son, Prince Edward, later Edward V, and was with him when he and his younger brother Richard were waylaid at Stony Stratford and taken to the Tower of London by their uncle, Richard, Duke of Gloucester, later Richard III. Alcock was clearly not just able but honest, for although he worked closely with Richard III he was also trusted by Henry VII, who took his advice to marry Edward IV's daughter Elizabeth of York, thus uniting the York and Lancastrian royal houses. In 1485, after the Battle of Bosworth Field, Alcock was appointed Lord Chancellor by the new king and opened Henry VII's first parliament.

Ribbesford

St Leonard's

Arcade of Oak

The setting here is sylvan and idyllic. The 12th-century church, with three long, gabled roofs and a small timbered bell turret, glows mellow pink amongst the green lawns and trees. The domes and turrets of historic Ribbesford House peek through the leaves and the silvery Severn shimmers peacefully below. We enter the church via the Norman north door, which is sheltered by a crooked white-painted wooden porch bearing the date 1633. Above the door itself is a tympanum, crudely carved in the 12th century but most appealing, showing a hunter in a Norman helmet aiming his bow and arrow at a strange, bulky creature with short legs and a tail.

The big surprise inside are the arcades. The north one is of stone, while the SOUTH ARCADE IS OF WOOD, STURDY OCTAGONAL OAK PILLARS THAT HAVE STOOD THERE SINCE 1450. Lightning struck the church in 1877, destroying the wooden north arcade, which was then remade in stone. John Ruskin himself had to fight to save the wooden south arcade from the restorers.

Preserved in the modern pulpit are

some jolly carvings from the original 15th-century rood screen, amongst them such delights as a pig playing the bagpipes, a sly fox beguiling some geese, a couple of piglets on their hind legs reaching for acorns, and a big-eared fellow, possibly a Green Man, sticking his tongue out. How rude.

At the west end is a more recent wonder, a gorgeous WILLIAM MORRIS WINDOW of 1875 created from a design by EDWARD BURNE-JONES. It is dedicated to Burne-Jones's mother-in-law, HANNAH MACDONALD, who lies beside her husband in the churchyard.

The MacDonald Sisters

Hannah and the Reverend George MacDonald had 11 children, seven daughters and four sons. Four of their daughters married prominent Victorians.

ALICE (1837–1910) married JOHN LOCKWOOD KIPLING and became the mother of RUDYARD KIPLING (named after Lake Rudyard, near Leek in Staffordshire, where John Lockwood proposed to her). Lord Dufferin, Viceroy of India, said of Alice, 'Dullness and Mrs Kipling cannot exist in the same room.'

GEORGIANA (1840–1920) married the Pre-Raphaelite artist EDWARD BURNE-JONES.

AGNES (1843–1906) married the artist and President of the Royal Academy, EDWARD POYNTER.

LOUISA (1845–1925) married ironmaster and industrialist ALFRED BALDWIN and became the mother of three-time Prime Minister STANLEY BALDWIN, the ONLY BRITISH PRIME MINISTER TO SERVE UNDER THREE DIFFERENT MONARCHS (George V, Edward VIII and George VI).

Alfred was the owner of the Wilden Ironworks, and in 1880 he funded the construction of a church, All Saints in Wilden, for his work-force and the local community, on a plot of raised land overlooking fields and the canal just south of the ironworks.

Wilden

All Saints

A Family Affair

The modest red-brick exterior of this neat Victorian church, built by ALFRED BALDWIN in 1880, conceals a unique treasure-house, THE ONLY CHURCH IN ENGLAND TO HAVE ALL EDWARD BURNE-JONES DESIGNED WINDOWS. When the church was first built, the windows were all of plain glass, but between 1902 and

1914 these were replaced with the 14 richly coloured red, blue and green Burne-Jones windows we see today. Burne-Jones died in 1898 but had already worked on the design of these windows, many of which are dedicated to various members of the Baldwin family to whom Burne-Jones was related, being Alfred Baldwin's brother-in-law. The east window, donated by Alfred Baldwin in thanks for his happy married life, shows Stanley, his only son and future Prime Minister, setting out on life's adventure with his guardian angel.

There is also a gold-threaded altarpiece designed by William Morris and worked on by Alfred's wife Louisa and Burne-Jones's wife Georgiana.

By the gate into the churchyard from the road is a quaint little clock tower that was erected in memory of Alfred Baldwin in 1910, two years after his death.

Rock

St Peter & St Paul

A Lively Place

The gentle village of Rock sits quietly at a respectful distance from its stern, self-confident church, surrounded by lovely countryside. This is THE BIGGEST AND MOST IMPORTANT NORMAN CHURCH IN WORCESTERSHIRE, and knows it. It was built in 1150 by Roger de Tosny, grandson of Ralph of Normandy, standard-bearer to William the Conqueror at the Battle of Hastings, and boasts some of the finest Norman work in the Midlands.

The building appears to be stepping assuredly down the slope of the churchyard, from the high 16th-century west tower, to the nave, with its odd parade of blind arches and windows in pairs, and then the chancel. The north doorway, below a plain, pointed tympanum, is of six orders carved with chevrons, lozenges, scallops, zigzags and saltires.

But the most exciting feature of St Peter & St Paul is the huge and glorious, slightly leaning, NORMAN CHANCEL ARCH, which sports on its capitals some of the most imaginative and entertaining carvings anywhere, probably the work of the famous Herefordshire School of masons responsible for the wonders of Kilpeck to the south (*see* pages 188-19). There is a sad-faced chap with a goatee beard who appears to be being cuddled by a lion that is biting its own tail, a beautiful horse's head, a centaur firing a bow and arrow, a rather appealing pig face, a boatful of sailors being dragged underwater by the sea monster Aspido, and an extraordinary, eye-poppingly contorted individual engaged in what is probably an unmentionable act. Such figures are described in respectable guidebooks as 'exhibitionist'. All these carvings are so lifelike and full of exuberance and movement that you can almost hear the stonework rustling with their activity.

Well, I never knew this about

WORCESTERSHIRE CHURCHES

Besford – St Peter's. Here is WORCESTERSHIRE'S ONLY TIMBER-FRAMED CHURCH. The wooden nave dates from the 14th century, while the stone chancel is 13th century. Inside is ONE OF ENGLAND'S FEW SURVIVING PRE-REFORMATION ROOD LOFTS and a remarkable 16TH-CENTURY TRIPTYCH commemorating RICHARD HARWELL, who died in 1576 at the age of 15 and lies beneath a tomb in the chancel. He is seen kneeling in the centre panel above a dead child in a shroud with two very much alive children on either side of him, one blowing bubbles, the other holding a rose. Time and Death are on the inside of the doors, while angels are on the outside.

Bredon – St Giles'.

*'Then hey for covert and woodland,
and ash and elm and oak,
Tewkesbury inns and Malvern roofs
and Worcester chimney smoke,
The apple trees in the orchard,
the cattle in the byre,
And all the land from Ludlow Town
to Bredon church's spire'*
JOHN MASEFIELD, 'LONDON TOWN'

Ash and elm are not what they were, but Bredon church's spire still soars 160 feet (49 m) into the Worcestershire

sky, just as Masefield saw it and as it has done since the 14th century.

The rest of St Giles' is fundamentally Norman, with a Norman tower arch, three Norman doors and a very attractive and very unusual NORMAN STONE VAULTED PORCH over the north door, with two beautifully carved inner and outer arches. There are many treasures inside the church, but the one for which St Giles' is justly famous is the sumptuous black marble and alabaster memorial of SIR GILES REED, who died in 1611. This is regarded as ONE OF THE BEST 17TH-CENTURY MONUMENTS IN ENGLAND.

Croome D'Abitot – St Mary Magdalene. This church is the work of two of Britain's finest 18th-century craftsmen, LAUNCELOT 'CAPABILITY' BROWN, who designed the exterior, and ROBERT ADAM, who laid out the

St Michael & All Angels, Great Witley

interior. The result is an almost perfect example of Georgian taste and style. The church was commissioned, along with the great house and park, by the 6th Earl of Coventry in the 1750s. It was Brown's first landscape commission and Robert Adam's first architectural commission. House, garden and church are now run by the National Trust.

Great Witley – St Michael & All Angels.

Here is THE FINEST BAROQUE CHURCH IN ENGLAND. It adjoins GREAT WITLEY COURT, which was begun in 1655 by ironmaster THOMAS FOLEY, and which now stands as a ruin after a fire in 1937. The church, with its distinctive gold-topped cupola, was completed in 1735 to a design by James Gibbs for Foley's great-grandson, the 2nd Lord Foley. Inside is THE LARGEST 18TH-CENTURY CHURCH MEMORIAL AND TALLEST FUNERARY MONUMENT IN ENGLAND, sculpted by JOHN MICHAEL RYSBRACK AND commemorating Lord Foley's parents. In 1747 the interior of the church was transformed when Lord Foley commissioned Gibbs to incorporate windows, furnishings and ceiling paintings bought at auction from the chapel at Canons, the Duke of Chandos's house at Edgware in Middlesex. The magnificent ceiling paintings showing the Ascension of Christ along with the Nativity and the Descent are by the Italian artist ANTONIO BELLUCCI. Indeed, Great Witley's church contains THE ONLY PURE BAROQUE INTERIOR OF ANY CHURCH IN ENGLAND OUTSIDE LONDON.

YORKSHIRE

St Patrick's, Patrington – known as the Queen of Holderness and regarded by many as the most perfect village church in England

Adel

St John the Baptist

Norman Carvings

Here is one of the England's Norman gems, a small 12th-century church untouched by our Gothic builders, repaired but not altered or ruined by the Victorians, save for the addition of a bellcote. Leeds is closing in from the south, and yet all around are fields and woods that keep the urban sprawl at bay. Adel, once a Roman settlement, is still a village.

The church of St John the Baptist was built in 1150 and we enter it by THE FINEST NORMAN DOORWAY IN YORKSHIRE. It has four orders, with the two outer arches, one of zigzag mouldings and one of rolled mouldings, both resting on pillars, while the two inner arches, carved with zigzags and beakheads, reach the ground. In the gable

and beasts. They are all different and all delightfully humorous, and a pleasant few minutes can be enjoyed by walking around the building and studying them.

In 1946 St John the Baptist hosted the marriage of Peter Middleton and Valerie Glassborow, paternal grandparents of Catherine, Duchess of Cambridge.

Boynton

St Andrew's

Talking Turkey

The mainly Georgian church of St Andrew stands at the gates of Boynton Hall, ancestral home of the Strickland family. The tower is 15th century but the main body of the church was restored by John Carr of York in the 18th century, after a fire. It's not particularly inspiring from outside, but the interior is a riot of colour and quirkiness, with green-painted pews and a swirling spiral staircase leading up to a gallery at the west end containing the Strickland family pew. The eye, however, is immediately drawn to the lectern, which rests, not on the outspread wings of an eagle, as one might expect, but upon the rounded tail of a turkey – this is in fact THE ONLY LECTERN IN THE WORLD SUPPORTED BY A TURKEY. And this is not the end of the turkey motif. This king of poultry can also be found adorning the impressive Strickland family tombs that fill the east end behind the altar.

The turkey, it turns out, is the crowning glory of the Strickland family

above is a worn depiction of Our Lord and the Holy Lamb. The whole is sheltered beneath a modern wooden porch. The door handle, in the form of a lion's head holding the sanctuary ring in its jaws while swallowing a man, is a replica of the bronze original, cast in York in 1200, and stolen in 2002.

Inside is a supremely well-preserved Norman chancel arch of three lavishly carved orders. The inner order is zigzag, the next resembles a stone ladder running round the arch, and the outer order consists of 37 grotesque beak-heads showing a variety of salivating faces eating or spitting out human prey. The capitals are equally well carved with angels and monsters, a jousting knight and a centaur firing a bow and arrow, this last being a favourite device of William the Conqueror's grandson King Stephen, who visited the area around the time that the church was being built.

Back outside, running all the way round the church under the eaves, are 78 corbels carved with the faces of men

crest. In 1497, WILLIAM STRICKLAND of Boynton travelled in the good ship *Matthew* to America, with the Cabot brothers, looking for gold. There is even some claim that he was THE FIRST ENGLISHMAN EVER TO SET FOOT IN THE NEW WORLD. He didn't find gold, but he did find turkeys, and he brought some back with him, introducing turkeys to Britain for the first time. William Strickland became rich thanks to turkeys, and when he applied for a coat of arms he requested that 'a turkey cock in his pride proper' be incorporated into the design. The crude sketch of a turkey that he made to illustrate what he wanted, is THE FIRST KNOWN DRAWING IN THE WORLD OF A TURKEY – it can still be seen at the College of Arms in London.

Hemingbrough

Collegiate Church of
St Mary the Virgin

Oldest Misericord

The slender spire of Hemingbrough Minster is one of the loveliest spires in England. It beckons to you from miles

away across England's biggest vale, the Vale of York, and it comes as quite a shock when you get there to find that it crowns a country church and not a cathedral. The 15th-century spire is twice the height of the modest 14th-century tower upon which it rests, soaring to 191 feet (58 m), and such is its height that the church looks as though it has been squeezed from both ends, causing the spire to shoot upwards, all to splendid effect.

Carved on the mouldings of the tower is a row of washing 'tuns', or tubs, put there as a visual pun on the name of the man who built it, JOHN WASHINGTON, PRIOR OF DURHAM from 1416 to 1446, 'whose family has won an everlasting name in lands unknown to him', as it says on a plaque in the cloisters of Durham Cathedral. He was an ancestor of the first President of the United States, George Washington.

The cathedral-like interior of Hemingbrough is a happy mix of different styles and ages from Norman to Victorian. The chief glory is the woodwork, with seating and a marvellous screen by Robert 'Mouseman' Thompson in the War Memorial Chapel and some exquisitely carved bench ends in the nave portraying demons, dragons, dogs and monkeys as well as a capering jester with cap and bells.

Hemingbrough's most venerable treasure can be found in the choir stalls, which boast of just one misericord, but what a one. It dates from about 1200 and is the oldest misericord in England.

Kirkdale

St Gregory's Minster

'Orm, the son of Gamal, bought St Gregory's Church when it was all utterly broke and fallen and caused it to be

made anew from the ground, to Christ and St Gregory, in the days of King Edward and in the days of Earl Tosti. Hawarth wrought me and Brand the Prior'

So reads the longest inscription of Saxon English in Britain. It can be found on the most complete example of a Saxon sundial in England, above the plain Norman door inside the porch of St Gregory's Minster in Kirkdale. The wording helps us to date the sundial to about 1055, when Edward the Confessor was king and Earl Tostig, brother of Harold Godwin, later King Harold, was Earl of Northumbria. Tostig was a bad egg and would later be banished from England by his brother for the murder of the Gamal mentioned in the inscription. He returned, thirsting for vengeance, in 1066, along with Harold Hardrada of Norway, but was defeated and killed at the Battle of Stamford Bridge.

St Gregory's has been much knocked about since Orm's day, but inside he would recognise the narrow tower arch and something of the chancel arch and the walling of the nave. The arcade leading to the aisle is late Norman, as is the font, protected by a Jacobean cover.

From the outside the Minster looks a bit topsy-turvy, with a very thin, unconvincing tower rebuilt in the 19th century, a square porch with wooden gates and gable, tall Saxon-style nave with Tudor windows and an oversized 13th-century chancel, made new in the 19th century. The setting, however, is splendid, the church resting in a sunlit dell with a green wall of trees as a backdrop.

And this is an ancient place. Below the church, on the other side of the stream that runs through a deep quarry behind the trees, there is a sunless, hidden cave, stumbled upon by a quarryman in 1821. Inside, along with Stone Age tools and weapons, lay the bones of animals no longer found in Britain: elephants, tigers, wolves, and there was even evidence of a hippopotamus – THE MOST NORTHERLY LOCATION OF HIPPO REMAINS EVER DISCOVERED.

Lastingham

St Mary's

Oldest Norman Crypt

ST CEDD, a monk from Lindisfarne, first came to this little wooded fold of the North Yorkshire moors in AD 654 to found a monastery as a last resting-place (Laestingua) for Ethelwald, King of Deira. A little wooden church was made and Cedd became the first abbot, a position he held until his death even while working as a missionary amongst the East Saxons (*see* page 92). In AD 664, after attending the Synod of Whitby, he returned to Lastingham where he died of the plague and was buried beside his church. His brother St Chad, who went on to become Archbishop of York, took over as abbot.

At the start of the 8th century a stone church was built on the site and Cedd's body was relocated to under the altar. No one knows what happened to this Saxon church; possibly it was sacked by the Danes, or maybe it just fell into disrepair, but in 1078 a prior from Whitby called Stephen arrived with a band of monks intending to raise a new abbey at Lastingham. He built a crypt over St Cedd's burial place and above it began a grand church, but his plans were constantly thwarted by marauding raiders, for Lastingham was a wild place, and Stephen eventually retired to the safety of York, where he founded St Mary's Abbey.

Stephen's crypt, however, remains as he left it, an entire church in miniature, THE OLDEST SURVIVING NORMAN CRYPT IN ANY PARISH CHURCH ANYWHERE IN THE WORLD and THE ONLY ONE COMPLETE WITH A NAVE, AISLES AND AN APSIDAL CHANCEL. There are fat round pillars with carved capitals holding up the vaulted roof, and the altar beneath which St Cedd is buried is made from a block of worked stone that was once a Roman incense altar.

The church above the crypt was completed for use as a parish church in 1228. The apse and chancel arch are Stephen's work, the nave and aisles 13th century, and the perpendicular tower 15th century. The spacious interior is pleasing enough, with bare stonework and a surprising uniformity.

But it is the crypt at Lastingham that is truly memorable, sprinkled with the dust of an English saint who was present at the dawn of England and who brought Christianity to the very first peoples of the English race. His shrine is today perhaps the most peaceful place to be found anywhere in the England he helped to form.

Lead

St Mary's

Rivers of Blood

It may be YORKSHIRE'S SMALLEST CHURCH, but St Mary's has experienced an awful lot of drama, the only building that was there to witness the turmoil swirling around 'the bloodiest battle ever fought on English soil', the BATTLE OF TOWTON. Today the church stands alone with its memories in the middle of a meadow, with just sheep, and possibly the bodies of men slain in battle, for company.

The date was 29 March 1461, Palm Sunday. It was snowing heavily. On the bare hillside above the church some 90,000 men, 50,000 Lancastrian followers of Henry VI and 40,000 Yorkist supporters of Edward IV, fought from dawn to dusk until the fields were drenched in blood. The Lancastrians were utterly defeated and fled, many of them running past the church or even desperately trying to find shelter within its walls. Some of the 10,000 who died that day are thought to be buried in the fields surrounding the church. Others were left to rot where they lay.

Cock Beck, the little stream that runs by the church, was said to run red with blood for days after the battle.

By then, St Mary's was already over 100 years old. In 1934 a Viking 'hog-back' gravestone was discovered beneath the church, suggesting that this was a religious site from the 9th century or earlier, while on the floor in front of the altar there are several gravestones from the 13th century, indicating that there was a church here then, probably made from timber. The graves, which are beautifully carved with heraldic signs, belong to the Tyas family, who owned the manor-house that once stood in the next-door field, and who were most likely responsible for the present stone church.

St Mary's has undergone various restorations over the centuries but is essentially unchanged since the Battle of Towton, a simple rectangular building with bellcote and doorway, with a solid wooden door. The interior is plain and un-ornamented, with some rough benches, a timber roof, a stone altar and a lovely 18th-century three-deck pulpit in the north-east corner.

By 1931 the church was almost a ruin until rescued by a group of ramblers, since when it has been known as the RAMBLERS' CHURCH.

In recognition of its role during a famous Yorkist victory, St Mary's became THE FIRST EVER RECIPIENT OF A GRANT FROM THE RICARDIAN CHURCHES RESTORATION FUND, set up

by members of the Richard III Society, who also hold a service here annually.

Patrington

St Patrick's

Queen of Holderness

St Patrick's in Patrington is regarded by many as THE MOST PERFECT VILLAGE CHURCH IN ENGLAND. Made of honey-coloured stone flecked with silver, the Queen shimmers in the pale watery light of the Humber where it bleeds into the cold North Sea. Her graceful spire, 189 feet (58 m) high, ascends in luminous beauty above the bare fields of Yorkshire's far east, serving as a landmark since it was raised in the 14th century – indeed, Captain Bligh (of the *Bounty*) used it as a reference point when he was conducting a nautical survey of the Humber in 1797.

St Patrick's is a supreme example of Decorated Gothic architecture and has a wonderful harmony of style and proportion thanks to the fact that it was built almost in its entirety in the first half of the 14th century, before the Black Death struck and brought such work to a halt. The interior of St Patrick's is light and spacious, with 30 elegant arches on clustered columns and a wealth of excellent stone carving, including foliage on the capitals and some 200 human and animal faces. An example of where the Black Death disrupted things can be found in the transepts, where the aisles of the south transept are vaulted while those of the north transept were never completed. THE POSITION OF THE LADY CHAPEL, IN THE EAST AISLE OF THE SOUTH TRANSEPT, IS UNIQUE IN ENGLAND.

There is also a rare surviving example of a stone EASTER SEPULCHRE, most having been destroyed in the Reformation or during the Civil War. An Easter Sepulchre is an arched recess normally found in the north wall, beside the altar, where the Crucifix and other sacred elements of the Easter story are placed during the Easter weekend. EASTER SEPULCHRES ARE FOUND ONLY IN ENGLAND. The one at Patrington is considered amongst the finest, with its exquisite carvings of Roman soldiers guarding the Tomb, from which Jesus is emerging flanked by angels.

From more modern times, at the base of the east window there is a fine reredos showing figures of kings and saints, installed in 1936 in memory of King George V, who was lord of the manor of Patrington.

The large tomb slab by the altar rail is probably that of ROBERT DE PATRYNGTON, master mason at York Minster from 1369, who is thought to be largely responsible for the creation of this sublime church – a remarkable

treasure to find in such a distant and unassuming village. It must once have been a prosperous market place serving the rich farmlands around it, to deserve such a monument.

Yorkshire by Numbers

Two Pews

Yorkshire is fortunate to possess TWO OF THE MOST OPULENT AND UNUSUAL FAMILY PEWS IN ENGLAND. In the north aisle of ST PETER'S, CROFT, on the River Tees, is the extraordinary MILBANKE PEW, a huge wooden edifice with red curtains that sits on Tuscan columns and is reached via a grand staircase with swirling balusters. It is thought to date from around 1680. CHARLES LUTWIDGE DODGSON's father became rector here in 1843, when the young Dodgson (later known as Lewis Carroll) was 11, and there is a crude carving of a smiling cat on the east wall of the chancel that may have inspired the Cheshire Cat from *Alice's Adventures in Wonderland*.

Inside HOLY TRINITY, WENSLEY, the 'Queen of Wensleydale', is the equally remarkable SCROPE PEW, installed by the 3rd Duke of Bolton for his wife Lavinia. She was an opera singer, and the pew is the very opera box in which the duke was sitting when he fell in love with her while watching her perform. The back of the pew is part of a carved 16th-century screen, brought here from the Scrope Chantry at Easby Abbey near Richmond after the Dissolution. It is adorned with the coat of arms of George III, while on the back is the SCROPE COAT OF ARMS,

RECKONED TO BE THE OLDEST COAT OF ARMS IN ENGLAND AFTER THAT OF THE ROYAL FAMILY.

Four Doors

North Newbald – St Nicholas. Described by some as THE MOST

COMPLETE NORMAN CHURCH IN YORKSHIRE, St Nicholas is unique in having FOUR SUPERB NORMAN DOOR-WAYS, one in each wall. Almost unchanged since it was built in 1135, the church has a massive tower resting on four mighty Norman arches and a long, lofty nave. Outside on the village green is a flat stone known as the Whipping Stone, where in 1624 a man was whipped to death in what was possibly THE LAST PUBLIC FLOGGING IN ENGLAND.

Four Fonts

Lying within 10 miles of each other in the Yorkshire Wolds are four churches that can boast FOUR OF ENGLAND'S FINEST NORMAN FONTS. The font in ST NICHOLAS, NORTH GRIMSTON, is THE ONLY FONT IN BRITAIN TO SHOW A

CARVED ILLUSTRATION OF THE DESCENT FROM THE CROSS. Resting in the tiny church of ST MARY'S, COWLAM, tucked away in a farmyard, is ONE OF ONLY TWO FONTS IN ENGLAND TO HAVE A CARVING THAT ILLUSTRATES THE MASSACRE OF THE INNOCENTS. Another

superb font can be found in ST MARY'S, KIRKBURN, which also has a UNIQUE STONE STAIRCASE at the west end, climbing steeply up two of the inside walls of the tower before turning into a spiral stair.

The fourth font is now in ST PETER'S, LANGTOFT, after being saved from the ruined church at nearby COTTAM, a deserted village ravaged by the Black Death in 1350.

Well, I never knew this about

YORKSHIRE CHURCHES

Aldborough – St Andrew's. Aldborough is a handsome village standing on the foundations of an important Roman city, Isurium Brigantum, capital of the largest tribe in Roman Britain, the Brigantes. St Andrew's Church, which sits right at the heart of the village on the site of the Roman temple to Venus, mostly dates from the 15th century but has Roman stones in its walls. In the north aisle the splendid brass of a knight with shield is of WILLIAM DE ALDEBURG, a high court judge who died in 1360. It is THE LAST KNOWN BRASS TO SHOW A SHIELD CARRIED ON THE ARM. The clock in the church tower was made in 1783 and has THE LONGEST PENDULUM IN ENGLAND, at 30 feet and 7 inches (9.32 m), which passes from the first floor, through the ringing chamber on the

ground floor and into a specially built pit, five feet (1.5 m) deep.

Bardsey – All Hallows. 'Music has charms to soothe a savage breast'. 'Heaven has no rage, like love to hatred turned / Nor Hell a fury, like a woman scorned'. These are quotes from the playwright and poet WILLIAM CONGREVE (1670–1729), who was born in Bardsey and baptised in All Hallows, a somewhat ungainly church in a beautiful hillside setting with a tall, narrow tower that is thought to be THE SECOND OLDEST SAXON CHURCH TOWER IN BRITAIN. The lower half was begun as a porch some time before AD 950, with the upper portion added later in the same century. Just down the road is the BINGLEY ARMS, mentioned in the church records of AD 905 as the Priest's Inn, possibly a rest house for craftsmen working on building the church, and a claimant for the title of ENGLAND'S OLDEST PUB.

Flamborough – St Oswald's. There is an intriguing monument in this lovely Norman church that may just be the inspiration for that delicious English dish toad-in-the-hole. It can be found in the chancel, to the left of the altar, on the tomb of 'LITTLE' SIR MARMADUKE CONSTABLE, who fought at Flodden aged 70 and died in agony in 1518 after swallowing a toad while drinking a glass of water. The toad then proceeded to make its way out of Sir Marmaduke by eating through his heart. This cautionary tale is graphically illustrated on the tomb by a sculpture showing the ribcage laid open to reveal a bulbous heart. The church also possesses ONE OF YORKSHIRE'S TWO REMAINING ROOD SCREENS COMPLETE WITH LOFT.

Garton-on-the-Wolds – St Michael's. From the outside this is every inch a medieval country church of Norman origins (1132), a massive, satisfyingly four-square tower on Norman foundations with a lovely west door of four

chevron-carved round arches and a Norman window above. Between them is a worn carving of the Archangel Michael slaying a dragon. Go in, however, through the equally delightful Norman south door of four deep arches and you enter another world, a Victorian world of vivid colours and stunning, larger-than-life murals. The walls of the nave, the splays of the windows and the roof are completely covered with colourful scenes from the Old Testament, in green, blue, red and gold. Displayed on the chancel walls are stories from the New Testament. Even the floor is picked out in mosaics of black and white and yellow. The effect is dazzling and overwhelming. The church was restored in Norman style in the 19th century by John Pearson with the interior decoration by G.E. Street, all at the behest of Sir Tatton Sykes of nearby Sledmere. It is on the Sykes Churches Trail, which takes in all the East Riding churches restored or rebuilt by the Sykes family – some 20 churches.

Lissett – St James's. During renovations in 1972 it was discovered that one of the bells hanging in the bellcote of this small church near the coast in

St Augustine's, Skirlaugh

Yorkshire's far east was dated MCCLIIII (1254). It immediately assumed the title of ENGLAND'S OLDEST DATED BELL, wresting the accolade from Lancashire's long-time champion, a bell in St Chad's, Claughton, dated 1296.

Skirlaugh – St Augustine's. Sitting quietly amongst the bungalows of this unassuming Yorkshire village is a most remarkable treasure, a stately building of pinnacles and battlements, unaltered since it was built in 1403, that has often been described as THE MOST PERFECT PERPENDICULAR PARISH CHURCH IN ENGLAND. The interior, unusually, has no chancel arch or screen to interrupt the view and is filled with natural light streaming in through huge Perpendicular windows of clear glass, six on each side and an even larger one at the east end, containing fragments of the original medieval stained glass. This glorious church was given to his home village by WALTER OF SKIRLAW, BISHOP OF DURHAM, who was responsible, amongst other fine buildings, for the central tower of York Minster.

Glossary

Ambulatory: An aisle for walking around three sides of a chancel or apse.

Anchorite: A hermit or religious recluse walled up, usually for life, in a cell attached to a chancel.

Apse: A recess, usually semi-circular, at the east end of a church. Most commonly found on Norman and occasionally Saxon churches.

Arcade: A series of arches, supported by pillars or columns normally found between nave and aisle. Blind arcades have no openings or windows and are usually used for decorative purposes.

Architectural styles:

Saxon: From the period c. AD 600 to mid 11th century. Characterised by rounded arches, triangular-headed windows and doors, lesenes (decorative vertical stone strips), long-and-short work (alternate horizontal and vertical stones at corners).

Norman: Also known as Romanesque. From the period mid 11th century to 1200. Characterised by rounded arches, heavy round pillars and massive vaulting.

Transitional: The period between Norman and Early English when round arches were changing to pointed arches.

Gothic, Early English: From period c.1200 to 1250. Characterised by pointed arches, plain lancet windows, stiff-leaf carving, Purbeck marble pillars.

Decorated: From period 1250-1350. Characterised by pointed arches, intricate window tracery, more flowing, naturalistic carvings.

Perpendicular: From post Black Death period (1350) to post Reformation (1540). Characterised by an emphasis on vertical lines, large windows, plain tracery, flattened arches, battlemented roofs and towers.

Aumbry: Small cupboard, usually on the wall of the chancel, for holding sacred vessels.

Bay: Area between two pillars of a window or an arch.

Beak-heads: Style of Norman decorative carving found on arches – heads of birds or beasts biting at the moulding on which they are carved.

Bellcote: Gabled turret, tower or framework, usually on a church roof, in which to hang a bell or bells.

Boss: Decorated projection of stone or wood, covering the point where the ribs of a vault meet.

Box pew: Wooden bench or seat in a church enclosed by wooden panels and entered by a door.

Broach spire: Spire with a square base

that tapers into an octagonal spire by means of triangular faces.

Buttress: Structure in stone or brick built against a wall as support. A flying buttress is shaped like a half arch with the buttress connected to the wall by an arm.

Canopy: Decorative cover over a feature such as an altar, statue, niche or tomb.

Capital: The top of a pillar or column, often decoratively carved (see stiff-leaf).

Chancel: Area at the east end of a church reserved for the clergy and containing the choir, altar and sanctuary.

Chantry: Medieval chapel attached to or inside a church where prayers are said for the soul of the chapel's founder.

Chevrons: Inverted 'V' shape decoration found on Norman arches.

Choir: Section of a church between the altar and the nave, occupied by the choir and clergy.

Clerestory: Upper storey of windows to give light to the nave.

Corbel: Projecting support of wood or stone, often carved with human heads, for a roof or arch. A series of corbels running around under the external eaves of a church is a corbel-table.

Cruciform: Church built in the shape of a cross.

Crypt: Underground room beneath the east end of a church, used as a chapel or burial place.

Doom: Painting of the Last Judgement found on the nave walls of medieval churches.

Effigy: Sculptured image of a person, usually lying down, on a tomb.

Foliated: Decorated with carvings of leaves.

Frieze: A length of sculpted or painted decoration.

Hatchment: Diamond-shaped plaque featuring the heraldic arms of a deceased person, hung on a church wall.

Lady Chapel: A chapel attached to or inside a church dedicated to the Virgin Mary.

Lancet: Tall, slender window with a pointed arch and no tracery found in early Gothic architecture.

Lectern: Reading desk in a church, often shaped like an eagle with spread wings, on which the Bible is placed and from which it is read during services.

Misericord: Small projection under a hinged choir stall seat on which the occupant can rest while standing. Often decorated with carving.

Mullion: Vertical divide between panes of glass in a window.

Nave: Main body of a church, between the west end and the chancel, where the congregation sits, excluding aisles.

Parclose screen: Separates a chapel from the rest of the church.

Parvise: Room above a porch, usually for a priest.

Pier: Pillar or column dividing the nave or chancel from the aisles.

Piscina: Basin for washing Communion vessels, usually found in recess in the wall of the chancel.

Poppy-head: Carved bench end (not necessarily carved with poppies, often with heads, animals, birds, religious symbols).

Pulpit: Enclosed rostrum or stand from where the sermon is delivered. The sides of the pulpit are often carved or painted.

Pyx: Container in which the consecrated Communion bread is kept.

Quire: Alternative spelling for choir.

Reredos: Screen behind the altar.

Rood: Carved figure of Jesus on the Cross flanked by the Virgin Mary and St John, once found above the 'rood screen' between the nave and chancel. Most were destroyed at the Reformation.

Rope-work carving: Stone carving designed to look like a rope.

Sedilia: Recessed seats for the clergy found in the south wall of the chancel. Normally a group of three.

Sanctuary: The section of the chancel that contains the altar, distinct from the choir.

Squint: Opening cut through an internal wall enabling priests at side altars to see the main altar in the sanctuary.

Stiff-leaf: Carvings of foliage, usually found on a capital.

String course: Projecting band of brickwork or stone running around a building.

Tester: Flat canopy above a pulpit. Also known as a sounding board.

Tracery: Stone ribs decorating the upper part of a window used in Gothic architecture.

Transept: The north and south arms of a cruciform church.

Tympanum: Triangular or semicircular panel above a doorway and below its arch. Often carved.

Vault: Stone roof. Can be barrel or tunnel vault (semicircular). Vault ribs are projecting bands of stone that can be structural or purely decorative. In fan vaulting the ribs form a fan shape. In lierne vaulting, otherwise known as stellar vaulting, some of the ribs (the lierne ribs) cross other ribs without touching the main piers and form a stellar shape.

Zigzag: 'Z' shape decoration of a Norman arch.

Gazetteer

Most of the churches featured are open during daylight hours or provide information on-site as to where a key may be collected.

I have provided post codes for those with satnav and Ordnance Survey Landranger map references for those who prefer to map-read.

P = Parish church or owned and run by the parish as a chapel or other place of worship. For further information see www.achurchnearyou.com

CCT = Churches Conservation Trust. For further information see www.visitchurches.org.uk

EH = English Heritage. For further information see www.english-heritage.org.uk

BEDFORDSHIRE

CARDINGTON –
ST MARY THE VIRGIN P

324 Church Lane, Cardington,
Bedfordshire MK44 3SR
OS: TL 088 478

COCKAYNE HATLEY –
ST JOHN THE BAPTIST P

Cockayne Hatley, Bedfordshire
SG19 2EA
OS: TL 260 496

ELSTOW – ABBEY CHURCH OF
ST MARY & ST HELENA P

6 Abbey Close Elstow, Bedfordshire
MK42 9XX
OS: TL 048 474

BLETSOE – ST MARY THE VIRGIN P

64 The Avenue, Bletsoe, Bedfordshire
MK44 1QQ
OS: TL 023 583

FELMERSHAM – ST MARY'S P

Church End, Felmersham,
Bedfordshire MK43 7JP
OS: SP 991 578

NORTHILL – ST MARY'S P

Bedford Road, Northill, Bedfordshire
SG18 9AA
OS: TL 149 465

BERKSHIRE

ALDWORTH – ST MARY'S P

Bell Lane, Aldworth, Berkshire
RG8 9SB
OS: SU 554 794

AVINGTON – ST MARK & ST LUKE

(Privately owned – keyholder
    lives nearby)
Avington Road, Avington,
    Berkshire RG17 0UL
    OS: SU 372 679

LOWER BASILDON – ST
BARTHOLOMEW'S CCT

Lower Basildon, Berkshire RG8 9NH
    OS: SU 612 791

APPLEFORD –
ST PETER & ST PAUL P

Church Street, Appleford,
    Oxfordshire OX14 4QE
    OS: SU 530 937

BOXFORD – ST ANDREW'S P

Winterbourne Road, Boxford,
    Berkshire RG20 8DP
    OS: SU 428 715

BUCKLEBURY – ST MARY'S P

Bucklebury, Berkshire RG7 6PL
    OS: SU 553 708

BUCKINGHAMSHIRE

HILLESDEN – ALL SAINTS P

Church End, Hillesden,
    Buckinghamshire MK18 4DB
    OS: SP 685 286

STOKE POGES – ST GILES' P

Church Lane, Stoke Poges,
    Buckinghamshire SL2 4NZ
    OS: SU 975 827

WING – ALL SAINTS P

Church Street, Wing,
    Buckinghamshire LU7 0NX
    OS: SP884233

CLIFTON REYNES –
ST MARY THE VIRGIN P

Church Lane, Clifton Reynes,
    Buckinghamshire MK46 5DT
    OS: SP 901 513

FINGEST – ST BARTHOLOMEW'S P

Fingest, Buckinghamshire RG9 6QE
    OS: SU 777 912

WEST WYCOMBE –
ST LAWRENCE'S P

West Wycombe Hill, West Wycombe,
    Buckinghamshire HP14 3AP
    OS: SU 826 947

CAMBRIDGESHIRE

BARTON – ST PETER'S P

School Lane, Barton, Cambridgeshire
    CB23 7BD
    OS: TL 407 557

ICKLETON –
ST MARY MAGDALENE P

Church Street, Ickleton,
    Cambridgeshire CB10 1SR
    OS: TL 494 438

SWAFFHAM PRIOR –
ST MARY'S P, ST CYRIAC &
ST JULITTA CCT

High Street, Swaffham Prior,
    Cambridgeshire CB5 0LD
    OS: TL 568 638

WESTLEY WATERLESS –
ST MARY THE LESS P

Church Lane, Westley Waterless,
Cambridgeshire CB8 0RL
OS: TL 617 562

GUYHIRN CHAPEL CCT

High Road, Guyhirn,
Cambridgeshire PE13 4EF
OS: TF 402 040

ISLEHAM PRIORY CHURCH EH

Church Street (B1104), Isleham,
Cambridgeshire CB7 5RX
OS: TL 642 743

WILLINGHAM – ST MARY &
ALL SAINTS P

Church Street, Willingham,
Cambridgeshire CB4 5HS
OS: TL 404 705

CHESHIRE

ASTBURY – ST MARY'S P

Astbury Village, Astbury, Cheshire
CW12 4RQ
OS: SJ 846 615

DARESBURY – ALL SAINTS P

Daresbury Lane, Daresbury, Cheshire
WA4 4AE
OS: SJ 580 828

MOBBERLEY – ST WILFRID'S P

Church Lane, Mobberley, Cheshire
WA16 7RD
OS: SJ 790 801

LOWER PEOVER – ST OSWALD'S P

Barrow's Brow, Lower Peover,
Cheshire WA16 9PZ
OS: SJ 743 741

MARTON – ST JAMES & ST PAUL P

Congleton Road, Marton, Cheshire
East SK11 9HE
OS: SJ 850 679

ACTON – ST MARY'S

Monk's Lane, Acton, Cheshire
CW5 8LE
OS: SJ 631 531

BUNBURY – ST BONIFACE P

Wyche Road, Bunbury, Cheshire East
CW6 9PH
OS: SJ 569 580

GAWSWORTH – ST JAMES'S P

Church Lane, Gawsworth, Cheshire
East SK11 9RJ
OS: SJ 890 696

MELLOR – ST THOMAS'S P

Church Road Mellor, Stockport,
Greater Manchester SK6 5LX
OS: SJ 982 889

CORNWALL

LANDEWEDNACK –
ST WINWALOE'S P

Church Cove Road, Landewednack,
Cornwall TR12 7PH
OS: SW 711 126

LAUNCELLS – ST SWITHIN'S P

Launcells, Cornwall EX23 9NQ
OS: SS 243 057

MORWENSTOW –
ST MORWENNA'S P

Morwenstow, Cornwall EX23 9SR
OS: SS 205 153

TREBETHERICK – ST ENODOC'S P

Access via St Enodoc Golf Club
above Daymer Bay, Trebetherick,
Cornwall PL27 6SA
OS: SW 932 773

ST ENDELLION –
ST ENDELIENTA'S P

B3314, St Endellion, Cornwall PL29 3TP
OS: SW 997 786

ST JUST IN ROSELAND –
ST JUST & ST MAWES P

St Just Roseland, Cornwall TR2 5JD
OS: SW 848 356

ZENNOR – ST SENARA'S P

B3306, Zennor, Cornwall TR26 3BY
OS: SW 454 385

CUMBRIA

BARTON – ST MICHAEL'S P

B5320, Barton, Cumbria CA10 2LR
OS: NY 487 263

BROUGHAM –
ST NINIAN'S, NINEKIRKS CCT

Brougham, Cumbria CA10 2AD
OS: NY 559 299

BURGH BY SANDS –
ST MICHAEL'S P

Ludgate Hill, Burgh by Sands,
Cumbria CA5 6BQ
OS: NY 328 591

CARTMEL – PRIORY CHURCH OF
ST MARY & ST MICHAEL P

Cartmel, Cumbria LA11 6QD
OS: SD 379 787

ST BEES – PRIORY CHURCH OF
ST MARY & ST BEGA P

B5345, St Bees, Cumbria CA27 0DS
OS: NX 968 121

BASSENTHWAITE – ST BEGA'S P

Bassenthwaite, Cumbria CA12 4QE
NY 226 287

WASDALE HEAD – ST OLAF'S P

Nether Wasdale, Cumbria CA20 1EX
OS: NY 188 086

ALDINGHAM – ST CUTHBERT'S P

Coast Road, Aldingham, Cumbria
LA12 9RT
OS: SD 283 710

BOLTON – ALL SAINTS P

Edenfold, Bolton, Cumbria
CA16 6AL
OS: NY 639 234

BOLTONGATE – ALL SAINTS P

B5299 Boltongate, Cumbria
CA7 1DA
OS: NY 229 408

BRAMPTON – ST MARTIN'S P

Front Street, Brampton, Cumbria
CA8 1NU
OS: NY 528 610

BRIDEKIRK – ST BRIDGET'S P

Bridekirk, Cumbria CA13 0NY
OS: NY 116 336

WARWICK ON EDEN –
ST LEONARD'S P

Warwick on Eden, Cumbria
CA4 8PG
OS: NY 466 569

DERBYSHIRE

ASHOVER – ALL SAINTS P

Church Street, Ashover, Derbyshire
S45 0AB
OS: SK 348 631

HATHERSAGE – ST MICHAEL'S P

Church Bank, Hathersage, Derbyshire
S32 1AJ
OS: SK 233 818

REPTON – ST WYSTAN'S P

Willington Road, Repton, Derbyshire
DE65 6FH
OS: SK 303 271

YOULGREAVE – ALL SAINTS P

Mawstone Lane, Youlgreave,
Derbyshire DE45 1WN
OS: SK 212 643

DALE ABBEY – ALL SAINTS P

The Village, Dale Abbey, Derbyshire
DE7 4PN
OS: SK 437 385

DETHICK – ST JOHN THE
BAPTIST P

Mill Lane, Holloway, Derbyshire
DE4 5GG
OS: SK 327 579

FOREMARK – ST SAVIOUR'S P

Foremark, Derbyshire DE65 6EJ
OS: SK 329 264

NORBURY – ST MARY &
ST BARLOCK P

Norbury Hollow, Norbury,
Derbyshire DE6 2ED
OS: SK 125 423

TIDESWELL – ST JOHN
THE BAPTIST P

Commercial Road, Tideswell,
Derbyshire SK17 8NU
OS: SK 152 757

DEVON

BRENTOR – ST MICHAEL'S P

Brentor, Devon PL19 0NP
OS: SX 470 804

SHEEPSTOR – ST LEONARD'S P

Portland Lane, Sheepstor, Devon
PL20 6PF
OS: SX 560 676

STAVERTON – ST PAUL DE LEON P

11 Woodland Close, Staverton, Devon
    TQ9 6PG
    OS: SX 793 639

TORBRYAN – HOLY TRINITY CCT

Torbryan Hill, Torbryan, Newton
    Abbot, Devon TQ12 5UR
    OS: SX 820 669

WIDECOMBE IN THE MOOR –
ST PANCRAS P

B3387, Widecombe in the Moor,
    Devon TQ13 7TA
    OS: SX 718 767

HARTLAND – ST NECTAN'S P

Hartland, Devon EX39 6DU
    OS: SS 235 247

MOLLAND – ST MARY'S P

Molland, Devon EX36 3NG
    OS: SS 807 283

PARRACOMBE – ST PETROCK'S CCT

Church Lane, Parracombe, Devon
    EX31 4PE
    OS: SS 674 449

SWIMBRIDGE – ST JAMES'S P

Church Lane, Swimbridge, Devon
    EX32 OPR
    OS: SS 620 299

DORSET

BERE REGIS –
ST JOHN THE BAPTIST P

Church Lane, Bere Regis, Dorset
    BH20 7HA
    OS: SY 847 947

STINSFORD – ST MICHAEL'S P

Church Lane, Stinsford, Dorset
    DT2 8PT
    OS: SY 714 915

STUDLAND – ST NICHOLAS P

Church Road, Studland, Dorset
    BH19 3AR
    OS: SZ 036 825

WINTERBORNE TOMSON –
ST ANDREW'S CCT

Marsh Lane, Winterborne Tomson,
    Dorset DT11 9HA
    OS: SY 883 973

WORTH MATRAVERS –
ST NICHOLAS OF MYRA P

Pikes Lane, Worth Matravers, Dorset
    BH19 3LQ
    OS: SY 972 774

WORTH MATRAVERS –
ST ALDHELM'S (PARISH CHAPEL)

Worth Matravers, Dorset BH19 3LR
    OS: SY 960 755

MORETON – ST NICHOLAS P

Moreton Drive, Moreton, Dorset
    DT2 8RJ
    OS: SY 805 892

OSMINGTON – ST OSMUND'S P

Church Lane, Osmington, Dorset
 DT3 6EJ
 OS: SY 724 829

WIMBORNE ST GILES – ST GILES' P

Park Lane, Wimborne St Giles,
 Dorset BH21 5LZ
 OS: SU 031 119

DURHAM

BOWES – ST GILES' P

Back Lane, Bowes, Durham
 DL12 9LG
 OS: NY 992 135

DALTON-LE-DALE – ST ANDREW'S P

B1285, Dalton-le-Dale, Durham
 SR7 8QA
 OS: NZ 407 480

ESCOMB – ST JOHN'S P

Escomb, Durham DL14 7SY
 OS: NZ 188 300

SEAHAM – ST MARY THE VIRGIN P

B1287, Seaham, Durham SR7 7AD
 OS: NZ 422 505

HART – ST MARY MAGDALENE P

6 Clevecoat Walk, Hart, Hartlepool
 TS27 3BU
 OS: NZ 470 351

HIGH CONISCLIFFE – ST EDWIN'S P

A67, High Coniscliffe, Darlington
 DL2 2LJ
 OS: NZ 226 153

KELLOE – ST HELEN'S P

Kelloe, Durham DH6 4PT
 OS: NZ 345 365

NORTON-ON-TEES –
ST MARY THE VIRGIN P

A1027, Stockton-on-Tees TS20 1EJ
 OS: NZ 442 221

WINSTON – ST ANDREW'S P

6 Church Mews, Winston, Durham
 DL2 3RL
 OS: NZ 143 168

ESSEX

BRADWELL ON SEA – ST PETER'S
ON THE WALL (PARISH CHAPEL)

Eastend Road, Bradwell-on-Sea, Essex
 CM0 7PW
 OS: TM 031 081

DANBURY – ST JOHN THE BAPTIST P

53 Main Road, Danbury, Essex
 CM3 4DJ
 OS: TL 779 051

GREENSTED-JUXTA-ONGAR –
ST ANDREW'S P

Church Lane, Greensted, Essex
 CM5 9LD
 OS: TL 538 030

HADSTOCK – ST BOTOLPH'S P

Hadstock, Essex CB21 4NX
 OS: TL 558 447

LANGFORD – ST GILES' P

Witham Road, Langford, Essex
    CM9 6QA
    OS: Tl 837 090

LITTLE MAPLESTEAD –
ST JOHN THE BAPTIST P

Little Maplestead, Essex CO9 2SL
    OS: Tl 822 339

NEWPORT – ST MARY THE VIRGIN P

    Church Street, Newport, Essex
    CB11 3RS
    OS: TL 520 341

TOLLESHUNT D'ARCY –
ST NICHOLAS P

Church Street, Tolleshunt D'Arcy,
    Essex CM9 8TS
    OS: TL 928 117

GLOUCESTERSHIRE

COBERLEY – ST GILES' P

Coberley, Gloucestershire GL53 9RA
    OS: SO 965 158

COWLEY – ST MARY'S P

Cowley, Gloucestershire GL53 9NL
    OS: SO 965 146

DEERHURST – ST MARY'S P

Deerhurst, Gloucestershire GL19 4BX
    OS: SO 870 299

DEERHURST – ODDA'S CHAPEL EH

Deerhurst, Gloucestershire GL19 4BX
    OS: SO 869 298

KEMPLEY – ST MARY'S EH

Kempley, Gloucestershire GL18 2AT
    OS: SO 669 312

DUNTISBOURNE ROUSE –
ST MICHAEL'S P

Duntisbourne Rouse, Gloucestershire
    GL7 7AP
    OS: SO 985 060

ELKSTONE – ST JOHN'S P

    Elkstone, Gloucestershire GL53 9PD
    OS: SO 967 122

SELSLEY – ALL SAINTS P

Selsley, Gloucestershire GL5 5LG
    OS: SO 829 037

HAMPSHIRE

BREAMORE – ST MARY'S P

Breamore, Hampshire SP6 2DF
    OS: SU 152 190

EAST MEON – ALL SAINTS P

Church Street, East Meon,
    Hampshire GU32 1NJ
    OS: SU 680 222

HAYLING ISLAND – ST MARY'S P

34 Church Road, Hayling Island,
    Hampshire PO11 0NT
    OS: SZ 723 001

HAYLING ISLAND – ST PETER'S P

St Peter's Road, North Hayling,
    Hampshire PO11 0RT
    OS: SZ 731 032

NATELY SCURES – ST SWITHUN'S P

Blackstocks Lane, Nately Scures,
  Hampshire RG27 9PH
  OS: SU 696 530

CORHAMPTON CHURCH P

Warnford Road, Corhampton,
  Hampshire SO32 3ND
  OS: SU 610 203

ITCHEN STOKE – ST MARY'S P

B3047, Itchen Stoke, Hampshire
  SO24 0QZ
  OS: SU 559 324

SELBORNE – ST MARY'S P

B3006, Selborne, Hampshire
  GU34 3JH
  OS: SU 741 337

HEREFORDSHIRE

BACTON – ST FAITH'S P

Bacton, Herefordshire HR2 0AR
  OS: SO 370 323

EATON BISHOP – ST MICHAEL &
ALL ANGELS P

Rectory Meadow, Eaton Bishop,
  Herefordshire HR2 9QJ
  OS: SO 443 391

KILPECK – ST MARY & ST DAVID P

Castle Park, Kilpeck, Herefordshire
  HR2 9DN
  OS: SO 445 305

LEINTWARDINE –
ST MARY MAGDALENE P

1 Church Street, Leintwardine,
  Herefordshire SY7 0LB
  OS: SO 404 740

WHITBOURNE –
ST JOHN THE BAPTIST P

Whitbourne, Herefordshire WR6 5RS
  OS: SO 725 569

CLIFFORD – ST MARY THE VIRGIN P

The Priory, Clifford, Herefordshire
  HR3 5EY
  OS: SO 251 450

SHOBDON – ST JOHN THE
EVANGELIST P

Shobdon, Herefordshire HR6 9NA
  OS: SO 401 628

STOKE LACY – ST PETER &
ST PAUL P

A465, Stoke Lacy, Herefordshire
  HR7 4HH
  OS: SO 620 494

HERTFORDSHIRE

FURNEUX PELHAM – ST MARY'S P

The Street, Furneux Pelham,
  Hertfordshire SG9 0LD
  OS: TL 431 279

KING'S LANGLEY – ALL SAINTS P

Church Lane, King's Langley,
  Hertfordshire WD4 8JP
  OS: TL 073 024

OLD HATFIELD –
ST ETHELDREDA'S P

Fore Street, Hatfield, Hertfordshire
AL9 5LP
OS: TL 235 084

ST PAUL'S WALDEN –
ALL SAINTS P

B651, St Paul's Walden, Hertfordshire
SG4 8BP
OS: TL 192 222

ESSENDON – ST MARY
THE VIRGIN P

West End Lane, Essendon,
Hertfordshire AL9 6HX
OS: Tl 273 087

LITTLE HORMEAD –
ST MARY'S CCT

Worsted Lane, Hormead,
Hertfordshire SG9 0LS
OS: TL 398 291

SHENLEYBURY –
ST BOTOLPH'S (PRIVATE)

Shenleybury, Shenley, Hertfordshire
WD7 9DL
OS: TL 183 018

WIDFORD –
ST JOHN THE BAPTIST P

B1004, Widford, Hertfordshire
SG12 8RL
OS: TL 413 157

HUNTINGDONSHIRE

BARNACK – ST JOHN THE BAPTIST P

Main Street, Barnack,
Huntingdonshire PE9 3DN
OS: TF 079 050

FENSTANTON – ST PETER &
ST PAUL P

Hampton Close, Fenstanton,
Huntingdonshire PE28 9JW
OS: TL 320 687

KIMBOLTON – ST ANDREW'S P

1 St Andrews Lane, Kimbolton,
Huntingdonshire PE28 0HB
OS: TL 099 678

LITTLE GIDDING –
ST JOHN THE EVANGELIST P

Little Gidding, Huntingdonshire
PE28 5RJ
OS: TL 127 816

ALWALTON – ST ANDREW'S P

Church Street, Alwalton,
Huntingdonshire PE7 3UU
OS: TL 133 959

CASTOR – ST KYNEBURGHA'S P

18 Church Hill, Castor,
Huntingdonshire PE5 7AX
OS: TL 124 985

GREAT PAXTON – HOLY TRINITY P

Church Lane, Great Paxton,
Huntingdonshire PE19 6RJ
OS: TL 209 641

KENT

Barfreston – St Nicholas P

Barfreston, Kent CT15 7JQ
    OS: TR 261 501

Brabourne – St Mary's P

The Street, Brabourne, Kent
    TN25 5LR
    OS: TR 103 416

Brookland – St Augustine's P

High Street, Brookland, Kent
    TN29 9QR
    OS: TQ 989 258

Cobham – St Mary Magdalene P

The Street, Cobham, Kent DA12 3BX
    OS: TQ 669 683

Tudeley – All Saints P

Tudeley, Kent TN11 0NZ
    OS: TO 622 454

Capel-le-Ferne – St Mary's CCT

Capel-le-Ferne, Kent CT18 7EX
    OS: TR 257 400

Chilham – St Mary's P

Church Hill, Chilham, Kent
    CT4 8DA
    OS: TR 068 536

Mereworth – St Lawrence's P

The Street, Mereworth, Kent
    ME18 5LU
    OS: TQ 660 537

LANCASHIRE

Heysham – St Peter's P

Main Street, Heysham, Lancashire
    LA3 2RN
    OS: SD 410 616

Ribchester – St Wilfrid's P

Church Street, Ribchester, Lancashire
    PR3 3YE
    OS: SD 649 350

Stydd – St Saviour's (Parish chapel)

Stydd, Lancashire PR3 3YQ
    OS: SD 653 359

Sefton – St Helen's P

Bridges Lane, Sefton L29 7WG
    OS: SD 356 012

Tunstall – St John the Baptist P

Church Lane, Tunstall, Lancashire
    LA6 2RQ
    OS: SD 614 739

Bleasdale – St Eadmer's P

Bleasdale, Lancashire PR3 1UZ
    OS: SD 573 455

Claughton – St Chad's P

A683, Claughton, Lancashire
    LA2 9LA
    OS: SD 566 665

Langho – Old Church of St Leonard CCT

Old Langho Road, Old Langho,
    Lancashire BB6 8AW
    OS: SD 701 357

PILLING – OLD ST JOHN THE
BAPTIST'S CHURCH CCT

Pilling, Lancashire PR3 6AA
   OS: SD 404 487

RIVINGTON CHURCH P

Horrobin Lane, Rivington, Lancashire
   BL6 7SE
   OS: SD 624 144

LEICESTERSHIRE

BOTTESFORD – ST MARY'S P

Church Lane, Bottesford,
   Leicestershire NG13 0DA
   OS: SK 807 391

BURTON LAZARS – ST JAMES'S P

Burton Lazars, Leicestershire
   LE14 2UH
   OS: SK 767 169

GADDESBY – ST LUKE'S P

Church Lane, Gaddesby,
   Leicestershire LE7 4WG
   OS: SK 689 130

TWYCROSS – ST JAMES'S P

16 Church Street, Twycross,
   Leicestershire CV9 3RN
   OS: SK 338 049

BREEDON ON THE HILL –
ST MARY & ST HARDULPH P

Main Street, Breedon on the Hill,
   Leicestershire DE73 8HF
   OS: SK 405 233

QUORN – ST BARTHOLOMEW'S P

Church Lane, Quorn, Leicestershire
   LE12 8DP
   OS: SK 561 165

STAUNTON HAROLD –
HOLY TRINITY P

Staunton Harold, Leicestershire
   LE65 1RT
   OS: SK 379 208

LINCOLNSHIRE

NORTON DISNEY – ST PETER'S P

Church Lane, Norton Disney,
   Lincolnshire LN6 9JX
   OS: SK 889 589

KINGERBY – ST PETER'S P

Kingerby, Lincolnshire LN8 3PF
   OS: TF 057 928

SEMPRINGHAM – ST ANDREW'S P

Pointon Road, Sempringham,
   Lincolnshire NG34 0LU
   OS: TF 106 328

STOW – MINSTER CHURCH OF
ST MARY P

Church Road, Stow, Lincolnshire
   LN1 2DE
   OS: SK 881 819

CONINGSBY – ST MICHAEL'S P

A153, Coningsby, Lincolnshire
   LN4 4RF
   OS: TF 222 580

HECKINGTON – ST ANDREW'S P

St Andrew's Street, Heckington,
    Lincolnshire NG34 9RF
    OS: TF 142 441

HOUGH ON THE HILL –
ALL SAINTS P

High Road, Hough on the Hill,
    Lincolnshire NG32 2AZ
    OS: SK 923 464

SCOPWICK – CHURCH OF
THE HOLY CROSS P

B1191, Scopwick, Lincolnshire
    LN4 3NR
    OS: TF 069 580

NORFOLK

BINHAM PRIORY EH

Warham Road, Binham, Norfolk
    NR21 ODQ
    OS: TF 980 399

HOUGHTON ON THE HILL –
ST MARY'S P

North Pickenham, Norfolk
    PE 37 8LJ
    OS: TF 868 053

LITTLE SNORING – ST ANDREW'S P

Little Snoring, Norfolk NR21 OHT
    OS: TF 952 325

WEST WALTON –
ST MARY THE VIRGIN P

Mill Road, West Walton, Norfolk
    PE14 7ET
    OS: TF 471 133

BLAKENEY – ST NICHOLAS P

Blakeney, Norfolk NR25 7NW
    OS: TG 033 435

BOOTON – ST MICHAEL &
ALL ANGELS CCT

Booton, Norfolk NR10 4NT
    OS: TG 122 223

EAST LEXHAM – ST ANDREW'S P

Lexham, Norfolk PE32 2QJ
    OS: TF 859 171

GUNTON – ST ANDREW'S CCT

Gunton Hall, Cromer, Norfolk
    NR11 7HJ
    OS: TG 227 342

NORTHAMPTONSHIRE

BRIXWORTH – ALL SAINTS P

Church Street, Brixworth,
    Northamptonshire NN6 9DB
    OS: SP 747 712

EARL'S BARTON – ALL SAINTS P

B573, Earl's Barton,
    Northamptonshire NN6 ONA
    OS: SP 851 638

FOTHERINGHAY – ST MARY &
ALL SAINTS P

Fotheringhay, Northamptonshire
    PE8 5HZ
    OS: Tl 059 931

GRAFTON REGIS – ST MARY
THE VIRGIN P

Bozenham Mill Lane, Grafton Regis,
Northamptonshire NN12 7SS
OS: SP 758 469

GREAT BRINGTON – ST MARY
THE VIRGIN P

59 Main Street, Brington,
Northamptonshire NN7 4JB
OS: SP 667 652

BRIGSTOCK – ST ANDREW'S P

12 Church Street, Brigstock,
Northamptonshire NN14 3EX
OS: SP 946 852

KING'S SUTTON – ST PETER &
ST PAUL P

Church Avenue, King's Sutton,
Northamptonshire OX17 3RF
OS: SP 497 361

WOODNEWTON – ST MARY'S P

Main Street, Woodnewton,
Northamptonshire PE8 5EB
OS: TL 032 945

NORTHUMBERLAND

BAMBURGH – ST AIDAN'S P

B1342, Bamburgh, Northumberland
NE69 7AB
OS: NU 178 349

BELLINGHAM – ST CUTHBERT'S P

Westland, Bellingham,
Northumberland NE48 2HE
OS: NY 837 832

BOLAM – ST ANDREW'S P

Bolam, Northumberland NE61 3UX
OS: NZ 095 825

BRANXTON – ST PAUL'S P

Branxton, Northumberland
TD12 4SW
OS: NT 892 374

BYWELL – ST ANDREW'S CCT
AND ST PETER'S P

Bywell, Northumberland NE43 7AE
OS: NZ 048 614

KIRKNEWTON – ST GREGORY'S P

B6351, Kirknewton, Northumberland
NE71 6XQ
OS: NT 913 302

NORHAM – ST CUTHBERT'S P

Church Lane, Norham,
Northumberland TD15 2LF
OS: NT 896 474

CHILLINGHAM – ST PETER'S P

Chillingham, Northumberland
NE66 5NJ
OS: NU 062 259

OVINGHAM – ST MARY'S P

Castle View, Ovingham,
Northumberland NE42 6BW
OS: NZ 084 637

WARKWORTH – ST LAWRENCE'S P

Dial Place, Warkworth,
Northumberland NE65 0UR
OS: NU 246 061

NOTTINGHAMSHIRE

BLYTH – ST MARY & ST MARTIN P

1 Priory Close, Blyth,
 Nottinghamshire S81 8HF
 OS: SK 624 872

CLUMBER – ST MARY'S NT

Clumber Park, Worksop,
 Nottinghamshire S80 3AZ
 OS: SK 626 746

EDWINSTOWE – ST MARY'S P

B6034, Edwinstowe, Nottinghamshire
 NG21 9QA
 OS: SK 625 669

BABWORTH – ALL SAINTS P

Babworth, Nottinghamshire DN22 8ES
 OS: SK 686 808

SCROOBY – ST WILFRID'S P

Church Lane, Scrooby,
 Nottinghamshire DN10 6AR
 OS: SK 652 907

EAST LEAKE – ST MARY'S P

1 Station Road, East Leake,
 Nottinghamshire LE12 6LW
 OS: SK 551 262

ELSTON CHAPEL CCT

Old Chapel Lane, Elston,
 Nottinghamshire NG23 5NY
 OS: SK 761 482

ELSTON ALL SAINTS P

Top Street, Elston, Nottinghamshire
 NG23 5NP
 OS: SK 758 479

HAWTON – ALL SAINTS P

Hawton, Nottinghamshire NG24 3RP
 OS: SK 788 511

KINGSTON ON SOAR – ST WILFRID'S P

The Green, Kingston on Soar,
 Nottinghamshire NG11 0DA
 OS: SK 501 277

LITTLEBOROUGH – ST NICHOLAS CCT

Littleborough, Nottinghamshire
 DN22 0HD
 OS: SK 824 825

OXFORDSHIRE

DORCHESTER – ABBEY OF ST PETER & ST PAUL P

Henley Road, Dorchester,
 Oxfordshire OX10 7HN
 OS: SU 579 941

EWELME – ST MARY P

Parson's Lane, Ewelme, Oxfordshire
 OX10 6HP
 OS: SU 646 914

IFFLEY – ST MARY THE VIRGIN P

Church Way, Iffley, Oxfordshire
 OX4 4EJ
 OS: SP 526 036

BRIGHTWELL BALDWIN – ST BARTHOLOMEW'S

Cadwell Lane, Brightwell Baldwin,
 Oxfordshire OX49 5PG
 OS: SU 653 950

CAVERSFIELD – ST LAWRENCE'S P

B4100, Caversfield, Oxfordshire
OX27 8TQ
OS: SP 580 252

CLIFTON HAMPDEN –
ST MICHAEL & ALL ANGELS P

High Street, Clifton Hampden,
Oxfordshire OX14 3EQ
OS: SU 547 955

KIDLINGTON – ST MARY
THE VIRGIN P

Church Street, Kidlington,
Oxfordshire OX5 2BB
OS: SP 497 148

RUTLAND

NORMANTON –
ST MATTHEW'S (MUSEUM ACCESS)

Rutland Water, Rutland LE15 8RP
OS: SK 932 062

STOKE DRY – ST ANDREW'S P

Main Street, Stoke Dry, Rutland
LE15 9JG
OS: SP 855 967

TEIGH – HOLY TRINITY P

Teigh, Rutland LE15 7RT
OS: SK 864 160

TICKENCOTE – ST PETER'S P

Tickencote, Rutland PE9 4AE
OS: SK 990 094

ASHWELL – ST MARY'S P

Ashwell, Rutland LE15 7LJ
OS: SK 865 137

BURLEY – HOLY CROSS CCT

Church Road, Burley, Rutland
LE15 7FP
OS: SK 883 102

MARKET OVERTON –
ST PETER & ST PAUL P

Church Lane, Market Overton,
Rutland LE15 7PR
OS: SK 885 164

SHROPSHIRE

HEATH CHAPEL (PARISH CHAPEL)

Heath, Shropshire SY7 9DS
OS: SO 557 856

PITCHFORD – ST MICHAEL'S P

Pitchford, Shropshire SY5 7DP
OS: SJ 527 042

TONG – ST BARTHOLOMEW'S P

Newport Road, Tong, Shropshire
TF11 8PW
OS: SJ 795 073

MELVERLEY – ST PETER'S P

Church Lane, Melverley, Shropshire
SY10 8PJ
OS: SJ 332 165

HALSTON HALL CHAPEL (PRIVATE
CHAPEL – ACCESS FROM HALL)

Ellesmere Road, Halston, nr.
Whittington, Shropshire SY11 4NS
OS: SJ 338 312

LLANYBLODWEL –
ST MICHAEL THE ARCHANGEL P

Llanyblodwell, Shropshire SY10 8NQ
OS: SJ 239 228

CARDESTON – ST MICHAEL'S P

B4393, Cardeston, Shropshire
SY5 9AH
OS: SJ 358 144

HODNET – ST LUKE'S P

7 Church Street, Hodnet, Shropshire
TF9 3NL
OS: SJ 612 286

ASTON EYRE (PARISH CHAPEL)

B4368, Aston Eyre, Shropshire
WV16 6XD
OS: SO 653 940

ATCHAM – ST EATA'S P

Malthouse Lane, Atcham, Shropshire
SY5 6QH
OS: SJ 540 091

BARROW – ST GILES' P

B4376, Barrow, Shropshire TF12 5BW
OS: SO 657 999

CLAVERLEY – ALL SAINTS P

Church Street, Claverley, Shropshire
WV5 7BY
OS: SO 792 934

MINSTERLEY – HOLY TRINITY P

B4387, Minsterley, Shropshire
SY5 0BE
OS: SJ 373 050

SOMERSET

COMPTON MARTIN –
ST MICHAEL'S P

The Batch, Compton Martin,
Somerset BS40 6JQ
OS: ST 545 570

CULBONE – ST BEUNO'S P

Porlock, nr Minehead, Culbone,
Somerset TA24
OS: SS 844 485

EAST COKER – ST MICHAEL'S P

East Coker, Somerset BA22 9JG
OS: ST 538 121

MELLS – ST ANDREW'S P

6 New Street, Mells, Somerset
BA11 3PW
OS: ST 727 492

ORCHARDLEIGH – ST MARY'S P
(ACCESS FROM PUBLIC FOOTPATH)

Orchardleigh, Somerset
BA11 2PH
OS: ST 773 509

CHEWTON MENDIP –
ST MARY MAGDALENE P

Church Lane, Chewton Mendip,
Somerset BA3 4GP
OS: ST 596 531

OARE – ST MARY'S P

New Road, Oare, Somerset
EX35 6NU
OS: SS 802 473

STOKE ST GREGORY –
ST GREGORY'S P

Huntham Lane, Stoke St Gregory,
 Somerset TA3 6HA
 OS: ST 348 271

WEARE – ST GREGORY'S P

Sparrow Hill Way, Weare, Somerset
 BS26 2LA
 OS: ST 414 526

STAFFORDSHIRE

ALSTONEFIELD – ST PETER'S P

Church Street, Alstonefield,
 Staffordshire DE6 2FX
 OS: SK 132 553

CLIFTON CAMPVILLE –
ST ANDREW'S P

Church Street, Clifton Campville,
 Staffordshire B79 0AR
 OS: SK 252 107

INGESTRE – ST MARY THE VIRGIN P

Ingestre, Staffordshire ST18 0RF
 OS: SJ 976 246

TUTBURY – ST MARY'S PRIORY P

Church Street, Tutbury, Staffordshire
 DE13 9JF
 OS: SK 211 291

ASHLEY – ST JOHN THE BAPTIST P

Church Road, Ashley, Staffordshire
 TF9 4LQ
 OS: SJ 762 363

HANBURY – ST WERBURGH'S P

Church Lane, Hanbury, Staffordshire
 DE13 8TF
 OS: SK 170 279

MAER – ST PETER'S P

Haddon Lane, Maer, Staffordshire
 ST5 5EE
 OS: SJ 792 383

RUSHTON SPENCER –
ST LAWRENCE'S P

Rushton, Staffordshire SK11 0QU
 OS: SJ 934 620

SUFFOLK

BOULGE – ST MICHAEL'S P

Boulge, Suffolk IP13 6BW
 OS: TM 254 528

DENNINGTON – ST MARY'S P

B1116, Dennington, Suffolk IP13 8JF
 OS: TM 281 669

EAST BERGHOLT –
ST MARY THE VIRGIN P

The Street, East Bergholt, Suffolk
 CO7 6TH
 OS: TM 070 344

IKEN – ST BOTOLPH'S

Iken, Suffolk IP12 2ES
 OS: TM 413 564

WETHERINGSETT – ALL SAINTS P

Church Street, Wetheringsett, Suffolk
 IP14 5PP
 OS: TM 127 668

BLYTHBURGH – HOLY TRINITY P

Priory Road, Blythburgh, Suffolk
IP19 9LR
OS: TM 450 753

LAVENHAM – ST PETER & ST PAUL P

Potland Lane, Lavenham, Suffolk
CO10 9QT
OS: TL 912 490

LONG MELFORD – HOLY TRINITY P

19 Church Walk, Long Melford,
Suffolk CO10 9DL
OS: TL 865 467

UFFORD – THE ASSUMPTION
OF OUR LADY P

6 Church Lane, Ufford, Suffolk
IP13 6DS
OS: TM 298 521

SURREY

ALBURY – ST PETER &
ST PAUL CCT

Church Lane, Guildford, Surrey
GU5 9AJ
OS: TQ 050 476

COMPTON – ST NICHOLAS P

45 The Street, Compton, Surrey
GU3 1EB
OS: SU 954 470

OCKLEY – ST MARGARET'S P

B2126, Ockley, Surrey RH5 5LT
OS: TQ 156 406

STOKE D'ABERNON – ST MARY'S P

Stoke D'Abernon, Cobham, Surrey
KT11 3PX
OS: TQ 129 584

WOTTON – ST JOHN THE
EVANGELIST P

St Johns Church Road, Wotton,
Surrey RH5 6HS
OS: TQ 125 479

ABINGER – ST JAMES'S P

Abinger Lane, Abinger, Surrey
RH5 6PY
OS: TQ 114 459

BLETCHINGLEY – ST MARY'S P

High Street, Bletchingley, Surrey
RH1 4PD
OS: TQ 327 508

BURSTOW – ST BARTHOLOMEW'S P

Church Road, Burstow, Surrey
RH6 9RG
OS: TQ 312 412

CHALDON – ST PETER &
ST PAUL P

Ditches Lane, Whyteleafe, Surrey
CR3 5AL
OS: TQ 308 556

DUNSFOLD – ST MARY &
ALL SAINTS P

Church Road, Dunsfold, Surrey
GU8 4LT
OS: SU 998 363

EFFINGHAM – ST LAWRENCE'S P

Church Street, Effingham, Surrey
   KT24 5NA
   OS: TQ 118 536

OCKHAM – ALL SAINTS P

Ockham, Surrey GU23 6NQ
   OS: TQ 066 565

WARLINGHAM – ALL SAINTS P

Ward Lane, Whyteleafe, Surrey
   CR6 9AT
   OS: TQ 355 589

SUSSEX

BOXGROVE – PRIORY CHURCH OF ST MARY & ST BLAISE P

Church Lane, Boxgrove, Sussex
   PO18 0ED
   OS: SU 908 075

CLAYTON – ST JOHN'S P

Underhill Lane, Clayton, Sussex
   BN6 9PJ
   OS: TQ 300 139

COOMBES CHURCH P

Coombes Road, Coombes, Sussex
   BN15 0RS
   OS: TQ 190 081

HARDHAM – ST BOTOLPH'S P

Church Lane, Hardham, Sussex
   RH20 1LB
   OS: TQ 038 176

PLUMPTON – ST MICHAEL'S P

B2116, Plumpton, East Sussex
   BN7 3AF
   OS: TQ 356 135

RUSPER – ST MARY MAGDALENE P

High Street, Rusper, West Sussex
   RH12 4PX
   OS: TQ 205 373

WORTH – ST NICHOLAS P

Church Road, Crawley, West Sussex
   RH10 7RT
   OS: TQ 301 361

OVINGDEAN – ST WULFRAN'S

Greenways, Ovingdean, Sussex
   BN2 7BA
   OS: TQ 355 035

SOMPTING – ST MARY'S P

Church Lane, Sompting, Sussex
   BN15 0AZ
   OS: TQ 161 056

WARWICKSHIRE

ASTLEY – ST MARY'S P

4 Castle Drive, Astley, Warwickshire
   CV10 7QS
   OS: SP 311 894

BERKSWELL – ST JOHN THE BAPTIST P

Church Lane, Berkswell, Solihull
   CV7 7BJ
   OS: SP 243 791

WOOTTON WAWEN – ST PETER'S P

Stratford Road, Wootton Wawen,
    Warwickshire B95 6BD
    OS: SP 153 632

BINTON – ST PETER'S P

Church Bank, Binton, Warwickshire
    CV37 9TN
    OS: SP 145 539

BRAILES – ST GEORGE'S P

Butchers Lane, Brailes, Warwickshire
    OX15 5NB
    OS: SP 315 393

TEMPLE GRAFTON – ST ANDREW'S P

Church Bank, Temple Grafton,
    Warwickshire B49 6PA
    OS: SP 123 548

WHICHFORD – ST MICHAEL'S P

    Ascott Road, Whichford,
    Warwickshire CV36 5PG
    OS: SP 312 346

WILTSHIRE

EDINGTON – PRIORY CHURCH
OF ST MARY, ST KATHERINE
& ALL SAINTS P

Monastery Road, Edington, Wiltshire
    BA13 4QR
    OS: ST 926 533

INGLESHAM – ST JOHN
THE BAPTIST CCT

Inglesham, Wiltshire SN6 7RD
    OS: SU 205 984

LACOCK – ST CYRIAC'S P

21 Church Street, Lacock, Wiltshire
    SN15 2LB
    OS: ST 917 685

LYDIARD TREGOZE – ST MARY'S P
(KEY IN LYDIARD PARK HOUSE)

Lydiard Park, Lydiard Tregoze,
    Wiltshire SN5 3PA
    OS: SU 103 847

CLYFFE PYPARD – ST PETER'S P

7 Wood Street, Clyffe Pypard,
    Wiltshire SN4 7PZ
    OS: SU 074 769

EAST KNOYLE – ST MARY'S P

Hindon Road, East Knoyle, Wiltshire
    SP3 6AE
    OS: ST 880 305

SEVENHAMPTON – ST JAMES'S P

Sevenhampton, Wiltshire SN6 7QA
    OS: SU 209 904

WORCESTERSHIRE

LITTLE MALVERN PRIORY P

Little Malvern, Worcestershire
    WR14 4JN
    OS: SO 770 403

RIBBESFORD – ST LEONARD'S P

Ribbesford, Worcestershire
    DY12 2TQ
    OS: SO 786 740

WILDEN – ALL SAINTS P

Wilden Lane, Stourport-on-Severn,
  Worcestershire DY13 9LP
  OS: SO 824 722

ROCK – ST PETER & ST PAUL P

Rectory Lane, Rock, Worcestershire
  DY14 9RX
  OS: SO 731 711

BESFORD – ST PETER'S P

1 Harewell Lane, Besford,
  Worcestershire WR8 9AT
  OS: SO 910 447

BREDON – ST GILES' P

Church Street, Bredon,
  Worcestershire GL20 7LF
  OS: SO 920 369

CROOME D'ABITOT – ST MARY MAGDALENE CCT

Croome D'Abitot, Worcestershire
  WR8 9DW
  OS: SO 886 450

GREAT WITLEY – ST MICHAEL & ALL ANGELS P

Great Witley, Worcestershire
  WR6 6JT
  OS: SO 769 649

YORKSHIRE

ADEL – ST JOHN THE BAPTIST P

Church Lane, Adel, West Yorkshire
  LS16 8DW
  OS: SE 274 404

BOYNTON – ST ANDREW'S P

Main Street, Boynton, East Riding of
  Yorkshire YO16 4XJ
  OS: TA 136 679

HEMINGBROUGH – COLLEGIATE CHURCH OF ST MARY THE VIRGIN P

6 Main Street, Hemingbrough,
  North Yorkshire YO8 6QE
  OS: SE 673 306

KIRKDALE – ST GREGORY'S MINSTER P

Kirkdale, North Yorkshire
  YO62 7TZ
  OS: SE 676 858

LASTINGHAM – ST MARY'S P

Anserdale Lane, Lastingham, North
  Yorkshire YO62 6TN
  OS: SE 728 904

LEAD – ST MARY'S CCT

B1217, Saxton, North Yorkshire
  LS24 9QN
  OS: SE 464 368

PATRINGTON – ST PATRICK'S P

Church Lane, Patrington, East Riding
  of Yorkshire HU12 0RE
  OS: TA 315 225

CROFT – ST PETER'S P

Tees View, Croft-on-Tees, North
  Yorkshire DL2 2NR
  OS: NZ 288 098

WENSLEY – HOLY TRINITY P

Low Lane, Wensley, North Yorkshire
   DL8 4HJ
   OS: SE 092 895

NORTH NEWBALD – ST NICHOLAS P

South Newbald Road, Newbald, East
   Riding of Yorkshire YO43 4SE
   OS: SE 911 365

NORTH GRIMSTON –
ST NICHOLAS P

North Grimston, North Yorkshire
   YO17 8AX
   OS: SE 841 677

COWLAM – ST MARY'S
(KEY FROM MANOR FARM)

Manor Farm, Cowlam, Yorkshire
   YO25 9RT
   OS: SE 965 655

KIRKBURN – ST MARY'S P

Main Street, Kirkburn, East Riding
   of Yorkshire YO25 9DY
   OS: SE 979 550

LANGTOFT – ST PETER'S P

Church Lane, Langtoft, East Riding
   of Yorkshire YO25 3TP
   OS: TA 008 670

COTTAM – ST MARY'S (RUIN)

Cottam, East Riding of Yorkshire
   YO25 3AE
   OS: SE 966 655

ALDBOROUGH – ST ANDREW'S P

Back Street, Boroughbridge, North
   Yorkshire YO51 9ER
   OS: SE 405 664

BARDSEY – ALL HALLOWS P

Church Lane, Bardsey, Leeds
   LS17 9DR
   OS: SE 365 431

FLAMBOROUGH – ST OSWALD'S P

Lily Lane, Flamborough, East Riding
   of Yorkshire YO15 1PW
   OS: TA 226 701

GARTON-ON-THE-WOLDS –
ST MICHAEL'S P

1 Station Road, Garton, East Riding
   of Yorkshire YO25 3EU
   OS: SE 981 593

LISSETT – ST JAMES'S P

Main Street, Lissett, East Riding of
   Yorkshire YO25 8HY
   OS: TA 144 581

SKIRLAUGH – ST AUGUSTINE'S P

Church Lane, Skirlaugh, Yorkshire
   HU11 5EU
   OS: TA142 396

Index of People

Index of Places